osteria

Also by the author
Fantastico!
Tru
Amuse-Bouche
American Brasserie
Butter Sugar Flour Eggs

Broadway Books   New York

hearty italian fare
from rick tramonto's kitchen

osteria

RICK TRAMONTO

with Mary Goodbody

PHOTOGRAPHS BY TIM TURNER

PUBLISHED BY BROADWAY BOOKS

Published in the United States by Broadway Books,
an imprint of The Doubleday Publishing Group,
a division of Random House, Inc., New York.
www.broadwaybooks.com

BROADWAY BOOKS and its logo,
a letter B bisected on the diagonal,
are trademarks of Random House, Inc.

Book design by Elizabeth Rendfleisch

Library of Congress Cataloging-in-Publication Data
Tramonto, Rick.
    Osteria : hearty Italian fare from Rick Tramonto's kitchen /
Rick Tramonto; with Mary Goodbody; photographs by Tim
Turner. — 1st ed.
        p.   cm.
    Includes index.
1. Cookery, Italian. I. Goodbody, Mary. II. Title.

    TX723.T7357 2008
    641.5945—dc22

2007045441

ISBN 978-0-7679-2771-0

PRINTED IN CHINA

10 9 8 7 6 5 4 3 2 1

First Edition

I dedicate this book to my Lord and Savior Jesus Christ, who always leads me down the right road and who brings me through every storm every time. One verse in particular guides me through my life: "I can do all things through Jesus Christ which strengthens me." Philippians 4:13

To my best friend and wife, Eileen Tramonto, who helps keep me loved, humble, and close to God.

To my sons, Gio, Sean, and Brian, who kept me cooking and eating all the time. I love you guys.

And finally to my mom and dad, Frank and Gloria Tramonto, who have both gone home to be with the Lord. This book would not be possible without all of these great food memories with my crazy, loving, Italian family. I love you and miss you.

contents

acknowledgments

from rick tramonto

Thanks to my friend and co-writer, Mary Goodbody, who for the fourth time has helped me put all of my thoughts and recipes into a book. Thanks for your attention to detail and for making me sound so good.

Thanks to my longtime friend and brilliant photographer, Tim Turner, who keeps me focused and challenges me to make every dish the best it can be during those long but fun photo shoots. Thanks for sharing my passion for Italian cuisine and culture.

Thanks to my supportive and loving family: Eileen Tramonto; Gio Tramonto; Sean and Brian Pschirrer; Paul and Dorothy Tramonto; Ed and Mary Carroll; Kathleen (Carroll), Lenny, Jesse, and Hannah Williams; and Joe and Bridget Carroll, who continue to show me how to live and breathe outside the culinary world. Thanks for the breath of fresh air. Also thanks to the Tramonto family, the Lepore family, the Gentile family, the Sansone family, the Abbamonte family, and the Faga family.

Thanks to my spiritual family, Pastors Gregory and Grace Dickow of Life Changers International Church, for their love, blessings, teachings, and prayers, and for feeding me the Word of God. I can't thank you enough. . . . Also to Van and Doni Crouch; Dr. Creflo and Taffi Dollar; Bishop T. D. Jakes; Jesse and Cathy Duplantis; Joel and Victoria Osteen; and Pastor James MacDonald at Walk in the Word for his teachings and wisdom of the Word.

Thanks to my loyal agent and friend, Jane Dystel; my editor, Jennifer Josephy; and the great team at Broadway Books for their trust and faith in this book and me.

Special thanks to Chef Chris Pandel. Thanks for your friendship, all of your long hours, the extra time you put into this project, and your great Italian palate. I couldn't have done it without you. I'd also like to thank my chefs as well as the rest of the teams at Osteria di Tramonto and Tramonto's Steak & Seafood, for all your extra time and care that went into this project.

A special thanks to my director of PR Jeffrey Ward and my assistant Christina Fox, who keep me organized, on time, and laughing.

Thanks to Belinda Chang, for her great wine notes in this book.

I would also like to thank the City of Chicago, Mayor Richard Daley, and the food press for supporting me and allowing me to hone my craft in this great city.

Thanks to those who inspire me on a daily basis and who support my culinary efforts: Rich Melman, my partner and friend, John Folse, Tom Coliccio, Chris Bianco, Pierre Gagnaire, Emeril Lagasse, the late Julia Child, Oprah Winfrey, José Andrés, Lidia Bastianich, Jean-Georges Vongerichten, Alain Ducasse, Bobby Flay, Alfred Portale, Mario Batali, Max MacCalman, David Bouley, Danny Wegman, Ina Pinkney (the breakfast queen), Randy Zweiban, Gray Kunz, Norman Van Aken, Martin Berasategui, Michael Lomonaco, Daniel Boulud, Michael Chiarello, Wolfgang Puck, Francois Payard, Greg Bromen, the late Jean-Louis Palladin, Alan Wong, Roger Vergé, Eric Ripert, Anton Mosimann, Raymond Blanc, and Max Riedel.

Thanks to my supportive friends whom I rarely get to see because I'm always working. I love you guys. Thanks to Ron, Jill, Zeke, and Olivia Losoya; Jim and Linda Murdough; Ken and Marla Hines; Peter Lepore; Larry and Julie Binstein; Vinnie and Theresa Rupert; and Wendy Payton. Last but not least to my culinary partner and pastry chef extraordinaire, Gale Gand, who continues to travel this journey with me and provides daily inspiration—both in and out of the kitchen.

A very special thanks to the vendors and the farmers across the country whom I work with every day. They work so hard to find and grow the best-of-the-best ingredients and products for me to use in my restaurants. This book would not be possible without you. Thank you and God bless you, big time.

from mary goodbody

What fun this book has been! And the food is just so, so good—as anyone would expect from a chef with Rick's talent. The journey just gets more remarkable and satisfying, and I am grateful to Rick and his team for taking me along. Thanks, too, to our agent, Jane Dystel, for her guidance and support during this project, and to Jennifer Josephy, our editor at Broadway, who believed in us and this book from the very beginning. I also want to thank Lisa Thornton for her help with the manuscript and my daughter, Laura, for her steadfast belief in me.

osteria

introduction

I wrote this book from my heart. Nothing inspires yet comforts me as much as the homey family-style Italian cooking presented on these pages. It is the food I grew up with and the food cooked at osterias both here and in Italy. It truly is the food of my childhood, the refuge of my adult life, and the key to my heritage.

I revel in the honest, robust flavors, the straightforward cooking techniques, and the emphasis on seasonal, fresh food all celebrated by this style of Italian cooking. This is how I like to cook at home for my family, and it's how I learned to cook from my Italian-American parents and immigrant grandparents. But because I am a professional chef, I did not think about compiling a book of osteria-style recipes until now. Perhaps I thought them too uncomplicated or unrefined, or perhaps I simply had to reach this point in my culinary odyssey. The time is right for me to turn my attention to more casual cooking, and it's right for this book.

Believe me, learning how to cook these dishes is a delicious and stimulating journey well worth taking! I hope you will join me.

a little about me

Currently I devote my energy to owning and managing a group of restaurants in Chicagoland, which is what we midwesterners call the greater Chicago metropolitan area. One of the restaurants is Tru and the other is an osteria. When I am not running from one of my professional kitchens to another, I like nothing more than to spend time in my home kitchen, cooking alongside my wife for our family.

I am best known as the executive chef and partner of the award-winning restaurant Tru, one of Chicago's high-end restaurants located a block from Michigan Avenue. My years at Tru have allowed me to showcase the cutting-edge cuisine I have studied most of my life. I never went to cooking school, but instead worked in some of New York's and Chicago's best restaurants, absorbing all I could. I also cooked in England for several years, and from there visited the Continent, particularly France, Spain, and Italy, to learn all I could from some of the world's greatest chefs. When I lived in England, I was the chef at a country house hotel, but I also worked with Raymond Blanc and Anton Mosimann and in France with Pierre Gagnaire and Michel Guerard. I traveled as much as I could, observing, learning, and eating anything and everything as a way to broaden my informal but wide-reaching culinary education.

I pour this hands-on knowledge into my career. The menu at Tru is filled with caviar and confit, truffles and lobster. The food is wonderful and I am extremely proud of the high standards we aim for and meet every night of the year. Our customers share our enthusiasm.

The food I cook at the osteria and at home is quite different from the food served at Tru. Both are faithful to quality and the seasons, and both are prepared with exacting care and attention, but the difference is in the experience, like putting on a tuxedo versus a pair of jeans. Both have to fit, but they are poles apart.

the osteria

An *osteria* is defined as a "tavern or humble restaurant" where the food is designed to accompany the wine. I love this concept! The cooking is simple—but never simplistic—and straightforward, and over the years it has evolved so that now most Italians think of it as any casual fare with a smart nod to its rich culinary history. At its best, nothing surpasses it, and I aspire to this authenticity at Osteria di Tramonto and when I cook at home.

Our customers happily embrace what we try to do at the osterias every day. As is typical of an osteria, we are open seven days a week for breakfast, lunch, and dinner. Customers sense that this is the "real deal," whether they order veal shank osso buco, a plate of garlic-and-oil pasta, a meatball salad, or braised monkfish. Our food is a welcome alternative to Italian-American restaurants; it's a breath of fresh air because its genuineness is a gentle reminder of how comforting and stupendous real Italian food can be, especially when it follows the seasons.

During the last five years, since I opened the osterias, I have rediscovered my Italian heritage in exciting ways. I have made numerous trips to Italy to soak up all I can about the food, the raw ingredients, the cooking, the culture, and the people. Not surprisingly, I found that hospitality is the glue that holds it all together. Italians welcome everyone to their restaurants, large and small, fancy and casual, with open arms—often quite literally—and are just as likely to invite you into their homes if the opportunity arises.

I recognize this impulse. I have been drawn to the hospitality and restaurant business since I got a job at Wendy's at age sixteen when I dropped out of high school to help out with the family finances—and I have been cooking in professional kitchens ever since. I grew up in a large Italian family in Rochester, New York, where home-cooked meals were a daily occurrence and on Sundays could last all afternoon, with as many people as possible squeezed around the table.

My two grandmothers spent as much time in our kitchen as their own. I learned to make marinara sauce from my grandmother from Naples, and risotto from my grandmother from Abruzzi. Both my grandfathers cured meat and aged wine in their basements. My aunts baked large casseroles of eggplant Parmesan, and my parents used gigantic pans for rectangular pizzas. (I still have those battered old pizza pans, and guess what? The pizzas I make in them are outstanding!) My parents tended a large vegetable garden and we all eagerly awaited spring's first peas and lettuces, summer's plump, juicy tomatoes, and autumn's mellow butternut squash. We piled skillets high with greens such as chard and spinach and watched as they shrank to a quarter of their mass while they soaked up the garlic and olive oil in the hot skillet.

We shopped at Wegmans, the wonderful family-owned supermarket chain that has its roots in Rochester, and also bought bread and pasta from the nearby Italian markets, although we never hesitated to make our own. I remember sitting at the kitchen table with my mother and grandmother, rolling pasta dough and running the silken sheets through the hand-cranked pasta machine. It's no coincidence that my fondest memories of childhood revolve around the kitchen, cooking and eating. We were a typical Italian-American family and food was at the center of our existence.

Cooking the food on the pages of this book is a natural outgrowth of what I recall from those early days. Though I never forget the old-world traditions that demand such enormous respect, in a number of cases I have refined a dish to meet contemporary tastes. When I have been inspired by an unfamiliar cooking technique or ingredient discovered in Italy, I have created a dish to keep up with the normal evolution of any great and organic cuisine.

my favorite places

When I travel in the country of my ancestors, I keep copious notes. My companions sometimes joke that my nose is poked in my notebook more than it's directed toward a beautiful plate of pasta or selection of salumi. Or they kid me about taking hundreds of pictures.

I can't help it. On every visit, I fall more in love with the place. I am thrilled to be there and yet can't wait to get home to Chicago and turn my customers and my family on to what I have learned. I document everything so that I can re-create the food in my American kitchen with the first-rate ingredients I have available here. And each new experience reinforces my excitement at being in Italy.

If you're looking for a relaxing amble through Tuscany or Calabria, don't sign up to travel with me! I am up before dawn, waiting for the fishermen to return with their morning catch, and then it's on to a small bakery to eat great bread, butter, and cheese with a steaming cup of coffee, and all before most American visitors are awake. Next, my wife, Eileen, and I, and whoever is with us from my restaurants walk through every market and food stall we can find before we stop for an early lunch at an osteria that has been recommended or that simply has caught my eye. An hour or two later, we have a second lunch at another osteria. In the afternoon, we might visit a winery or food producer, and then top off the day with two dinners at two different restaurants. We fall into bed about midnight and then I'm up before dawn, ready to do it all over again. I love it! It's grueling, no doubt about it, but I learn so much that every day is well worth the taxing schedule.

I love to wander the winding streets of cities such as Rome and Naples, or drive along the glittering sea of the Amalfi coast, but nothing pleases me more than a stop at Montalcino in Tuscany, a town that stole my heart when I first laid eyes on it. Not only is this medieval town famed for its exquisite red wine, Brunello di Montalcino, but it also offers amazing views of surrounding valleys, and its hilly, cobbled streets beg you to explore them. If I ever were to retire, this is where you would likely find me—eating, drinking wine, taking notes, and snapping pictures.

When I return from one of my two- or three-week sojourns to Italy, I sort through the photos and choose the best to hang in the restaurants. Others I keep in albums or electronic files for quick reference. The pictures tell the story of my trips. I don't know if anyone would call them especially good photography, but they capture the essence of the country I love so well—from simple pictures of sun-baked stone walls or a dog asleep in a doorway to more lively shots of bustling vegetable markets and prosperous wineries. I especially like to take photos of old doors in Italy—ancient wooden doors with peeling paint and big brass or iron hinges and knockers.

my favorite food

I could not wait to open an osteria. As I have said, the food we serve is reminiscent of the food I ate as a child, but it is so much more. It's hearty, robust fare, instantly recognizable to the customer and yet sophisticated enough to appeal to adventurous diners.

I could cook this kind of food all day, every day and very often that's exactly what I do! And both my wife and I prepare many of these recipes at home, too, for our three boys. As you can well imagine, the boys have ever-expanding appetites, and so cooking for them is pure pleasure.

When you leaf through the pages to come, you will find a pizza topped with four cheeses, my mom's old-fashioned lasagna, and a simple spinach-and-cheese omelet. Yet, you will also come across a salad of heirloom beets with mascarpone cheese and thin capellini pasta with six kinds of tomatoes. Sound good? Read on!

Osteria cooking is all about fresh, seasonal ingredients, great cheeses, quality pasta, fresh herbs, and exceptional olive oils and vinegars. It also is about taking your time when you cook, and this "slow and steady" cooking is something I appreciate.

When you prepare the braised short ribs served with garlic mashed potatoes, perhaps, or the pork shanks braised with borlotti beans, you will be compelled to enter the kitchen hours before dinner. You won't have to stay there for hours, but the dish does require some preparation and later tending. The end result? Try it! Fall-off-the-bone tender meat with rich, intense flavors that can be achieved only by long, slow cooking.

It's not all slow cooking, though. I have a recipe for grilled pork chops with broccoli rabe and one for grilled veal chops with a light apple-and-mint salad. I have a seductive dish of olive oil–crushed potatoes and another of creamed onions with Parmesan cheese.

Italy is home to world-class cheeses and world-class wines. I like to end a meal with cheese, such as the simple preparation for Gorgonzola, one of Italy's treasures, with a balsamic jelly. For something more upscale, try Robiola Bosina cheese with a radish salad drizzled with white truffle oil.

My sommeliers helped write the wine notes that accompany the chapters and many of the recipes. They have traveled to Italy with me, along with other members of the team, and their memory of the wines is invaluable. Italian wine reflects the attitude of the Italian people: The wine is as good as it gets but lacks pretension. Drinking great wine and eating great food is always a celebration infused with a keen sense of good fun and cheer.

Finally, the desserts in this book are simple and easy, too. I am not a trained pastry chef and make no pretense of being one, but I have a few tried-and-true desserts in my repertoire. For example, an osteria meal could very well end with a rustic apple crostada served with caramel gelato, or, if they are in season, peaches poached in red wine and then festooned with airy whipped mascarpone.

Osteria food is nothing if not reliable, and it is always tasty. It's the food I love to cook and celebrate, and I hope you, too, will develop an affection for it. Because I hold this food in such esteem, I dedicate the book to my parents, Frank and Gloria Tramonto, and to my grandparents, who I wish could have seen the publication of *Osteria*. I would have loved nothing more than to share my success with them. I feel honored to have their recipe cards, some of their cooking implements, and, most of all, their passion and spirit. It infuses all the food in the book and speaks to the love and admiration I have for my family and my heritage.

breakfast

When I travel in Italy, I often get up very early to visit the vegetable and fish markets when they are bustling and welcoming the day with their freshest and best. This means that by eight o'clock I am sitting down somewhere for breakfast, ravenously hungry and enjoying caffè latte, some fresh-baked rolls with sweet butter and homemade berry jam, and amazing fresh fruit. This is the Italian breakfast—so simple and straightforward and so wonderful. It's all about the best ingredients and the freshest brewed coffee, just-baked bread, and perfectly ripe fruit. But I love American breakfasts, too, and look forward to the weekends when I cook big, hearty meals for my family. I love eggs, particularly, and am not afraid to pair them with meat and cheese. And so, in this chapter, I bring both worlds together with omelets and frittatas that speak the Italian language and hash and eggs and smoothies that are all-American.

Breakfast is a wonderful meal to cook and eat together as a family. Many of us teach our kids to cook by starting with breakfast food. We scramble eggs or make an omelet late at night when we're in need of comfort, nourishment, or both. We whip up smoothies as treats, and sneak strips of crisp bacon when no one is looking. Even if you think of yourself as someone who "never eats breakfast," chances are you enjoy it just as much as I do!

notes from the sommelier
bubbles for breakfast

Nothing makes Chef Tramonto happier than a glass of something bubbly to pair with breakfast dishes. Thankfully, Italian winemakers accommodate our decadent proclivities with their bountiful choice of sparkling wines. If a glass of méthode champenoise in the A.M. sounds a little too wild for you, try one of Italy's bottled nonalcoholic fizzy delights like Limonata or Aranciata from San Pellegrino with breakfast. A spritzy fruit juice poured into a fluted glass makes even a simple breakfast a celebration of life.

If, however, you ascribe to the idea that "it's five P.M. somewhere in the world," then pop the cork on a bottle of aromatic Prosecco from the Veneto, peachy Moscato d'Asti from Piedmont, or rich, toasty Franciacorta from Lombardy. Although these are the more traditional beginnings for an Italian meal, there are others that the adventurous drinker should not neglect. There are sparkling Gavi and Erbaluce di Caluso, made from the Cortese and Erbaluce grapes, respectively, in Piedmont. You will also find interesting red sparkling wines made from the Brachetto grape, also in Piedmont, and the Lambrusco variety in Emilia-Romagna. One of our favorite pairings at the Osteria is rich, meaty salumi and eggs with a chilled glass of fruity, red Lambrusco. *Perfetto!*

The classic brunch beverage, the bellini, is another sparkling delight blending Prosecco with white peach nectar, and this drink has infinite possibility and variations. Blood orange, pear, apple, blueberry—we have tried using all of these fruits to make nontraditional bellini, and when the fruits are in season, the result is delicious. Forget what you have been taught about French sparkling wine dominance, and come play with the Italians!

omelets and frittatas

Omelets, like soufflés and cream sauces, confound some home cooks. They begin with a sure hand, but too easily the contents of the pan turn into flavorful scrambled eggs instead of a tender egg casing folded over a flavorful filling, firm and smooth on the outside and soft and creamy on the inside. Of course, there is nothing wrong with scrambled eggs, but if you want an omelet, they become a poor second. I like Montagné's advice in the renowned *Larousse Gastronomique*: He advises to use a clean frying pan "in which nothing else is ever cooked . . . Beat the eggs . . . and add them only at the last moment. . . . Finally," he writes, "have confidence in yourself."

I agree with this last admonishment above all others and suggest you learn to make omelets in the privacy of your kitchen when you have time to concentrate and hone your skills. Julia Child makes the same point: "Learning to make a good omelette is entirely a matter of practice," she writes in *Mastering the Art of French Cooking.*

Classic omelets are made with three eggs and in these modern times should be cooked in a 7- to 8-inch nonstick omelet pan or frying pan. I like to whisk the eggs enthusiastically just before I pour the mixture into the pan, because the incorporated air helps make the omelet light and fluffy. Also, nonstick pans or well-buttered omelet pans are important because the eggs must be able to slide along the bottom of the pan and fold over on themselves before they slip from pan onto plate.

Omelets are undeniably French in origin, not Italian, although there is evidence that the Romans made a similar dish and the origin of the word is Latin. I include them here because they are so delicious and intrinsic to breakfast and brunch (and are just as good for lunch and supper). Also, omelets are basic to any good cook's repertoire. I ask every cook who applies for a job in one of my restaurants to make an omelet. A chef's proficiency with this simple dish tells me a lot about his or her training and overall skill level.

Every Italian home cook makes frittatas, which are eaten any time of day and often are served at room temperature as antipasti. In Spain, tortillas, the Spanish version of frittatas, are frequently served as tapas. In the United States we think of eggs as breakfast or brunch foods and so I include frittatas in this chapter, although they could show up in others with total authenticity.

Although frittatas and omelets could be called close cousins, based as both are on eggs cooked with aromatic cheeses, vegetables, herbs, and meats, the difference is how the savory ingredients are married to the eggs. For omelets, cooked eggs are folded over these ingredients and then the whole thing glides gracefully onto a plate. For frittatas, these same ingredients are mixed with the raw eggs and then poured into the pan, partially cooked on top of the stove, and then finished in the oven or under the broiler. Frittatas are cooked as one large "pie," never folded, and are cut into wedges for serving, whereas omelets are meant to be individual servings. This means frittatas might be considered more family friendly than omelets, unless you are cooking for a very small family or just one or two people.

My grandmother added a pinch of baking powder to the raw egg mixture to ensure that the frittata puffed up a little. I still do this, as well as whisking a good amount of air into the eggs just before I pour them into the pan for the lightest frittatas anywhere.

florentine-style omelet

omelette fiorentino

Two 2-ounce bunches fresh baby spinach, stems
   removed
¼ cup olive oil
12 large eggs
Pinch of baking powder
Kosher salt and freshly ground black pepper
4 tablespoons unsalted butter
½ cup diced smoked fontina cheese (about
   2 ounces)
½ cup diced plum tomatoes (1 plum tomato)

This is the omelet of my childhood. My
mother and grandmothers usually made them
with a combination of spinach, fontina,
tomatoes, and basil. When I think "omelet,"
this is what comes to mind. ❀ *serves 4*

1 Wash the spinach very well. In a frying
   pan, heat the olive oil over medium heat
   and cook the spinach, stirring often, for
   1 to 2 minutes, or until most of the liquid
   evaporates and the spinach wilts thoroughly.
   Set aside.

2 Crack the eggs into a mixing bowl, add the
   baking powder, and season to taste with
   salt and pepper. Using a wire whisk, beat
   until smooth and airy.

3 In a large nonstick sauté or 7- or 8-inch
   omelet pan, melt 1 tablespoon of butter
   over medium heat. Pour about a quarter of
   the eggs into the pan, sprinkle with a little
   more salt and pepper, and cook for 30
   seconds, or until the bottom begins to set.

4 Gently flip the eggs and cook for about
   30 seconds longer, or until the bottom sets
   but the eggs do not brown.

5 Sprinkle about a quarter of the cheese, a
   quarter of the tomatoes, and a quarter of
   the spinach just off center on the omelet.
   Fold in half, cook for about 1 minute to
   soften the cheese and warm the tomatoes,
   and slide from the pan onto a plate and
   serve. Repeat to make 3 more omelets.

roman-style omelet

omelette romano

½ pound hot or sweet Italian sausage
12 large eggs
Pinch of baking powder
Kosher salt and freshly ground black pepper
4 tablespoons unsalted butter
¼ cup julienned roasted red bell pepper (see Note)
2 tablespoons fresh basil, washed, stems removed, julienned
2 ounces goat cheese, crumbled (about 2 tablespoons)

I call this a Roman omelet because of its ingredients, particularly the fresh sausage. Every supermarket in the United States sells Italian sausage labeled "sweet" or "hot and spicy." The choice is yours. When I think of the sausage I have eaten in Italy and especially in Rome, I think of the classic fennel-infused fresh pork sausage, which adds flavor that is just bold enough for this simple omelet whose flavor is further boosted with roasted peppers and basil. The goat cheese is the finishing touch. *serves 4*

1 In a sauté pan, cook the sausage over medium-high heat until nicely browned and cooked through. Drain on paper towels until cool enough to handle, and then crumble the sausage meat. Set aside.

2 Crack the eggs into a mixing bowl, add the baking powder, and season to taste with salt and pepper. Using a wire whisk, beat until smooth and airy.

3 In a large nonstick sauté or 7- or 8-inch omelet pan, melt 1 tablespoon of butter over medium heat. Pour about a quarter of the eggs into the pan, sprinkle with a little more salt and pepper, and cook for 30 seconds, or until the bottom begins to set.

4 Gently flip the eggs and cook for about 30 seconds longer, or until the bottom sets but the eggs do not brown.

5 Sprinkle about a quarter of the bell pepper, a quarter of the basil, and a quarter of the cheese just off center on the omelet. Fold in half, cook for about 1 minute to soften the cheese and warm the bell pepper, and slide from the pan onto a plate and serve. Repeat to make 3 more omelets.

note To roast bell peppers, char them over a grill or gas flame or under a broiler until blackened on all sides and soft. Turn them as they char to ensure even blackening. Remove from the heat and transfer to a bowl. Cover with plastic wrap and set aside for about 20 minutes to steam as they cool. Lift the peppers from the bowl and rub or peel off the blackened skin.

frittata with oven-dried cherry tomatoes and mozzarella

frittata con pomodorini secchi e mozzarella

12 large eggs

1 cup freshly grated Parmigiano-Reggiano cheese

¼ cup whole milk

Pinch of baking powder

Kosher salt and freshly ground black pepper

4 tablespoons unsalted butter

32 Oven-Dried Cherry Tomato halves (recipe follows)

16 baby mozzarella balls, each about ½ ounce, halved

4 large fresh basil leaves, washed, stems removed, torn (about 2 ounces)

1 Preheat the oven to 350°F.

2 Crack the eggs into a mixing bowl and add ¾ cup of Parmigiano-Reggiano, the milk, and the baking powder and season to taste with salt and pepper. Using a wire whisk, beat until smooth and airy.

3 In a 10- to 14-inch ovenproof nonstick sauté pan, melt 1 tablespoon of butter over medium heat. Reduce the heat to low and pour a quarter of the eggs into the pan. Cook, stirring constantly, for 1 to 2 minutes, or until they begin to scramble but are only partially cooked.

4 Evenly distribute 8 tomato halves, 4 mozzarella balls, and a quarter of the basil over the eggs in the pan. Sprinkle a little salt and pepper over the frittata. Transfer the pan to the oven and let the frittata cook for 3 to 5 minutes longer, or until the eggs are set and cooked through.

5 Remove from the oven and sprinkle the hot frittata with about a tablespoon of grated Parmigiano-Reggiano. Using a large, broad spatula, lift the frittata from the pan and serve. Repeat to make 3 more frittatas.

Italians love to cook with tomatoes, mozzarella cheese, and basil—no surprises there. I love them in a simple frittata, with salty Parmigiano-Reggiano cheese serving as the underlying flavor. Because the cheese provides a good dose of salty flavor, don't add too much kosher salt to the eggs. I make these as individual frittatas, but you could take a more traditional approach and cook this as a single frittata in a large pan, cut into wedges for serving. *serves 4*

oven-dried cherry tomatoes
makes 32 tomato halves

16 cherry tomatoes

About ¼ cup extra virgin olive oil

Kosher salt and freshly ground black pepper

1 Preheat the oven to 250°F.

2 Cut the tomatoes in half lengthwise. Set each half, cut side up, on a baking pan and drizzle with enough olive oil to coat. Season lightly with salt and pepper.

3 Let the tomatoes "dry" in the oven for about 20 minutes, or until they are slightly softened and the edges are slightly crispy.

4 Let the tomatoes cool and use immediately or refrigerate in an airtight container, covered with olive oil, for up to 7 days.

val d'aosta–style frittata
frittata val d'aosta

fingerling potatoes
4 ounces fingerling potatoes, sliced about ¼ inch thick
Kosher salt and freshly ground black pepper

escarole
2 tablespoons olive oil
1 medium yellow onion, sliced
1 head escarole, washed and cut into 1-inch pieces
1 teaspoon kosher salt
Freshly ground black pepper

frittata
12 large eggs
¾ cup freshly grated Parmigiano-Reggiano cheese
¼ cup whole milk
Pinch of baking powder
5½ teaspoons kosher salt
Freshly ground black pepper
4 tablespoons unsalted butter
½ cup shredded Fontina Val d'Aosta cheese

to serve
2 tablespoons snipped fresh chives
½ cup Rick's Homemade Crème Fraîche (page 15)

1 Preheat the oven to 350°F.

2 To prepare the fingerling potatoes, toss the sliced potatoes in a small bowl with salt and pepper to taste.

3 Spread the potatoes in a small baking pan and roast for about 25 minutes, or until fork tender. Remove from the oven and set aside.

4 To prepare the escarole, in a large sauté pan, heat the olive oil over medium-high heat. Add the onion and cook for 4 to 5 minutes, or until translucent. Add the escarole and cook for 3 to 4 minutes, or just until slightly wilted. Season to taste with salt and pepper. Remove from the pan and set aside.

5 To prepare the frittata, crack the eggs into a mixing bowl and add the Parmigiano-Reggiano, milk, and baking powder and season to taste with salt and pepper. Using a wire whisk, beat until smooth and airy.

6 In a 10- to 14-inch ovenproof nonstick sauté pan, melt 1 tablespoon of butter over medium heat. Add about a quarter of the potatoes and ¼ cup of the escarole and cook for about 2 minutes, or until any moisture has evaporated.

7 Reduce the heat to low and pour a quarter of the eggs into the pan. Cook, stirring constantly, for 1 to 2 minutes, or until they begin to scramble but are only partially cooked. Sprinkle a teaspoon of salt and a little pepper over the frittata.

I tasted a frittata made with glorious Fontina Val d'Aosta cheese, potatoes, and braised escarole when I was in Venice. There it was served as an antipasto at lunchtime, as is common in Italy, but I put it in the breakfast chapter, where Americans would expect to find it. This frittata is made with tender fingerling potatoes and dressed up with smooth, indulgent crème fraîche and some snipped chives. Again, I prepare these as individual frittatas, but you could make one large frittata and serve it cut into wedges. *serves 4*

(continued)

8 Once the eggs begin to set, cover the frittata with a quarter of the fontina. Transfer the pan to the oven and let the frittata cook for 3 to 4 minutes longer, or until the eggs are set and cooked through but not browned. Remove from the oven.

9 Sprinkle the hot frittata with about a quarter of the snipped chives and a dollop of the crème fraîche. Using a large, broad spatula, lift the frittata from the pan and serve. Repeat to make 3 more frittatas.

rick's homemade crème fraîche
makes about 2 cups

1 cup heavy whipping cream
2 tablespoons buttermilk
2 tablespoons fresh lemon juice

1 Stir the cream, buttermilk, and lemon juice in a glass bowl or jar. Cover and let stand at room temperature for 24 hours, or until very thick.

2 Stir to make sure the crème fraîche is thick enough. It should be the consistency of sour cream.

3 Cover and refrigerate for at least 24 hours before using. It will keep for up to 10 days in the refrigerator.

note While this is an easy way to make it, and I hope you do so, you can buy really good crème fraîche that is ready to use instead.

eggs in hell
uova all'inferno

1 tablespoon olive oil
1 teaspoon crushed red pepper flakes, or more
4 cups Pomodoro Sauce (recipe follows)
8 large eggs
½ cup freshly grated Parmigiano-Reggiano cheese

1 In a large sauté pan, heat the olive oil and red pepper until the flakes begin to warm through and their aroma blooms. Pour the Pomodoro Sauce into the pan and stir to create a diavolo sauce.

2 Heat the diavolo sauce over medium heat until hot and bubbly. Crack the eggs and slide them into the sauce. Cover and simmer on low heat for 7 to 10 minutes, or until the egg whites are firm and opaque and the yolks are still soft and runny.

Unless you grew up in an Italian family that always had red sauce in the refrigerator or freezer, you may not be familiar with this easy egg dish. Easy, that is, as long as the sauce is made already, because all you do is poach the eggs in the sauce and serve them sprinkled with Parmigiano-Reggiano cheese. It gets its name from the heat of the red pepper flakes and the red color of the sauce; if you want to make it slightly more angelic, decrease the amount of pepper flakes. Serve this with crusty Italian bread or thick slices of toast.

❀ *serves 4*

3 Using a large spoon, scoop 2 eggs and a quarter of the sauce into each of 4 serving bowls. Sprinkle each with a quarter of the grated cheese and serve.

pomodoro sauce
makes about 4 cups

2 tablespoons olive oil
2 to 3 garlic cloves, minced
¾ cup white wine
Pinch of crushed red pepper flakes
2½ pounds whole, peeled canned tomatoes
Kosher salt and freshly ground black pepper
¾ teaspoon sugar
¼ teaspoon chopped fresh basil

1 In a saucepan, heat 1 tablespoon of olive oil over low heat. Add the garlic and cook gently for 3 to 4 minutes, or until golden brown. Add the wine and red pepper, raise the heat to medium-high, and bring the wine to a brisk simmer. Cook for about 2 minutes, or until the liquid reduces by half.

2 Meanwhile, put the tomatoes in a mixing bowl and crush with a fork or potato masher. Add to the pan and season to taste with salt and pepper. Stir in the sugar.

3 Bring the sauce to a simmer over medium heat and cook for 50 to 60 minutes.

4 Stir 1 tablespoon of olive oil and the basil into the sauce and taste. Add more salt and pepper if needed.

salami and eggs

salumi e uova

½ pound salami
1 tablespoon olive oil
1 cup diced onions
12 large eggs
2 tablespoons unsalted butter
Kosher salt and freshly ground black pepper

1 Dice the salami into ¼- to ½-inch dice. Cook in a sauté pan over medium-high heat until browned and the fat is rendered. Drain on paper towels and set aside.

2 In a sauté pan, heat the olive oil over medium-high heat and sauté the onions for 3 to 4 minutes, or until translucent and lightly browned. Set aside.

3 Crack the eggs into a mixing bowl and whisk until smooth.

4 In a nonstick sauté pan, melt the butter over medium heat. Add the reserved salami and cook for about 30 seconds. Add the eggs and stir with a spatula until scrambled to the consistency you prefer. Season to taste with salt and pepper, keeping in mind that the salami is salty.

5 Spoon the salami and eggs onto each of 4 serving plates, garnish each portion with the reserved onions, and serve.

I could probably write a book on Italian salami, of which there are hundreds of varieties. Very often they are seasoned with fennel or anise, or both. Salami are not fresh sausage but instead are cured, which means they have been smoked or dried and don't need any more cooking, although you may heat them up, as I do here. Use any salami you like for this dish; I generally make it with fennel salami, but if you have Genoa or another type, use it, and it's good, too, with hot buttered toast. It's an indulgent dish, along the lines of ham and eggs, and perhaps because of that it's a big treat on Father's Day. My dad always asked for it on that special day in June. *serves 4*

blood orange crêpes with vanilla mascarpone

crepes d'arancio sanguigno

crêpes
1 cup all-purpose flour
¾ teaspoon sugar
About 1 teaspoon kosher salt
3 large eggs
¾ cup milk

4 teaspoons unsalted butter

to serve
32 sections blood oranges (about 6)
4 tablespoons Vanilla Mascarpone (page 21)
1 cup Blood Orange Sauce (page 21)

1 To prepare the crêpe batter, mix the flour, sugar, and salt in a large bowl.

I am intensely fond of the combination of mascarpone, vanilla, and oranges and go a little crazy when I can make this with blood oranges. Available from late December through mid-March or thereabouts, the oranges with their distinctive crimson flesh are sweeter than other oranges and taste a little bit of berries. Blood oranges are originally from Sicily; today they are easy to find in Italy and Spain and, I am happy to say, increasingly in the United States, where growers from California and Texas are producing very good specimens.

   If you add a splash of Grand Marnier to the orange sauce, the rich, sweet crêpes are instantly transformed into dessert. ❀ *serves 4*

2 In a separate bowl, whisk the eggs and milk. Pour into the bowl with the flour and whisk just until combined. Do not overmix the batter. Set aside for at least 1 hour at room temperature and up to 48 hours in the refrigerator. Let the batter return to room temperature before cooking the crêpes.

3 To prepare the crêpes, heat an 8-inch non-stick skillet or crêpe pan over medium heat and melt ½ teaspoon of butter in it. When it melts, ladle 6 tablespoons (about ⅔ cup) of the batter into the pan. Swirl and tip the pan so that the batter spreads in a thin layer over the bottom of the pan and about half an inch up the sides. If there seems to be an excess of batter, pour it back into the bowl. As it cooks, the crêpe will form bubbles and start to set around the edges.

4 Use a thin spatula to loosen the crêpe and when the bubbles pop, lift the crêpe at the edges to see if the underside is nicely browned. If so, flip the crêpe and cook for about 30 seconds longer, or just until set but before it crisps too much around the edges. Adjust the heat as necessary.

5 Remove the crêpe from the pan and set aside on a plate covered with a clean, dry kitchen towel. Repeat until you have 8 crêpes.

6 To serve, spread about 1 teaspoon of the Vanilla Mascarpone over each crêpe. Fold 2 crepes in half and then in half again to form triangles. Put them on a serving plate. Garnish each plate with 8 orange segments, 1 tablespoon of the Vanilla Mascarpone, and ¼ cup or less, depending on your taste, of the Blood Orange Sauce. Repeat for a total of 4 servings. *(continued)*

vanilla mascarpone
makes 1 cup

8 ounces mascarpone cheese
Finely grated zest of ½ orange
1 tablespoon vanilla paste (see Note)

1 In a mixing bowl, whip all of the ingredients with a wire whisk until fully incorporated.
2 Reserve for use on crêpes.

note Vanilla paste, also called vanilla purée, is a mixture of finely ground vanilla beans suspended in natural gum and is preferred over vanilla extract when a recipe does not need liquid. Scrape the seeds from a whole vanilla bean into the mascarpone if you cannot find the paste. I do not recommend using extract here, because I don't like the flavor it imparts.

blood orange sauce
makes about 2½ cups

About 2 cups fresh blood orange juice (about 12 oranges)
1½ cups fresh or packaged orange juice, strained
2 tablespoons unsalted butter

1 In a saucepan, heat both juices over medium-high heat. Cook at a rapid simmer until reduced by half to about 1½ cups.
2 Add the butter to the pan and heat gently, stirring, until the butter melts and is fully incorporated. Cover and remove from the heat.

crêpes

Crêpes can be a challenge for the home cook, but if you have mastered pancakes, you can master crêpes. Here's a trick: Let the crêpe batter rest for at least 1 hour and up to 2 hours at room temperature. During this time, the flour expands in the liquid and allows the batter to cook up into light, airy cakes. Here's another trick: Don't pour too much batter into the pan. Crêpes are meant to be thin. To encourage this, let the batter cover the pan in a thin layer as you swirl the pan over the heat. This should not be too difficult with my crêpe batter, because I make it with milk. If you see a recipe that calls for cream, know that the crêpes will be a little thicker.

Finally, don't be discouraged if the first few crêpes don't come out perfectly. Keep trying. Even the most seasoned chef rarely uses the first crêpe of a batch.

panettone french toast
panettone tostato

french toast batter
6 large eggs
2 cups whole milk
2 cups half-and-half
2 tablespoons sugar
1 teaspoon ground cinnamon
¼ vanilla bean, split, or ¼ teaspoon pure vanilla
    extract
Kosher salt

cinnamon whipped cream
1 cup heavy cream
½ tablespoon sugar
Pinch of ground cinnamon

Turn loaves of panettone, which come in those hard-to-miss cubelike boxes, into French toast and you're in for an awesome treat. I got a few loaves for Christmas one year and when one turned mildly stale, I cooked it as French toast for my sons for breakfast. Instant success! I tried it with a fresh loaf and it was even better. Either way, it's over the top. If you don't have panettone on hand, use a high-quality raisin bread or brioche. 🍀 *serves 4*

french toast
8 slices panettone or good-quality raisin bread,
    cut about ½ inch thick
8 tablespoons unsalted butter
Maple syrup
Confectioners' sugar

1   To prepare the French toast batter, whisk the eggs, milk, half-and-half, sugar, cinnamon, and scraped vanilla seeds or extract in a large bowl. Season to taste with salt, transfer to a broad, shallow bowl, and set aside.

2   To prepare the cinnamon whipped cream, in a chilled mixing bowl or the bowl of an electric mixer fitted with the whisk attachment, whisk the cream and sugar until soft peaks form. Sprinkle the cinnamon over the whipped cream and whisk for a little longer, or until the whipped cream thickens a little further. Cover and refrigerate.

3   To prepare the French toast, lay at least 2 slices of bread in the batter and let them soak for 2 to 3 minutes.

4   Meanwhile, in a large nonstick skillet, melt 2 tablespoons of butter over medium heat. When the butter is melted, lift the bread from the batter, let the excess drip off, and cook for about 4 minutes on each side, or until lightly browned and cooked through.

5   Transfer to a serving plate and top with a dollop of whipped cream, a drizzle of syrup, and a sprinkling of confectioners' sugar. Repeat to make 4 servings.

goat cheese and ricotta pancakes

frittelle di caprino e ricotta

4 large eggs, separated
1 cup ricotta cheese
1 cup goat cheese
⅔ cup sour cream
1⅓ cups all-purpose flour
1 tablespoon baking powder
½ teaspoon baking soda
½ teaspoon kosher salt
1½ cups whole milk
Unsalted butter, softened
Maple syrup

Italians don't eat pancakes but Americans love them, whether they are called griddle cakes, flapjacks, or pancakes. I couldn't design a breakfast menu without them and so when I decided to create some, I came up with these, made with a batter rich with goat cheese and ricotta. If you like goat cheese, I promise you will be wild for these.

serves 4; makes about 40 pancakes

1 Preheat the oven to 250°F.

2 In a large mixing bowl, whisk the egg yolks, cheeses, and sour cream until blended.

3 In another bowl, whisk the flour, baking powder, baking soda, and salt. Add to the cheese mixture with the milk and whisk until blended.

4 In the bowl of an electric mixer fitted with the whisk attachment, beat the egg whites on medium speed until soft peaks form. Using a rubber spatula, fold the egg whites into the batter.

5 Heat a griddle or large skillet over medium heat and brush with a little butter.

6 Working in batches, spoon 2 tablespoons of batter for each pancake onto the griddle or into the skillet and cook for about 3 minutes on each side, or until golden brown. Remove to a platter and keep pancakes warm in the oven.

7 Put 10 pancakes on each plate and serve drizzled with syrup.

banana waffles with nutella

cialde di banana con nutella

2 cups all-purpose flour

4 tablespoons sugar

2 teaspoons baking powder

2 teaspoons kosher salt

Pinch of ground cinnamon

Pinch of freshly grated nutmeg

4 large eggs, separated

2 cups whole milk

4 ripe bananas, mashed

¾ cup unsalted butter, melted and cooled

1 cup Nutella

1. In a mixing bowl, whisk the flour, sugar, baking powder, salt, cinnamon, and nutmeg. Set aside.

2. In another mixing bowl, whisk the egg yolks and milk. Add the flour mixture and stir just until blended. Add the bananas and melted butter and mix well.

3. In the bowl of an electric mixer fitted with the whisk attachment, beat the egg whites until stiff peaks form. Gently fold the whites into the batter. Mix only until incorporated. Do not overmix or the egg whites will deflate.

4. Spray a waffle iron with nonstick vegetable cooking spray and heat the iron according to the manufacturer's instructions.

5. Ladle about a quarter of the batter onto the waffle iron and cook until the waffle is lightly browned and lifts easily from the waffle iron. Repeat to make 4 waffles. Serve topped with Nutella.

When I make these waffles, I cook them on a big waffle iron, so that each waffle is about 9 inches in diameter. Your waffle iron may be smaller, but the waffles will be just as addictive! Instead of syrup, I top them with Nutella, a heavenly mixture of chocolate and hazelnuts that was developed in Italy during World War II as a way to "extend" the limited amount of chocolate then available. It caught on in a big way and is enjoyed all over Europe. I am glad to report it is starting to establish a foothold here in the United States—and none too soon! When these banana-flavored waffles are liberally spread with Nutella, they become our version of chocolate chip waffles, in spirit if not literally. ❀ *serves 4*

pork shank hash with fingerling potatoes and fried egg

stinco di maiale con patate e uova fritte

½ pound fingerling potatoes
¼ cup olive oil
Kosher salt and freshly ground black pepper
4 tablespoons unsalted butter
1 large red bell pepper, julienned
2 yellow onions, diced
¾ pound Braised Pork Shank, shredded (recipe follows)
½ cup braising liquid from the pork (recipe follows)
4 large eggs
4 teaspoons chopped fresh flat-leaf parsley

1 Preheat the oven to 350°F.

2 Toss the potatoes with the olive oil and season to taste with salt and pepper. Spread the potatoes on a baking sheet and roast for about 25 minutes, or until tender. Let the potatoes cool to room temperature and then slice into ½-inch slices. Set aside.

3 In a large sauté pan, melt the butter over high heat.

4 Add the potatoes, bell pepper, and onions and sauté for about 5 minutes, or until the bell pepper softens and the potatoes begin to get crispy.

Classic hash and eggs has long been an American diner staple and is one of my all-time favorites. Making hash is also a good way to use meat left over from Saturday-night dinner. I never get up in the morning and say "Let's braise a shank for breakfast," but if one is in the refrigerator or freezer, I go for it!

serves 4

5 Add the pork shank and braising liquid to the pan, stir well, and cook just until heated through. Season to taste with salt and pepper.

6 Meanwhile, fry the eggs in a separate skillet, sunny side up.

7 Divide the hash evenly among 4 shallow bowls or plates and top each serving with 1 egg. Garnish with the chopped parsley and serve.

braised pork shank
makes about ¾ pound meat

2 pounds pork shank (2 shanks)
Kosher salt and freshly ground black pepper
½ onion, cut into large dice
1 small carrot, cut into thick rounds
½ celery rib, cut into large dice
2 tablespoons white wine
1 teaspoon olive oil
1 small garlic clove, smashed
2 black peppercorns
1 teaspoon chopped fresh flat-leaf parsley
1 sprig fresh thyme
½ fresh bay leaf
2 cups chicken stock
2 cups veal stock or chicken stock (see Note)

1 Preheat the oven to 300°F. Put an empty roasting pan in the oven to heat.

2 Season the pork shanks with salt and pepper and put them in the hot roasting pan. Transfer the pan to the stovetop and sear the pork shanks over medium-high heat until lightly browned on all sides,

turning them with tongs. Lift the pork shanks from the pan and set aside. Leave the fat in the pan.

3 Add the onion, carrot, celery, wine, olive oil, garlic, peppercorns, parsley, thyme, and bay leaf to the pan and cook over medium-high heat for about 2 minutes, or until the wine reduces by half. Return the pork shanks to the pan and add the stocks. Bring to a boil over high heat and as soon as the liquid boils, cover the pan and transfer to the oven. Roast for about 4 hours, until the meat is fork tender and just about falling off the bone.

4 Remove the pan from the oven and let the pork shanks cool in the braising liquid.

5 When they are cool, remove the pork shanks, pull the meat from them, and refrigerate the meat for at least 1 hour. You should have about 12 ounces, or ¾ pound. Discard the bone. Strain the braising liquid and refrigerate it.

note Although veal stock makes this especially rich, you can use chicken stock instead. You can buy veal stock in many supermarkets and gourmet markets, so if you see it, keep some on hand.

lardo on toast

bruschetta con lardo

8 thick slices ciabatta or country-style bread
6 tablespoons extra virgin olive oil
1 garlic clove
4 ounces lardo
Kosher salt

In Tuscany, lardo on warm toast is often served with coffee for breakfast. I like it equally well on crusty Italian bread. Lardo is hog fat laced with just a little meat, very similar to our fatback, and cured with salt and flavored with herbs and spices. Don't be put off by its name; lardo literally melts in the mouth with subtle, warm flavor—and is well worth trying! Lardo should always be sliced very thin. *serves 4*

1 Preheat the oven to 400°F.

2 Lay the bread slices on a baking tray and brush with olive oil. Toast in the oven for 2 to 3 minutes, or until lightly browned and crisp on the outside but still soft on the inside.

3 Turn the bread slices over and toast the other side. Rub that side with the garlic clove.

4 Lay the lardo on the warm bread. Season to taste with salt and serve.

cured salmon with potato cake
salmone con torta di patate

salt cure
1½ cups kosher salt
6 tablespoons sugar
¼ cup fennel seeds, toasted and ground
1 fresh bay leaf
1 sprig fresh tarragon
¼ cup olive oil

salmon
1¼-pound piece skinless, boneless salmon

to serve
1 cup sour cream
Kosher salt and freshly ground black pepper
8 caper berries
8 tablespoons diced red onion
4 wedges Potato Cake (page 30)

This is a very popular dish at Osteria di Tramonto. Here I tell you how to cure the salmon, but you can also buy sliced cured salmon (gravlax) at a good deli or specialty market. If you have the time, make your own. It's very easy and tastes just wonderful. And think how proud you will be to serve it!

serves 4

1 To prepare the salt cure, combine 1½ cups of salt with the sugar, fennel seeds, bay leaf, and tarragon in a mixing bowl. Pour the olive oil into the bowl and stir until the mixture resembles wet sand.

2 To prepare the salmon, spread about half of the salt cure in a thin layer on a baking sheet. Lay the salmon on the salt cure, skinned side down, and then pour the remaining salt cure over the salmon. Pat it around and over the salmon so that it is completely covered. Refrigerate for 15 to 24 hours.

3 After refrigerating, lift the salmon from the salt cure and rinse well under cool, running water. Pat dry.

4 Slice the salmon into about 20 thin slices.

5 In a small bowl, stir the sour cream with salt and pepper to taste and set aside.

6 Slice the caper berries in half lengthwise, leaving the stems on the berries.

7 Arrange about 5 slices of salmon on each of 4 plates. Garnish each serving with a quarter of the sour cream, caper berries, and diced onion. Serve with a wedge of warm Potato Cake.

(continued)

potato cake
serves 4

4 russet potatoes, peeled and grated (about 5 cups)
Kosher salt and freshly ground black pepper
1 cup (2 sticks) unsalted butter
½ cup unsweetened applesauce

1   In a mixing bowl, toss the potatoes with salt and pepper and set aside for about 5 minutes to allow the salt to pull moisture from the potatoes. Drain all excess liquid.

2   Melt all but 2 tablespoons of the butter. Pour over the potatoes, cover with plastic wrap, and set aside.

3   In a nonstick sauté pan, melt 2 tablespoons of butter over medium-high heat. Scoop half of the potato mixture into the pan and spread it into an even layer. Top with the applesauce, spreading it evenly over the potatoes. Finally, spread the rest of the potatoes over the applesauce. Press on the cake with the back of a spoon or a spatula to compress it.

4   Cook for about 15 minutes, or until the potatoes on the bottom are golden brown. Drain the excess butter from the pan, turn the cake over, and cook for about 5 minutes longer, draining excess butter as needed, until the cake is crisp.

5   Drain excess grease from the pan and flip the cake. Allow this side to cook until it is crisp and the potatoes on the bottom are golden brown. Drain excess grease as needed.

6   Drain the cake on paper towels, patting the top to sop up excess grease. Cut into quarters and serve warm.

half grapefruit with mint syrup

pompelmo con sciroppo di menta

1 white grapefruit
½ cup Mint Syrup (recipe follows)
2 Ruby Red grapefruit, halved
4 tablespoons sugar
12 fresh raspberries
4 fresh sprigs mint, stems removed

1   Peel the white grapefruit and divide it into segments. You will need 12 segments.

2   In a mixing bowl, toss the white grapefruit segments with the Mint Syrup and set aside.

3   Using a paring knife or serrated grapefruit knife, cut around the edges of each segment of the Ruby Red grapefruit halves to make the segments easy to remove from the shell with a spoon. Put each grapefruit half in a bowl.

4   Sprinkle each grapefruit half with 1 tablespoon of sugar. Run a small blowtorch over each grapefruit half for about 20 seconds, or until the sugar just starts to turn brown and caramelize. If you don't have a blowtorch, put the grapefruit under a hot broiler for a minute until the sugar melts and begins to caramelize. Watch carefully to avoid blackening the sugar.

5   Top each half with 3 of the white grapefruit segments and then garnish each with 3 raspberries and a mint sprig and serve.

mint syrup

makes about 1 cup

½ cup sugar
1 small bunch fresh mint leaves
¼ vanilla bean, split, or 1 teaspoon pure vanilla extract

1   In a saucepan, stir together 1 cup of water and the sugar and bring to a boil over high heat. Remove from the heat and add the mint leaves and vanilla bean or extract. Set aside for about 10 minutes.

2   Strain the syrup into a glass or plastic storage container and discard the mint leaves and vanilla bean. Cover and refrigerate for at least 1 hour, or until cold. Use right away or cover and refrigerate for up to 1 week.

Everyone likes a half grapefruit, served unadorned or perhaps with a sprinkling of sugar. Here's a slightly dressed-up version, with white grapefruit sections scattered over halved Ruby Red grapefruit. The naturally bitter citrus fruit is sweetened with a minty sugar syrup for an easy but elegant breakfast dish. ❈ *serves 4*

pear smoothies
frullato di pere ❀ *serves 4*

1½ pounds ripe pears, peeled and cored
1 cup chopped banana
2 cups apple juice
1 cup Simple Syrup (recipe follows)
¼ teaspoon pure vanilla extract
6 to 8 ice cubes
Juice of ½ lemon

Put the pears, banana, apple juice, syrup, and vanilla in the jar of a blender. Add the ice and purée until smooth. Add the lemon juice and pulse. Pour into 4 tall chilled glasses and serve.

plum smoothies
frullato di prugne ❀ *serves 4*

1½ pounds frozen plums, peeled and cored
2 cups Simple Syrup (recipe follows)
1 cup plain yogurt
1½ teaspoons finely minced ginger
6 to 8 ice cubes
Juice of ½ lime
2 tablespoons chopped fresh mint

Put the plums, syrup, yogurt, and ginger in the jar of a blender. Add the ice and purée until smooth. Add the lime juice and mint and pulse. Pour into 4 tall chilled glasses and serve.

berry smoothies
frullato di bosco ❀ *serves 4*

12 ounces strawberries (about 2 cups)
12 ounces blueberries (about 1¾ cups)
3 cups orange juice
½ cup Simple Syrup (recipe follows)
6 to 8 ice cubes
Juice of ½ lemon
½ cup chopped toasted almonds, optional

Put the strawberries, blueberries, orange juice, and syrup in the jar of a blender. Add the ice and purée until smooth. Add the lemon juice and pulse. Strain for seeds if needed. Pour into 4 tall chilled glasses, garnish with almonds, if desired, and serve.

peach vanilla smoothies
frullato di pesche e vaniglia
❀ *serves 4*

12 ounces peaches, peeled and cored
1 banana
2 cups pineapple juice
1 cup vanilla yogurt or ½ cup silken tofu mixed with ½ cup yogurt
6 to 8 ice cubes

Put the peaches, banana, pineapple juice, and yogurt in the jar of a blender. Add the ice and purée until smooth. Pour into 4 tall chilled glasses and serve.

simple syrup
makes about 2 cups

2 cups sugar
2 cups water

1 In a medium saucepan, combine the sugar and water over medium heat and stir until the sugar dissolves. Raise the heat, bring to a boil, and remove from the heat. Set aside to cool.

2 Transfer to a container with a tight-fitting lid and refrigerate for up to 1 week.

smoothies

Smoothies are a great breakfast opener and a delicious way to use fruit that might be reaching the end of its peak. In Italy, they may be called *frullati*.

Smoothies are fun and easy to make, and I often whip them up for the kids when I cook breakfast on Sundays. Because of the fruit, they are seasonal and make great little *amuses* before breakfast or brunch, or really any other meal.

I like to use the best ripe or slightly overripe seasonal fruit I can find, but if you just can't get hold of any, then high-quality, unsweetened, quick-frozen fruit is a great substitute. I think the best fruit to use is any with a few soft spots, which indicates it is slightly overripe and so the sugar content will be high. If the fruit is very sweet, you can eliminate the sugar syrup I call for in my recipes. In the end, rely on your own creativity and choose oranges, bananas, pineapples, cranberries, raspberries, blackberries, strawberries, or grapes. You can use any kind of fruit juice, too, such as apple, orange, or grape. There are no rules! Any soft fruit, even melon, works well.

If you don't have enough fresh fruit on hand, or to make the smoothie a little thicker, add a few more ice cubes to the blender. Although I like yogurt for most smoothies, you can replace it with another creamy substance such as coconut milk or soy milk. Even peanut butter is a good thickener. I sometimes add a few spoonfuls of protein powder or tofu to boost the healthful-ness of the drink. In fact, if anyone asks me if I like tofu, I answer, "Yes, but only in smoothies!"

The blender you use should be powerful enough to make the process a pleasure. Once they are whipped up in the blender, the smoothies must be served right away, cold and in chilled glasses. You can garnish them with fresh herbs, such as mint and basil, for an extra touch. I finish them with a little squirt of lemon or lime juice, as I find the acid brings up the flavor. If you feel like getting fancy, coat the rim of each glass with sugar, just as you would use salt for margaritas.

░ sandwiches

Sandwiches are happily playful, which is one of the reasons I love them so much. You can put just about anything between two slices of bread and enjoy it, and then pair it with little treats such as pickles, hot vinegared peppers, chips, and small salads.

In America, the sandwich is mostly about the filling, while in Italy every sandwich starts with great bread and the filling generally is lighter and simpler. Good Italian sandwiches are found all over. Even the Autogrill, the roadside chain along Italy's *autostrade,* serves outstanding panini—all its food is good, actually—and I never miss an opportunity to stop at one of these Italian versions of a fast-food restaurant and indulge.

The best Italian sandwiches, regardless of where they are made, use the finest salamis, vegetables, and cheeses. But still, it is critical to have good bread. Look for it at farmers' markets, specialty shops, and small bakeries. Even some supermarkets sell good, crusty bread these days. Once you find a loaf, try to eat it right away. It's best consumed on the day it is baked.

At the osteria, many customers come for lunch and eat at the bar. We serve numerous sandwiches, and I never tire of coming up with different ones. This chapter is a sampling of some of my favorites. It was hard to know where to stop!

notes from the sommelier
the gauntlet

We take writing our wine lists incredibly seriously. It is a family affair with Chef Tramonto and all our sommeliers, with my participation. We want to provide for our guests at the osteria the smartest, most comprehensive, and most value-driven collection of Italian wines possible, without overrunning every nook and cranny of storage space in the restaurant (fine with me, but not fine for the chef). Although it is easy to stock our cellars with verticals of the legendary, high-scoring, oft-written-about luxury wines such as Gaja Barbaresco, Conterno Barolo, and Super Tuscans such as Sassicaia and Masseto, we revel in the challenge of finding the most interesting and tasty Piedirosso, Pigato, and Procanico to tempt our guests.

To that end, when the restaurant was under construction and still uninhabitable, we found ourselves in a whirlwind of tasting appointments off site, often up to eight hours straight, auditioning hundreds of wines daily for several weeks. Each day, we asked our trusted wine sellers to bring only the wines of a particular region of Italy.

Alto Adige day seems to always be a bit easier, as these northern wines tend to have a nice palate-cleansing and reviving acidity that certainly helps when there are so many wines to taste. On that day we taste wines like crisp, clean Sauvignon Blanc from Zemmer and the elegant Chardonnays of Elena Walch, both made from international grape varieties, and Hofstatter Pinot Bianco and Mayr-Nusser Lagrein made from homegrown grapes.

On the other hand, Tuscany day can be a tough one, with all of the rich, high-octane reds that are typically presented, and for the tremendous number of high-quality wines that we just cannot bring ourselves to forgo swallowing. Tuscany provides us with glassfuls of the classic Sangiovese-based Chianti, Brunello di Montalcino, and Vino Nobile di Montepulciano, and their more reasonably priced facsimilies: Sangiovese Toscana, Rosso di Montalcino, and Rosso di Montepulciano. The neoclassic Tuscan reds include the blends in which Sangiovese is married with grapes like Cabernet Sauvignon, Merlot, and Syrah. These are the Super Tuscan wines.

We call these few weeks of intense wine tasting "The Gauntlet." As much fun as it sounds, you realize that tasting can actually be very hard work.

Thank goodness for the chef's sandwiches: Sicilian Tuna to revive the palate after all of that Sicilian Nero d'Avola, Bresaola and Arugula on Lombardy day when we have been drinking Sforzato di Valtellina and its simpler cousin, Rosso di Valtellina, both made from Chiavennesca—all perfect vehicles for bringing our palates and ourselves back to life!

open-face bresaola and arugula sandwich

ciabatta con bresaola e rucola

4 ciabatta rolls or other large crusty rolls

4 teaspoons extra virgin olive oil

3 cups arugula (about 2½ ounces)

4 teaspoons fresh lemon juice

Kosher salt and freshly ground black pepper

8 to 10 ounces Bresaola, thinly sliced

2 ounces Parmigiano-Reggiano cheese, shaved
   (about 2 tablespoons)

1 Preheat the oven to 300°F.

2 Split the rolls in half without cutting all the way through. The rolls should lie flat when opened but still be connected.

3 Lightly brush the cut portions of the rolls with olive oil. Transfer the rolls to a baking sheet, spread open and facing up, and warm them in the oven for about 5 minutes.

4 Meanwhile, in a mixing bowl, toss the arugula with the lemon juice and season to taste with salt and pepper.

5 Remove the warm bread from the oven and top the bottom half of each roll with an equal amount of Bresaola. Top the Bresaola with the arugula salad and then with shaved cheese. Serve as open-face sandwiches.

This is about as straightforward a sandwich as you will find. It has only a few ingredients, so they have to be the best of the best! I was inspired to create this after a trip to Italy when I stopped in nearly every small, family-run osteria and *enoteca* (wine bar) I came across. Very often these restaurants had been in the family for generations, and I loved sitting at the bar with a glass of wine and a few open-face sandwiches. Bresaola is air-dried, cured beef from Lombardy. The sandwich is so simple, yet so good! *serves 4*

lobster salad sandwich

panino con insalata d'aragosta

4 teaspoons kosher salt

2 cups dry white wine

4 sprigs fresh flat-leaf parsley

2 sprigs fresh thyme

1 teaspoon black peppercorns

One 1½-pound live lobster

¾ cup Rick's Homemade Aioli (recipe follows)

2 scallions (white and green parts), finely sliced

2 tablespoons finely diced celery

2 tablespoons Dijon mustard

2 tablespoons fresh lemon juice

1 tablespoon chopped fresh tarragon

Pinch of cayenne

8 slices soft white bread, crusts removed

Lobster rolls, especially those made in Maine during the summer months, are pure luxury even though they are simple fare, with good-sized chunks of fresh Atlantic lobster nestled in soft rolls. In Italy, you can buy slender sandwiches filled with seafood salads, wrapped in paper so that you can savor them as you walk along the glittering Mediterranean. This sandwich is my marriage of the two. Start with a live lobster if you can; otherwise, buy the best, freshest cooked lobster meat available. You could also substitute a pound or so of shrimp or crab for the lobster.

serves 4

1. In a large saucepan, bring 1 quart of water, 3 teaspoons of salt, and the wine, parsley, thyme, and peppercorns to a boil over high heat.

2. Drop the lobster into the boiling liquid, head first, and cover the pan. When the liquid returns to a boil, cook for 8 to 10 minutes, or until the shell turns bright red. Set aside to cool in the cooking liquid. When it is cool, refrigerate the lobster and its cooking liquid.

3. When the lobster is cold, drain the liquid from the lobster and discard it. Pull the meat from the lobster's tail and claws. Discard the shells. Dice the lobster meat into bite-sized pieces.

4. In a bowl, toss the lobster with the aioli, scallions, celery, mustard, lemon juice, tarragon, cayenne, and remaining teaspoon of salt until well mixed. Set aside at room temperature for 1 hour to allow the flavors to blend. If not using after 1 hour, refrigerate until ready to use.

5. Place a slice of bread on each of 4 serving plates. Divide the lobster salad evenly among the slices. Top each with another slice of bread and gently press on the bread to spread the lobster salad nearly to the edges. Crimp the edges of the bread with a fork or your fingers to seal the lobster inside.

6. Cut each sandwich in half and serve.

rick's homemade aioli
makes about 3 cups

2 large egg yolks
1 garlic clove, minced
2 cups extra virgin olive oil
1 cup vegetable oil
Juice of 3 lemons
Kosher salt

1 In a mixing bowl, whisk the egg yolks and garlic with 1 tablespoon of water. Begin adding the olive oil in a very thin, steady stream, whisking as you do so. When about half has been incorporated, you can add it a little more quickly. When the olive oil is incorporated, whisk in the vegetable oil in the same fashion. Alternatively, you could make the aioli in a blender and pour the oils through the feed tube.

2 Whisk in the lemon juice. Season to taste with salt. Cover and refrigerate until ready to use. The aioli will keep for up to 7 days.

sicilian tuna sandwich

panino con tonno siciliano

8 slices whole-grain bread
1 fennel bulb, trimmed and shaved
¼ cup drained capers, rinsed
Twelve ½-inch-thick tomato slices
8 leaves romaine lettuce, ribs removed and leaves
  halved
3 cups Tuna Salad (recipe follows)

1 Lightly toast the bread slices.
2 Place a slice of bread on each of 4 serving
   plates. On each slice, lay a quarter of the
   shaved fennel, 1 tablespoon of capers,
   3 tomato slices, and 2 romaine leaves. Top
   with equal amounts of the Tuna Salad and
   then the remaining slices of bread. Press
   down gently and then cut each sandwich in
   half and serve.

This sandwich is as much about the tuna as
anything else. The salad is pretty classic, made
with celery, scallions, and pickles, but when
you make it with imported Italian tuna, it
takes on a new dimension you may not have
experienced. Sure, you can make this with any
canned tuna you have in the cupboard, but
once you taste the imported Italian tuna,
which is far richer than other types, you will
recognize it for the treat it is!

   You could buy good pickles to use in the
tuna salad, but I hope you'll try making your
own. Get some really good cucumbers and go
to town. It's surprising how easy pickling is,
and yet it's almost a lost art. ❋ *serves 4*

tuna salad
makes about 3 cups

Three 6-ounce cans tuna packed in olive oil,
  drained and chopped (see Note)
3 tablespoons finely diced celery
3 tablespoons minced House-Made Pickles
  (page 42)
3 tablespoons sliced scallions
3 teaspoons chopped fresh flat-leaf parsley
3 teaspoons chopped fresh tarragon
3 teaspoons snipped fresh chives
6 tablespoons Rick's Homemade Aioli (page 39)
Kosher salt and freshly ground black pepper

1 In a large mixing bowl, combine the tuna,
   celery, pickles, scallions, parsley, tarragon,
   chives, and aioli. Season to taste with salt
   and pepper. Mix well.
2 Cover and refrigerate until ready to use.
   The Tuna Salad will keep for up to 1 day.

note I use imported Italian tuna packed in
olive oil, but not everyone has access to this
excellent canned product, nor do they want to
spend the money for it. Use your favorite
brand of domestic tuna, preferably packed in
oil, if you can't find an Italian brand. If you do
find it and can afford it, you will discover as I
have that the imported stuff is well worth the
extra cost! *(continued)*

house-made pickles
makes about 6 cups

12 Kirby cucumbers, sliced ¼ inch thick on the
    diagonal (about 6 cups)
3 yellow onions, sliced into half moons
6 tablespoons kosher salt
6 cups white vinegar
3 cups sugar
⅓ cup celery seeds
3 teaspoons mustard seeds
1½ teaspoons crushed red pepper flakes

1. In a large mixing bowl, combine the cucumbers and onions. Add the salt, toss to mix, and set aside for 1 hour.

2. In a large saucepan, combine 9 cups of water with the vinegar, sugar, celery seeds, mustard seeds, and red pepper and bring to a boil over high heat.

3. Meanwhile, rinse the salt off the cucumbers and onions and return to the bowl. As soon as the vinegar mixture boils, pour it over the cucumbers. Let it cool to room temperature.

4. Transfer the pickles to scrupulously clean jars. Screw on the lids. They will keep for up to 2 weeks in the refrigerator.

tramonto hero
hero di tramonto

Four 6-inch Italian hero rolls
½ cup Mustard Mayonnaise (recipe follows)
2 cups finely shredded romaine lettuce
8 ounces thinly sliced provolone cheese
8 ounces thinly sliced hard salami
8 ounces thinly sliced Calabrese salami
1 cup shaved fennel
2 Roma tomatoes, sliced ½ inch thick
Kosher salt and freshly ground black pepper
¼ cup Green Olive Tapenade (recipe follows)
½ cup Homemade Giardiniera (page 44)

1 Slice each roll lengthwise and lightly toast all halves. Spread each toasted half with Mustard Mayonnaise and then set the top halves aside.

2 On the bottom half of each roll, build the sandwich, dividing the romaine, provolone, salamis, fennel, and tomatoes evenly among them. Season to taste with salt and pepper. Top the tomatoes with equal amounts of Green Olive Tapenade and Homemade Giardiniera.

3 Put the top halves on the sandwiches, press together gently, and serve.

This is one great sandwich. Call it a hero or a sub, but you won't be disappointed when you build it. You can select different meats and cheeses to suit your taste, but those listed here are my favorites. When I was growing up, my friends and I got our subs from Rubino's, an old-style Italian sandwich shop in Rochester, New York, known for the best subs in town. They put black or green tapenade and homemade giardiniera on their sandwiches, and so that's the way I like to make them, too. My recipe for giardiniera makes about 6 cups, which is more than you will need, but it keeps very well and is a great condiment to have around. Add some good, crusty bread and you have a sandwich that can't be beat. Thank you, Rubino family! ❀ *serves 4*

mustard mayonnaise
makes about ⅔ cup

½ cup mayonnaise
2 tablespoons Dijon mustard
1½ teaspoons chopped fresh tarragon
1 teaspoon fresh lemon juice
Kosher salt and freshly ground black pepper

In a mixing bowl, whisk the mayonnaise, mustard, tarragon, and lemon juice. Season to taste with salt and pepper. Use immediately or cover and refrigerate for up to 3 days.

green olive tapenade
makes about 3 cups

2 roasted red bell peppers, peeled and finely diced (see page 11)
1 cup pitted and chopped green Cerignola olives
2 anchovy fillets, drained and crushed
2 tablespoons drained capers, rinsed and smashed
1 tablespoon red wine vinegar
6 tablespoons extra virgin olive oil   *(continued)*

¼ cup chopped fresh flat-leaf parsley
Freshly ground black pepper
Kosher salt

1 In a nonreactive glass or ceramic mixing bowl, combine the bell peppers, olives, anchovies, capers, and vinegar. Add the olive oil and parsley and about 1 teaspoon of black pepper and stir gently to mix well. Season to taste with salt.

2 Cover and refrigerate for up to 7 days.

homemade giardiniera
makes about 6 cups

1 teaspoon freshly ground black pepper
1 bay leaf
Pinch of crushed red pepper flakes
Pinch of dried oregano
2 cups apple cider vinegar
1 cup white wine vinegar
1 cup sugar
1 teaspoon kosher salt
1 fennel bulb, trimmed of fronds, diced
1 large red onion, diced
1 celery rib, diced
1 large carrot, peeled and diced
1 large red bell pepper, ribs removed, diced
1 large yellow bell pepper, ribs removed, diced
1 jalapeño pepper, halved and seeded
1 cup cauliflower florets
1 cup pitted and halved Queen green olives or other large green olives
3 pickled peperoncini, sliced (see Note)
1 fresh sprig thyme
1 cup extra virgin olive oil

1 In a small, dry skillet set over medium-high heat, toast the black pepper, bay leaf, red pepper, and oregano for about 1 minute, or until fragrant. Slide from the pan to a plate and allow to cool.

2 Lay a 5- to 6-inch square of cheesecloth on a work surface. When the herbs are cool, pile them in the center. Gather the corners together and tie with a length of string to make an herb sachet.

3 In a large pot, heat 2 cups of water and the cider vinegar, wine vinegar, sugar, salt, and herb sachet over high heat and bring to a boil.

4 Add the fennel, onion, celery, carrot, bell peppers, jalapeño, and cauliflower. Let the liquid return to a boil, reduce the heat to a simmer, and cook for 10 to 12 minutes, or until the firmer vegetables (carrots, peppers, cauliflower) are al dente.

5 Remove from the heat and let cool. When the mixture is cool, add the olives, peperoncini, and thyme. Stir to mix, and then stir in the olive oil. Use right away or cover and refrigerate for up to 1 month.

note Peperoncini are also called Tuscan peppers or sweet Italian peppers. They are 2 to 3 inches long and taper to a point. Peperoncini, which can be green or red when picked, have a mild flavor with just a hint of heat and are sold pickled in jars.

parmesan-crusted chicken pesto sandwich

ciabatta con pollo impanato in parmigiano e pesto

4 ciabatta rolls or other large crusty rolls
4 tablespoons unsalted butter, softened
2 cups freshly grated Parmigiano-Reggiano cheese
4 ounces sliced provolone cheese
2 cups Roasted Pesto Chicken (recipe follows)
4 cups Italian Vegetables (page 46)

1 Preheat the oven to 350°F.

2 Slice each roll in half lengthwise and spread the outside crusts of the rolls with butter. Pat the butter-coated sides of the rolls with the Parmigiano-Reggiano until they are fully coated. Toast lightly in a sauté pan, buttered sides down, over medium heat, until lightly browned.

3 Divide the provolone evenly among the bottom halves of each roll, laying it on the cut sides of the rolls.

4 If the Roasted Pesto Chicken and Italian Vegetables have been refrigerated, warm them in separate saucepans until nearly hot. Top each sandwich with a quarter of the chicken and a quarter of the vegetables.

5 Arrange the open-face sandwiches in a baking pan and bake for 3 to 4 minutes, or until the provolone melts. Sprinkle with any remaining grated Parmigiano-Reggiano and top with the remaining roll halves. Press lightly to compress, slice in half, and serve.

roasted pesto chicken
makes about 6 cups

One 3½-pound chicken
2 to 3 tablespoons olive oil
Kosher salt and freshly ground black pepper
¾ cup Basil Pesto (page 46)

1 Preheat the oven to 400°F.

2 Rub the chicken with the olive oil and then season liberally with salt and pepper. Transfer the chicken to a small roasting pan and roast for 40 to 60 minutes, until cooked through and the thigh juices run clear when pierced with the tip of a small knife. If you use an instant-read thermometer, the breast meat will register 170°F when done.

3 Remove the chicken from the roasting pan and set aside to cool. When it is cool enough to handle but still warm, pull the meat from the bones, discarding the skin and the bones. Tear or chop the meat into bite-sized pieces and transfer to a mixing bowl.

4 Toss the meat with the Basil Pesto. Use right away or cover and refrigerate until ready to use. The chicken can be prepared up to 24 hours ahead of time. *(continued)*

Don't worry, making this sandwich need not be a production where you start by cooking a chicken. You can easily use leftover chicken. If you do take the time to roast the chicken for the sandwich, you'll want to use homemade pesto, which is easy to whip up in the food processor and makes everything just a little better. What I like so much about this sandwich is that as much attention is paid to the outside of the sandwich as to the filling. The crusty sides of the rolls are coated with cheese for jolts of flavor with every bite. *serves 4*

basil pesto
makes about 2 cups

8 ounces fresh basil leaves (about 2 cups, packed)
1⅔ cups extra virgin olive oil, plus more to cover
1¼ cups freshly grated Parmigiano-Reggiano cheese
1½ teaspoons finely minced garlic
1½ teaspoons kosher salt
4 ounces (about ½ cup) toasted pine nuts (see Note)

1 Put all of the ingredients in the bowl of a food processor fitted with the metal blade and process until smooth.

2 Transfer to a storage container with a tight-fitting lid and cover with about ½ inch of olive oil, so the pesto does not oxidize. Cover and refrigerate for up to 10 days or until needed.

note To toast the pine nuts, spread them in a small, dry skillet and toast over medium-high heat, stirring occasionally, for 1 to 1½ minutes, or until they darken a shade or two and are fragrant.

italian vegetables
makes about 4 cups

2 tablespoons olive oil
1½ cups sliced button mushrooms
1 fennel bulb, trimmed of fronds, thinly sliced
2 yellow onions, thinly sliced
2 red bell peppers, thinly sliced
Kosher salt and freshly ground black pepper

1 Heat a large sauté pan over high heat. When the pan is hot, heat the olive oil. Add the mushrooms, reduce the heat slightly, and cook for 5 to 7 minutes, or until nicely browned and caramelized.

2 Add the fennel and onions and cook for about 5 minutes, or until fully wilted. Add the bell peppers and season to taste with salt and pepper. Cook for about 3 minutes, or until the bell peppers are just tender.

3 Remove from the heat and set aside, covered, to keep warm. Use hot or lukewarm.

caprese sandwich

panino caprese

4 tablespoons unsalted butter, softened

Eight ½-inch-thick slices ciabatta or Italian country-style bread

½ cup Basil Pesto (page 46)

12 ounces fresh mozzarella cheese, sliced ½ inch thick

Twelve ½-inch-thick tomato slices

Kosher salt and freshly ground black pepper

About 1 teaspoon olive oil

How could I write a sandwich chapter and not include this most classic of all Italian sandwiches, the *caprese*? My dad, Frank, loved to make this, although he added white anchovies to it and usually made it with tomatoes he grew himself every summer. If you do not have a panini press, use a heated cast-iron skillet as a weight placed on top of the sandwich as it cooks. When you have summer's best tomatoes, homemade pesto, and some really great mozzarella, you can't go wrong. *serves 4*

1 Butter one side of each slice of bread and top with 1 tablespoon of Basil Pesto. Top 4 of the bread slices with equal amounts of mozzarella and 3 tomato slices. Season to taste with salt and pepper and top with the remaining bread slices, pesto side down.

2 Heat the olive oil in a small skillet over medium-high heat, or brush a panini press with olive oil and preheat to high. If you use a skillet, grill each sandwich for 2 to 3 minutes on each side, or until the bread is golden brown and the cheese melts. During cooking, weight the sandwich with a heated cast-iron skillet. When one side of the sandwich is golden brown, turn it over and press the sandwich with a spatula. Weight it again. If you use a panini press, grill each sandwich for about 4 minutes, or until the bread is golden brown and the cheese melts.

3 Cut each sandwich in half and serve.

melted cheese panini with honey and mustard

panino con formaggio sciolto, miele e senape

4 tablespoons whole-grain mustard

Eight ½-inch-thick slices ciabatta or Italian country-style bread

6 ounces Scamorza cheese, cut into 8 thin slices (see Note)

4 ounces Burrata cheese, cut into 4 slices (see Note)

4 ounces fontina cheese, cut into 4 slices

1 ounce Parmigiano-Reggiano cheese, shaved (about 1 tablespoon)

Kosher salt and freshly ground black pepper

2 tablespoons unsalted butter, softened

About 1 teaspoon olive oil

2 tablespoons honey

1 Spread the mustard on 1 side of each slice of bread. Set 4 slices aside.

2 Top each of 4 slices with 2 slices of Scamorza, a slice of Burrata, and a slice of fontina. Distribute the Parmigiano-Reggiano among all 4 sandwiches. Season lightly to taste with salt and pepper. Top with the remaining 4 slices of bread, mustard side down.

3 Using a pastry brush, brush the butter over both sides of the sandwiches.

4 Heat the olive oil in a small skillet over medium-high heat, or brush a panini press with olive oil and preheat to high. If you use a skillet, grill each sandwich for 2 to 3 minutes on each side, or until the bread is golden brown and the cheese melts. When one side of the sandwich is golden brown, turn it over and press the sandwich with a spatula or weight with a heated cast-iron skillet. If you use a panini press, grill each sandwich for about 8 minutes, or until the bread is golden brown and the cheese melts.

5 Cut the sandwiches into rectangles and slice the rectangles into bricks, or bars, each about 1 inch long. Stack on plates for serving and drizzle with the honey.

note Scamorza cheese is a little like mozzarella but denser, drier, and chewier with a mild saltiness. It's often made from buffalo milk but just as often is made from cow's milk. If you've never tried it, try it now. It's delicious on its own with a little pepper and a drizzle of olive oil.

Burrata is another mozzarella-like cheese that may be hard to find outside Italy or large American cities, but if you see it, grab it! It is made from the creamy remnants of mozzarella; though the Scamorza is a little dry, this cheese is creamy and rich.

Smoked mozzarella is a good substitute for either of these cheeses.

I love how mustard accentuates the flavors of these mild, meltable cheeses and then the honey, drizzled over the panini before serving, brings the sandwich home. You experience a new sensation with every bite, akin to the sweet and sour flavors so loved by so many. Yet this is nothing more exotic than a grilled cheese sandwich! *serves 4*

eggplant parmesan sandwich

panino con melanzane alla parmigiana

2 cups all-purpose flour

Kosher salt and freshly ground black pepper

6 large eggs

2 cups panko

½ cup freshly grated Parmigiano-Reggiano cheese

2 large eggplant (about 2½ pounds), peeled and
    sliced lengthwise into 16 thin slices

½ cup olive oil

4 cups Pomodoro Sauce (page 16)

Sixteen ¼-inch-thick slices provolone cheese

Four 6-inch Italian hero rolls

Extra virgin olive oil

¼ cup finely sliced fresh basil

This is a classic Italian-American sandwich. The best way to make it is with leftover eggplant Parmesan, but because not everyone has it in the refrigerator, I explain how to make it from scratch. When I was a kid, my mom always made more than we needed and put half the pan away for sandwiches the next day or the day after. She put mayonnaise on her sandwich, which never appealed to me, but my dad and I made ours exactly as I describe here and always ate them hot. *serves 4*

1 Mix the flour with enough salt and pepper to season it in a mixing bowl. Whisk the eggs and ¾ of cup water in a second bowl. Mix the panko and half of the Parmigiano-Reggiano in a third bowl.

2 One at a time dredge each eggplant slice in the flour, dip it in the egg wash, and then coat with the panko mixture. Transfer to a baking sheet or rack.

3 Meanwhile, heat the olive oil in a nonstick skillet over high heat and cook each eggplant slice for 3 to 4 minutes on each side, or until golden brown on both sides. Drain the eggplant on paper towels. Do not crowd the pan with eggplant, add more olive oil as needed during cooking.

4 Preheat the oven to 350°F.

5 In a 9 × 13-inch baking pan, spread a layer of Pomodoro Sauce over the bottom. Layer the eggplant slices and provolone in the pan, spreading a layer of sauce between each layer of eggplant and cheese. End with a layer of sauce. Sprinkle the remaining Parmigiano-Reggiano over the top of the casserole.

6 Bake for 25 to 35 minutes, until the cheese melts and browns lightly.

7 While the casserole bakes, split each roll in half and brush each half with olive oil. Toast the rolls lightly in a sauté pan over medium heat, oiled sides down, until light brown.

8 Spoon the hot eggplant mixture over the bottom halves of the rolls and gently press the top halves of the rolls over the eggplant mixture. Garnish with the basil and serve.

grilled vegetable sandwich on focaccia

verdure grigliate su focaccia

½ small eggplant, peeled and sliced ½ inch thick

1 zucchini, sliced lengthwise ½ inch thick

3 tablespoons extra virgin olive oil, plus a little
more for dressing the arugula

2 teaspoons minced garlic

1 teaspoon chopped fresh oregano

¼ cup chopped fresh flat-leaf parsley

4 teaspoons fresh lemon juice, plus a little more
for dressing the arugula

Kosher salt and freshly ground black pepper

4 focaccia rolls (small squares of focaccia bread)

¼ cup sliced roasted red bell pepper (see page 9)

About 3 cups arugula

4 ounces provolone cheese, sliced ½ inch thick

Look for the freshest vegetables at your local farmers' market when you make this sandwich. If you see some that I don't list here, such as fennel, mushrooms, or peppers, grab them. Grilling brings out the flavor of these fresh ingredients, making a truly outstanding sandwich. *serves 4*

1 Prepare a charcoal or gas grill by spraying the grilling rack with nonstick vegetable spray. Heat the grill until medium-hot.

2 In a mixing bowl, toss the eggplant and zucchini with about 1 tablespoon of olive oil, 1 teaspoon of garlic, and the oregano. Transfer the vegetables to the grill and cook, turning once, for 2 to 3 minutes, or until softened and lightly browned. If necessary, use a grilling basket for the vegetables so that they don't slip through the grill rack.

3 Return the grilled vegetables to the bowl and while still warm toss with the parsley, lemon juice, and 1 teaspoon of garlic. Season to taste with salt and pepper.

4 To assemble the sandwiches, slice each focaccia roll in half lengthwise. Top the bottom half of each roll with equal amounts of the vegetables and the bell pepper. Dress the arugula with a touch of lemon juice and olive oil. Top the vegetables with equal amounts of arugula and cheese. Lay the top half of each roll over the cheese and press gently to close.

5 Heat 2 tablespoons of olive oil in a small skillet over medium-high heat, or brush a panini press with olive oil and preheat to high. If you use a skillet, grill each sandwich for 2 to 3 minutes on each side, or until the bread is golden brown and the cheese melts. When one side of the sandwich is golden brown, turn it over and press the sandwich with a spatula. If you use a panini press, grill each sandwich for about 4 minutes, or until the bread is golden brown and the cheese melts.

6 Cut each sandwich in half and serve.

genoa ham and green olive tapenade sandwich

panino con prosciutto di genova e tapenade di olive

One 6-inch ciabatta roll or baguette, or eight
   ½-inch-thick slices Italian country-style bread
10 ounces sliced smoked ham
8 ounces sliced fontina cheese
12 tablespoons Green Olive Tapenade (page 43)
½ cup unsalted butter, softened
1 teaspoon olive oil

Wait until you taste this classic ham sandwich from Turin, Italy! I used to work with a guy we called Uncle Phil who was from Turin, and he used to make these all the time. I had never heard of putting green olives in a ham sandwich, but why not? And are these good!

serves 4

1 Slice each roll in half lengthwise. Top the bottom half with equal amounts of ham, cheese, and Green Olive Tapenade. Lay the top half of each roll over the tapenade and press gently to close.

2 Brush both sides of each sandwich with butter.

3 Heat the olive oil in a small skillet over medium-high heat or brush a panini press with olive oil and preheat to high. If you use a skillet, grill each sandwich for 2 to 3 minutes on each side, or until the bread is golden brown and the cheese melts. When one side of the sandwich is golden brown, turn it over and press the sandwich with a spatula. If you use a panini press, grill each sandwich for about 8 minutes, or until the bread is golden brown and the cheese melts.

4 Cut each sandwich in half and serve.

soups and salads

For someone who has been cooking professionally for more than 30 years, choosing just four soups to include in this chapter was a challenge. Soup is always on a restaurant menu, and I am inspired by the seasons and the ingredients on hand to make scores of different soups. I could write an entire book on soup! In the end, I chose four tried-and-true soups that have long been among my favorites and that remind me of my childhood, when a bowl of piping hot soup and a chunk of bread meant life was safe, warm, and wonderful.

Unlike with soups, I didn't grow up eating salads, but I have learned to appreciate them as an adult. When I travel in Italy, I eat the most incredible salads and have come to understand that the freshness and quality of the ingredients is what makes a salad truly great. Many have just a few ingredients, so if they are not the best, what's the point? Obviously technique is important—and everyone should know how to mix a good vinaigrette, for instance—but without the ingredients, technique won't save you. There are lots of points of view about technique, but not many about a perfectly ripened tomato!

notes from the sommelier
trattamento equo

We wanted to find a simple and elegant solution to the common problem of which wine to drink with a meal at our osteria. Our guests are presented with an all-Italian wine list filled with everything that is good to drink from the boot-shaped country that produces almost a quarter of all of the wine produced on earth! The osteria wine list contains many pages with lots of text in a foreign language, and the selection process can be daunting when you are just not sure whether you are in the mood for a Sangiovese, a Nerello Mascalese, or a Nero d'Avola.

To make the wine ordering process just a little less stressful, in addition to offering a multitude of wines poured in the traditional *quartino* (0.25 liter) and *mezzolitro* (0.5 liter) decanters, we introduced a program for our guests named *Trattamento Equo*, which translates to "a fair deal." It is also fun for guests to customize their own deal with the many white, rosé, and red options. The beauty of the Italian wine-making sensibility is that every wine is intended to be enjoyed and to showcase what is on your plate.

Experiment—the butternut squash soup will shine with an oaked, white Tuscan Chardonnay, the "Batàr" cuvée from Querciabella or the simpler Torricella bottling; a fleshy, Lagrein Rosé from the Alto Adige; or even a spicy, fruity red Barbera from Clerico, Prunotto, or Rivetti in Piedmont. For those who just want to enjoy a few tastes of several wines, we offer an easy and pleasurable tasting nightly. We always learn a thing or two when we try to serve wines with a particular dish. We typically pour a few whites and a few reds, depending on the evening, and they are all designed to accommodate the meal. On any given evening, we invite you to start the progression with a taste of ebullient, sparkling Bisol Prosecco; followed by tastes of earthy, fragrant white Palazzone Grechetto from Umbria and La Valentina Montepulciano from Abruzzo; and finish with dark, juicy Malvasia Nera from San Marzano in Puglia.

Perhaps you will want to try this at home— offering your guests a choice of several wines that complement a soup or another dish. Experimenting with wine is fun and educational.

sausage and escarole soup

minestra di scarola e salsiccia

½ pound dried cannellini beans
½ cup olive oil
8 garlic cloves, minced
1 tablespoon ground fennel seeds
1 tablespoon crushed red pepper flakes
4 sprigs fresh thyme
1¼ pounds Italian sausage, crumbled
4 celery ribs, cut into large dice
2 carrots, cut into large dice
1 onion, cut into large dice
Kosher salt and freshly ground black pepper
2 quarts chicken stock
2 quarts Parmesan Broth (recipe follows)
2 heads escarole, washed and dried
2 quarts Stewed Tomatoes (recipe follows)
2 tablespoons sherry vinegar

I love this warm, homey soup, and because it's one I grew up eating, I am not surprised it hits the spot for so many. In Italy, the region where it's made dictates the kind of sausage used. In some parts they use pork, in others game or duck sausages. I rely on spicy pork sausage, but if you prefer sweet sausage or turkey sausage, for example, substitute it. The secret to this soup's special goodness lies with the Parmesan broth, which is a delicious way to use Parmesan rinds—those rock-hard ends on the cheese. It has a wonderful salty and cheesy flavor that makes it perfect for soups and pasta sauces. *serves 6 to 8*

1   In a bowl or pot, cover the beans with cold water by about 1 inch. Set aside to soak for at least 6 hours or overnight. Change the water two or three times during soaking, if possible.

2   In a large soup pot, heat the olive oil over medium heat. Add the garlic, fennel seeds, red pepper, and thyme and cook for 2 to 3 minutes, or until the garlic softens but does not color and the spices are fragrant.

3   Add the sausage and cook, breaking it into large chunks and stirring until browned. When the sausage is about halfway cooked through, add the celery, carrots, and onion, season to taste with salt and pepper, and cook for about 5 minutes longer, or until the vegetables soften and the sausage is nicely browned.

4   Drain the beans and discard the water. Put the beans in the pot with the sausage. Add the stock and Parmesan Broth and bring to a simmer over medium-high heat. Reduce the heat to low and cook for 1 to 1½ hours, until the beans are softened but still hold their shape. Do not overcook.

5   Add the escarole and tomatoes and season to taste with salt. Cook at a gentle simmer for about 10 minutes, or until the escarole is tender. Stir in the vinegar and season to taste with salt and pepper. Ladle into bowls and serve.

parmesan broth
makes 1 gallon

1 tablespoon black peppercorns
1 teaspoon crushed red pepper flakes
1 gallon chicken stock
1½ pounds Parmigiano-Reggiano cheese rind
1 bay leaf
1 sprig fresh thyme
2 tablespoons olive oil
Kosher salt

1 In a stockpot, toast the peppercorns and red pepper over medium heat for about 30 seconds, or until fragrant. Add the stock and cheese rind and bring to a simmer over medium-high heat. Add the bay leaf, thyme, and olive oil and simmer for about 1 hour.

2 Remove and discard the cheese rind and bay leaf. Season to taste with salt.

3 Using a handheld mixer or immersion blender, mix the broth until smooth. Strain through a fine-mesh sieve or chinois into a bowl.

4 Use immediately or let the broth cool, cover, and refrigerate for up to 5 days.

stewed tomatoes
makes 2 to 2½ cups

2½ pounds Roma tomatoes (8 to 10 tomatoes), cored and scored a few times with a small, sharp knife
5 tablespoons extra virgin olive oil
1½ garlic cloves, sliced
3 sprigs fresh rosemary
2½ sprigs fresh thyme
Pinch of crushed red pepper flakes
Kosher salt
8 fresh basil leaves

1 In a large pot filled with boiling water, blanch the tomatoes for about 7 seconds. Lift from the water and set aside to cool. (Do not shock in cold water.) When they are cool enough to handle, slip the skins off the tomatoes.

2 Halve the tomatoes lengthwise, hold them over a plate, and gently squeeze out the seeds and juice. Set the tomatoes aside and discard the seeds and juice.

3 In a sauté pan, heat 4 tablespoons of olive oil and the garlic, rosemary, thyme, and red pepper over medium heat. When very warm, remove from the heat and let the mixture stand for at least 10 minutes to give the garlic and herbs time to steep in the oil and flavor it.

4 Meanwhile, in a large saucepan, heat 1 tablespoon of olive oil over medium heat. When the olive oil is hot, add the tomatoes and salt to taste. Stir for 10 to 15 minutes, or until the tomatoes start to break down and become very dry.

5 Strain the herb-infused olive oil through a fine-mesh sieve or chinois into the tomatoes. Discard the garlic and herbs. Cook the tomatoes and olive oil for 4 to 7 minutes, stirring occasionally, or until the sauce has emulsified. The tomatoes will have a sheen from the oil and will turn a bright reddish-orange. The sauce also tastes very fresh. Stir in the basil and season to taste with salt; use as desired.

butternut squash soup with chestnut honey mascarpone

crema di zucca con mascarpone
di castagne e miele

4 tablespoons unsalted butter
1 yellow onion, sliced
2½ pounds butternut squash (about 2 medium squash), peeled and diced into 1-inch pieces
2 ounces Parmigiano-Reggiano cheese rind
2 sprigs fresh thyme
1 fresh bay leaf
Pinch of ground coriander
Small pinch of freshly grated nutmeg
Kosher salt
¼ cup mascarpone cheese, slightly softened
1 teaspoon chestnut honey or other mild honey
Freshly ground black pepper
6 cups chicken stock or vegetable stock
1 cup heavy cream
Juice of 1 orange
Crumbled amaretti cookies, optional

1   In a large saucepan, heat 1 tablespoon of butter over medium-high heat. When the butter is hot and melted, add the onion,

When my grandmother made butternut squash soup in the fall, she sprinkled crumbled amaretti cookies over the top, to give it a little crunch and extra sweetness. I still love to do this, but have made my version a little more sophisticated with a garnish of honey-sweetened mascarpone. I think most people like butternut squash; its mild yet distinctive flavor speaks to autumn. I make this soup all the time—it's that easy. *serves 4 to 6*

reduce the heat to medium-low, and cook slowly for 10 to 15 minutes, or until the onion is very tender but not browned. Add the squash, cheese rind, thyme, bay leaf, coriander, and nutmeg. Stir to mix, season to taste with salt, cover the pan, and cook over medium heat for about 10 minutes. Stir the mixture often.

2   Meanwhile, in the bowl of an electric mixer fitted with the whisk attachment, whip the mascarpone and honey until smooth. Season to taste with salt and pepper and continue to whip until stiff. Do not overwhip or the mascarpone will separate. Set aside.

3   Add the stock and cream to the squash mixture, raise the heat to medium-high, and bring to a simmer. Reduce the heat to medium and simmer for about 5 minutes, or until the squash is tender. Remove and discard the cheese rind, thyme, and bay leaf.

4   Transfer the soup to the jar of a blender and purée until smooth. You may have to do this in two batches. If you have an immersion blender, you can blend the soup right in the pot.

5   Strain the soup through a fine-mesh sieve or chinois. Return it to the pan and set it over medium heat. Season to taste with salt and pepper. Whisk in 3 tablespoons of butter and the orange juice.

6   Pour the hot soup into bowls and serve each with a heaping tablespoon of mascarpone. Garnish with crumbled cookies, if desired.

fennel-orange soup

zuppa di finocchio e arancia

1 tablespoon fennel seeds

1 star anise

1½ teaspoons coriander seeds

½ teaspoon crushed red pepper flakes

¼ cup olive oil

½ cup unsalted butter, cubed

3 fennel bulbs, sliced, fronds reserved

1 white onion, sliced

Kosher salt

6 garlic cloves, sliced

3 ounces Parmigiano-Reggiano cheese rind

Juice and grated zest of 1 orange

¼ cup extra virgin olive oil

2 ounces Parmigiano-Reggiano cheese, shaved
(about 2 tablespoons)

Since I first tasted it, I have been especially fond of fennel, with its fresh anise flavor. I braise it, add it raw to salads, and make soup with it. Tossing a cheese rind into the soup is a classic Italian technique to boost the flavor—and to satisfy the Italian home cook's penchant for never wasting a thing! *serves 6 to 8*

1 Lay a 5- to 6-inch square of cheesecloth on a work surface. Pile the fennel seeds, star anise, coriander seeds, and red pepper in the center. Gather the corners together and tie with a length of string to make a spice sachet.

2 In a heavy saucepan, heat the olive oil and butter over medium heat. When the butter melts, but before it starts to brown, add the sliced fennel, the onion, and the spice sachet. Season to taste with salt and let the vegetables cook for 7 to 10 minutes, or until they are completely translucent. Add the garlic and cook for 2 to 3 minutes longer, or until the garlic softens.

3 Add the cheese rind, orange juice, and 2 quarts of water and bring to a brisk simmer over medium-high heat. Simmer for 15 to 20 minutes to give the flavors time to develop. Remove the cheese rind and spice sachet.

4 Meanwhile, chop the reserved fennel fronds so that you have about 2 tablespoons. Discard the rest.

5 Transfer the soup to the jar of a blender and purée until smooth. You may have to do this in batches. While the soup is puréeing, slowly pour the extra virgin olive oil into the soup and blend until incorporated.

6 Ladle into warm soup bowls. Garnish with the shaved cheese, orange zest, and fennel fronds and serve.

minestrone

1 cup (2 sticks) unsalted butter
½ cup diced onion
½ cup diced carrot
½ cup diced celery
6 garlic cloves, chopped
½ cup potatoes, peeled and diced
2 cups tomato juice
1 quart chicken stock
½ pound dried tubetti pasta
½ cup diced zucchini
½ cup diced squash
1 cup cooked garbanzo beans (see Note)
1 cup cooked cannellini beans (see Note)
1 cup chopped fresh basil
Kosher salt and freshly ground black pepper
About 6 tablespoons Basil Pesto (page 46)

Minestrone is eaten all over Italy and, not surprisingly, varies from region to region. In Genoa it has cabbage and in Florence pork and chiles, but everywhere it has vegetables and usually pasta. My grandmother was from Naples and so my version is very close to hers. When I was a kid, my mom sometimes added leftover chicken to the vegetable soup for a main course. *serves 6 to 8*

1 In a large saucepan, heat the butter over medium heat. When the butter is hot, add the onion, carrot, celery, and garlic and cook over medium heat for 7 to 10 minutes, or until softened but not colored.

2 Add the potatoes and cook, stirring, for about 5 minutes, or until they begin to soften. Add the tomato juice, raise the heat to medium-high, and bring to a brisk simmer. Cook for 5 to 7 minutes, or until the liquid reduces by a third. Add the stock, return to a simmer, and cook for about 30 minutes.

3 Meanwhile, cook the pasta in lightly salted boiling water for 6 to 8 minutes, or until barely al dente. The cooking time may vary according to the pasta. Drain.

4 Add the zucchini, the squash, and both kinds of beans and stir. Simmer for about 5 minutes, or until heated through. Add the drained pasta and let it heat in the soup for about 5 minutes. Stir in the basil and season to taste with salt and pepper. Remove from the heat, garnish with Basil Pesto, and serve.

note To cook the beans, soak 8 ounces of each kind of bean in enough cold water to cover by about 1 inch for at least 6 hours or overnight. Change the water two or three times during soaking, if possible. Drain the beans and put them in a large pot. Cover with enough fresh water or chicken stock to cover the beans by 2 inches. Bring to a boil, reduce the heat to a simmer, and cook for 1 to 1½ hours, until the beans are softened but still hold their shape. Season to taste with salt and pepper. Do not overcook. Drain and set aside or cover and refrigerate for up to 24 hours.

ligurian seafood salad
insalata di pesce

marinade

1 cup extra virgin olive oil

2 tablespoons minced garlic

1 tablespoon chopped fresh flat-leaf parsley

1 tablespoon chopped fresh thyme

1½ teaspoons chopped fresh rosemary

1 teaspoon chopped Calabrian chile or another hot chile such as jalapeño or serrano

seafood salad

¾ pound mussels

½ pound littleneck clams

1 cup dry white wine

1 tablespoon chopped garlic

Pinch of crushed red pepper flakes

¾ pound calamari, the body sliced into ¼-inch-thick rings and the tentacles halved

1 cup diced celery

1 cup diced fennel

cannellini salad

1 quart cooked cannellini beans (see page 61)

1 cup Oven-Dried Cherry Tomatoes (page 12)

3 tablespoons chopped fresh flat-leaf parsley

3 tablespoons minced shallots

Juice of 3 lemons

2 tablespoons Calabrian chile oil or other hot chile oil

1½ cups extra virgin olive oil

Kosher salt and freshly ground black pepper

to serve

4 slices Rick's Basic Crostini (page 64)

2 lemons, halved

1 To prepare the marinade, in a large saucepan, heat the olive oil over low heat. Add the garlic and cook for about 4 minutes, or until the garlic begins to sizzle. Do not let it burn. Remove from the heat and set aside to cool.

2 When the oil is cool, stir in the parsley, thyme, rosemary, and chile and set aside.

3 To prepare the seafood salad, heat a large sauté pan over high heat. When the pan is hot, put the mussels and clams in the pan. Add the wine, garlic, and red pepper. Cover and steam for 5 minutes, or until the shells begin to open. Add the calamari, cover, and cook for 1 to 2 minutes longer, or until the shellfish are fully open. Remove the shellfish and the calamari from the pan and set aside.

4 To prepare the cannellini salad, mix the beans, tomatoes, parsley, shallots, lemon juice, chile oil, and olive oil in a large bowl. Season to taste with salt and pepper and set aside. *(continued)*

I fell for this style of salad when I was visiting the Ligurian coast many years ago and stopped at one osteria after another along the way to try their versions of a seafood salad. I washed them all down with glasses of crisp, chilled Italian white wine and have nothing but relaxing memories of the journey. Back home in Chicago, I work with top-notch fishmongers to get the best fish and shellfish I can find to make a salad redolent of lemons, herbs, and olive oil. When you make your own version, go with the market and the season when you select fish and shellfish. ❦ *serves 4*

5 Transfer the cooked seafood to a bowl and toss with the marinade and the celery and fennel. Season to taste with salt and pepper.

6 Spoon a quarter of the cannellini salad on each of 4 serving plates. Arrange a quarter of the seafood salad on top and serve with a crostini and lemon half.

rick's basic crostini

What is the difference between crostini and bruschetta? In general, crostini are more refined and smaller. The bread slices for my crostini measure about 2 inches across and are thinner than the bread for bruschetta, and when topped with great flavors, fit the definition of powerful tiny bites that by virtue of their size are less overwhelming than bruschetta. The little toasts are always toasted, never grilled.

serves 4

3 garlic cloves
Pinch of kosher salt
8 tablespoons unsalted butter, softened
1 teaspoon fresh lemon juice
Freshly ground black pepper
1 slender baguette, cut into eight ¼-inch-thick slices

1 On a cutting board, finely chop the garlic and sprinkle the salt over it. Keep chopping and smashing the garlic and salt together to make a paste. Use a wide-bladed knife so that you can smear the paste along its flat side. You could also accomplish this in a mortar and pestle.

2 In a small bowl, mix the butter, lemon juice, and garlic paste. Fold the softened butter over and onto the garlic mixture, mashing it down with the back of a spoon or spatula. Season to taste with pepper and continue folding.

3 Lay a sheet of plastic wrap on a work surface. Scrape the butter onto the plastic and use the plastic wrap to shape the butter into a log encased in the plastic wrap. Refrigerate for up to 3 days. You can also freeze the garlic butter for up to 2 months. Let the butter soften before using.

4 Preheat the oven to 375°F.

5 Lay the bread slices on a baking sheet and brush both sides of each slice with garlic butter. Bake for 6 to 7 minutes, turning once, or until golden brown but not too crispy. Let cool before using.

meatball salad
insalata di polpettine

1½ cups Pomodoro Sauce (page 16)

Eight 4-ounce Meatballs (recipe follows)

2 cups chopped iceberg lettuce

2 cups chopped romaine lettuce

1 generous cup diced cucumber

¾ cup finely sliced radicchio

½ cup chopped fresh tarragon

½ cup chopped fresh basil

½ cup snipped fresh chives

½ cup chopped fresh flat-leaf parsley

¼ cup julienned red onion

¾ cup Tramonto's House Dressing (page 67)

Kosher salt and freshly ground black pepper

3¾ cups Garlic Croutons (page 67)

½ cup freshly grated Parmigiano-Reggiano cheese

I ate this when I was growing up, although I don't believe you would ever find it in Italy. If you didn't want Sunday's leftover meatballs in a sandwich on Monday, you had them in a salad. And was it good! Our customers love this once they try it—they savor how the flavors of the meatballs, tomato sauce, vegetables, and dressing mingle on the plate.

When you make the meatballs, handle them with care; otherwise they will be tough rather than light and tender. The recipe for them makes more than you need here, but they are great leftovers and will hold in the refrigerator for about 5 days. ❀ *serves 4*

1. In a saucepan, heat the Pomodoro Sauce and the meatballs over medium heat until both are heated through. Cover and set aside to keep warm.

2. In a large mixing bowl, toss the lettuces, cucumber, radicchio, herbs, and onion. Pour the dressing over the salad and toss to mix. Season to taste with salt and pepper.

3. Put a quarter of the salad off center on each of 4 serving plates. Spoon 2 meatballs and some sauce next to the salad. Garnish the salad with Garlic Croutons and the meatballs with the grated cheese and serve.

meatballs
makes about 20 meatballs

6 large eggs, beaten

5 pounds ground beef (I like to mix chuck and sirloin in an 80/20 mix)

4 to 6 garlic cloves, minced

1 pound freshly grated Parmigiano-Reggiano cheese

4 cups seasoned dried bread crumbs (see Note)

2 cups chopped fresh flat-leaf parsley

1 tablespoon kosher salt

1 teaspoon freshly ground black pepper

1 cup (2 sticks) unsalted butter, melted and cooled to room temperature

1. Preheat the oven to 350°F.

2. In a large mixing bowl, lightly mix the eggs, ground beef, and garlic, preferably with your hands.

3. In another mixing bowl, mix the cheese, bread crumbs, parsley, salt, and pepper. Add the cheese mixture to the meat mixture with the melted butter. Mix with your

hands or a wooden spoon just until fully incorporated. Do not overmix.

4 Line a shallow baking pan with parchment paper. Roll the meat into large meatballs, about the size of a large scoop of ice cream, and put them on the pan. You should have about 20 meatballs.

5 Bake for about 15 minutes, or until cooked through. Use immediately or cover and refrigerate for up to 5 days.

note You can use store-bought seasoned bread crumbs or make your own. We season dried bread crumbs with salt, black pepper, onion powder, dried oregano, and garlic powder. One good-sized slice of bread yields about ½ cup of crumbs.

tramonto's house dressing
makes about 2 cups

¼ cup red wine vinegar
¼ cup Champagne vinegar
1 teaspoon sugar
1 teaspoon dry mustard, such as Colman's
1 teaspoon Dijon mustard
1 teaspoon minced garlic
1½ cups vegetable oil
Pinch of chopped fresh tarragon
Pinch of chopped fresh oregano
Pinch of dried oregano
Pinch of crushed red pepper flakes
Kosher salt and freshly ground black pepper

1 In the jar of a blender, combine the wine vinegar, Champagne vinegar, sugar, dry mustard, Dijon mustard, garlic, and 1 tablespoon of water and process until

blended. With the motor running, add the oil in a drizzle through the feed tube until the dressing emulsifies.

2 Add the tarragon, fresh and dried oregano, and red pepper. Season to taste with salt and pepper. Use immediately or cover and refrigerate for up to 1 week.

garlic croutons
makes about 4 cups

One 1½-pound loaf focaccia
1½ cups olive oil
½ cup freshly grated Parmigiano-Reggiano cheese
½ garlic clove, minced
2 tablespoons chopped fresh thyme
Leaves from ¼ sprig fresh rosemary
Kosher salt and freshly ground black pepper

1 Preheat the oven to 350°F.

2 Cut the bread into ½-inch cubes.

3 In a mixing bowl, stir together the olive oil, cheese, and garlic. Add the thyme and rosemary and season to taste with salt and pepper.

4 Add the bread cubes and toss gently until coated. Spread the bread cubes on a baking sheet, leaving space between the cubes, and bake for 12 to 15 minutes, or until they are golden brown and crisp.

5 Let the croutons cool to room temperature. Store in a lidded container at room temperature for up to 2 weeks.

arugula salad
insalata di rucola

8 ounces arugula
2 ounces Parmigiano-Reggiano cheese, shaved
  (about 2 tablespoons)
¼ cup fresh lemon juice
¼ cup extra virgin olive oil
Kosher salt and freshly ground black pepper
2 lemons, halved

1 In a salad bowl, toss the arugula with the cheese. Drizzle with the lemon juice and olive oil and toss gently. Season to taste with salt and pepper.

2 Divide the salad among 4 serving plates and garnish each with a lemon half.

This is a classic Italian salad you find everywhere in Italy; it can be made with baby arugula or more mature, and hence more peppery, leaves. It all depends on what you are in the mood for. Italians love arugula, and with good reason. Its bright, sharp flavor is never mistaken for any other green and brightens up any dish. In Florence, grilled steak nearly always is accompanied by baby arugula, whose sharp taste cuts through the rich meat, and so I often serve this salad with steak. *serves 4*

osteria chopped salad
insalata mista d'osteria

½ cup fresh corn kernels
1 tablespoon olive oil
1¼ cups shredded iceberg lettuce
1¼ cups finely green cabbage
1 cup finely shredded Napa cabbage
1 cup finey shredded red cabbage
1 cup diced jicama
1 cup cooked garbanzo beans (see page 61)
½ cup diced fennel
½ cup diced carrots
½ cup sliced radishes
½ cup crumbled blue cheese
⅓ cup diced seedless European cucumber
1 tomato, seeded and diced
2 tablespoons toasted pine nuts (page 46)
2 tablespoons chopped fresh basil
2 tablespoons chopped fresh tarragon
1 tablespoon snipped fresh chives
2½ cups Garlic Croutons (page 67)
2 cups Mustard-Herb Vinaigrette (recipe follows)
Kosher salt and freshly ground black pepper

When I started cooking in Chicago, I discovered chopped salads and soon grew to love them. We sometimes refer to them as antipasti salads, because they can have just about anything and everything in them, although there is no such thing in Italy, where antipasti salad would be an antipasti platter. A good chopped salad can't be beat, particularly when made with the mustardy salad dressing based on our house dressing. ✿ *serves 4*

1 Preheat the oven to 400°F.

2 In a small bowl, toss the corn kernels with the olive oil. Transfer to a small baking dish and spread out in a single layer. Roast for 4 to 6 minutes, or until lightly browned. Set aside to cool.

3 In a large mixing bowl, toss all the ingredients except the Mustard-Herb Vinaigrette and the salt and pepper. Pour the vinaigrette over the salad and toss well. Season to taste with salt and pepper. Divide among 4 serving plates.

mustard-herb vinaigrette
makes about 2½ cups

2 tablespoons Champagne vinegar
1 tablespoon plus 1 teaspoon red wine vinegar
¾ teaspoon Dijon mustard
1 tablespoon plus 1 teaspoon sugar
¾ teaspoon kosher salt
1½ tablespoons dry mustard, such as Colman's
1 to 2 garlic cloves, finely minced
Freshly ground black pepper
Pinch of crushed red pepper flakes
1½ cups extra virgin olive oil
Pinch of chopped fresh tarragon
Pinch of chopped fresh oregano
Pinch of dried oregano

1 In a mixing bowl, whisk 3 tablespoons of water with the vinegars, Dijon mustard, sugar, salt, dry mustard, garlic, black pepper, and red pepper. Slowly add the olive oil in a steady stream, whisking to emulsify.

2 Add the herbs and gently stir to mix. Cover and refrigerate until ready to use. The dressing will keep for up to 3 days in the refrigerator.

raw artichoke salad

insalata di carciofi crudi

½ cup plus 1 tablespoon fresh lemon juice
3 whole artichokes
3 cipolline onions, peeled but left whole
2 tablespoons aged balsamic vinegar
7 fresh basil leaves
10 tablespoons extra virgin olive oil
Kosher salt and freshly ground black pepper

The idea of a raw artichoke may not appeal to most people, who think of only cooked globe artichokes or perhaps marinated artichoke hearts, but when the vegetables are fresh and in season in the early spring, they are magnificent sliced very thin and dressed with olive oil and good balsamic. You are slicing only the choke—the leaves go into a soup or the compost. This is a classic Mediterranean salad; to thoroughly enjoy it, make sure the choke is well trimmed with all leaves and fuzzy bits removed. Buy heavy specimens with tightly closed leaves and moist stems.

serves 4

1 Fill a large bowl with cold water and add 1 tablespoon of lemon juice to make acidulated water.

2 Peel the artichokes by holding each one upside down, pulling the leaves toward you, and snapping the leaves at their natural breaking point, which is about two-thirds down toward the stem. When the light green interior leaves are exposed, use a paring knife to trim along the top of the artichoke. Work around the circumference of the heart and remove the remaining leaves. The choke will remain; if the outer edges of the heart are rough, trim them. Peel the stem and cut the artichoke in half from stem to heart. Remove the choke (heart) and make sure all leaves and fuzzy bits are removed.

3 Submerge the chokes in the water. They will keep without turning brown for up to 3 hours.

4 In a pot filled with lightly salted boiling water, cook the onions for about 4 minutes, or until tender. Drain and set aside to cool. When they are cool, cut them in half and let the layers separate naturally. Sprinkle the onions with the vinegar and let them marinate for about 5 minutes.

5 Using a mandoline, shave the chokes. Alternatively, use a sharp knife to slice them very thin.

6 Put the chokes in a mixing bowl and add the onions and basil.

7 Dress the salad with ½ cup of lemon juice and the olive oil. Toss and season to taste with salt and pepper.

bread salad

panzanella

1 head radicchio

2 tablespoons olive oil

Kosher salt and freshly ground black pepper

½ red onion, very thinly sliced

6 fresh basil leaves, torn

6 cups Garlic Croutons (page 67)

2 cups diced cucumbers

2 cups large-diced vine-ripened red, yellow, or
multicolored beefsteak or plum tomatoes

1 cup extra virgin olive oil

¼ cup sherry vinegar

Juice of ½ lemon

2 ounces Parmigiano-Reggiano cheese, shaved
(about 2 tablespoons)

This classic summer salad, called *panzanella* in Italy, originated in the central part of the country where tomatoes are plentiful and especially tasty. For this rustic bread salad, the tomatoes don't have to be seeded or peeled, just chopped. The bread may be soaked in water or wine and then squeezed dry, or it may be made into croutons, as I prefer. I also add radicchio to give this salad even more personality. ❀ *serves 4*

1 Prepare a charcoal or gas grill by spraying the grilling rack with nonstick vegetable spray. Heat the grill until medium-hot.

2 Cut the radicchio in half, leaving the core intact. Brush the olive oil over one half of the radicchio and sprinkle with salt and pepper. Set the other half aside.

3 Lay the oiled radicchio on the grill, flat side down, and grill for about 3 minutes, or until lightly charred. Flip and repeat on the other side. The radicchio will be raw in the center. Let the radicchio cool, slice it very thin, and transfer to a salad bowl. Add the onion and basil to the bowl.

4 Tear the reserved radicchio half into bite-sized pieces and add to the bowl. Add the Garlic Croutons, cucumbers, and tomatoes to the salad bowl.

5 Pour the extra virgin olive oil, vinegar, and lemon juice over the salad and toss to mix. Season to taste with salt and pepper and top with the shaved cheese.

farro salad with guanciale and medjool dates
farro con guanciale e datteri

farro

2 tablespoons unsalted butter
¼ cup minced onion
1 pound farro
1 gallon chicken stock
2 tablespoons olive oil

salad

3 ounces guanciale or pancetta, sliced into strips
About ½ cup sliced Medjool dates, pits removed
½ bunch fresh flat-leaf parsley, thick stems
   removed, chopped
⅔ cup extra virgin olive oil
¼ cup fresh lemon juice
¼ cup red wine vinegar
Kosher salt and freshly ground black pepper

I couldn't let this chapter end without including this wonderful salad made with farro and dates. Farro is an ancient grain similar to wheat but low in gluten and high in nutty flavor and good nutrition. It's the grain that kept the Roman army going for centuries, and as such is good enough for me! Sticky, sweet dates are just as ancient as farro, having been harvested since very early times from date palms that grow in North Africa and the Middle East. The salad is reminiscent of one I ate in the Piedmont region of Italy, which is famous for its pork, and so I include guanciale (pork cheeks), which is similar to pancetta. You can substitute prosciutto or pancetta.

serves 4

1 To cook the farro, melt the butter in a large pot over medium heat. Add the onion and cook for about 5 minutes, or until translucent. Add the farro and cook, stirring, for about 4 minutes, until lightly toasted and fragrant.

2 Add the stock and bring to a boil. Reduce the heat and simmer for about 40 minutes, until the farro kernels pop.

3 Drain the farro, toss with the olive oil, and transfer to a large mixing bowl.

4 To prepare the salad, in a sauté pan, cook the guanciale over low heat until the fat is rendered and the meat is crisp.

5 Add the cooked guanciale and rendered fat to the farro. Add the dates and parsley and stir to mix.

6 Add the olive oil, lemon juice, and vinegar and toss well. Season to taste with salt and pepper. Divide among 4 serving plates.

antipasti

Of all the chapters in the book, this one speaks the loudest to me. I love to eat this way: small bites of intense flavors and textures that run the gamut from soft and silken to crunchy and brittle. I could have gone on forever, coming up with recipes that could be served as a first course or an antipasto. I think most of us like to eat this kind of food, whether it's a surprising smooth savory custard with tomato sauce, asparagus spears served with a fried egg on top, or luscious little fingerling potatoes with garlicky bagna cauda. These dishes are casual, fun, and exciting. Nearly anything goes when it comes to antipasti—and I couldn't be happier.

notes from the sommelier
metal mavens and metal heads

From the sommelier's perspective, the antipasti course is all about purity. These first bites invariably highlight the focused, unfettered flavors of the season. Spring asparagus simply adorned with pecorino and a fried egg emanates simplicity. Heirloom tomatoes in all of their glory make the most delicious bruschetta in the summer, and the charred fall squash with balsamic could not be more clear.

At our osteria, the antipasti course inspires us to highlight the purest expression of the grapevine: the unoaked, single-varietal wine. Our wine lists highlight just this style, and grape juice exposed to metal instead of wood makes our hearts race, our mouths water, and our taste buds rejoice. With these wines, you will notice a lack of the oak-driven gamut of flavors like toast, vanilla, clove, and coconut. When you taste and drink wines from a "Metal Maven," you will never experience the sensation of sucking on an oak chip. Instead you will notice pristine expressions of the grape varietals being used, and wines whose flavors are driven by fruit and terroir-influenced characteristics that in other wines can be masked.

We have found that it is often in the northern regions of Italy that the winemakers dare to present their wines just about "oak free." Look for single-varietal wines made exclusively from one type of grape such as Sauvignon Blanc, Tocai Friulano, Pinot Bianco, Nosiola, Pinot Noir, Barbera, or Merlot. White, pink, and red wines can all be found in their pure, naked state. Some of our favorite practitioners of this style of wine include Valter Scarbolo in Friuli, Pojer e Sandri in Trentino, Zemmer in the Alto Adige, and last but not least, Giovanni Puiatti, whose motto is "Save a tree, drink Puiatti," in light of the fact that he does not age his wines in oak barrels.

bruschetta with pickled herring and lemon-chive crème fraîche

bruschetta con aringhe marinate

4 whole herring fillets
2 cups whole milk
1 cup sugar
1 cup white wine vinegar
2 teaspoons ground allspice
2 teaspoons crushed yellow mustard seeds
2 teaspoons coriander seeds, crushed
2 teaspoons black peppercorns
1 teaspoon caraway seeds
Grated zest of 1 lemon
1 small red onion, sliced
2 carrots, thinly sliced
½ bunch fresh dill
2 bay leaves

1 cup Rick's Homemade Crème Fraîche (page 15), or store-bought
Juice of ½ lemon
2 tablespoons snipped fresh chives
Kosher salt and freshly ground black pepper
8 slices Rick's Basic Bruschetta (recipe follows)
1 tablespoon chopped fresh flat-leaf parsley

If you are surprised to see a recipe for pickled herring in a book primarily about Italian food, it will help to know that I lived in England for several years. Before then, I didn't especially like pickled herring, but it was served at breakfast, at lunch, and with the evening pint, and I slowly came around. Today, I have a keen appreciation for it, although I like to control the pickling process so I do it myself rather than buying the herring already pickled. When you top the bread with the herring and then crème fraîche, the flavors and textures are creamy, crunchy, salty, and fatty. ❀ *serves 4*

1 In a shallow dish, soak the herring in the milk to cover. Cover with plastic wrap and refrigerate for 12 to 24 hours to draw out the impurities. Drain the herring, rinse, and pat dry. Cut off the fins and, using a boning knife, fillet the herring by taking it off the skeletal bones. Leave on the skin. Cut the fillets crosswise into 2-inch-wide strips.

2 In a saucepan, combine 1½ cups of water with the sugar, vinegar, allspice, mustard seeds, coriander seeds, peppercorns, and caraway seeds and bring to a boil, stirring to dissolve the sugar. Remove from the heat and cool completely. When the pickling mixture is cool, stir in half of the lemon zest.

3 Arrange the herring fillets, onion, carrots, dill, and bay leaves in a glass dish. Pour the cooled pickling mixture over them so that they are covered completely. Cover with plastic wrap and refrigerate for 24 hours before serving.

4 In a bowl, whisk the crème fraîche, lemon juice, remaining lemon zest, and chives. Season to taste with salt and pepper.

5 Put a few fillets of herring and some of the pickled vegetables on top of each bruschetta. Drizzle some of the lemon-chive crème fraîche over the top, garnish with parsley, and serve.

rick's basic bruschetta

This is the ultimate vehicle for any number of toppings and therefore extremely useful for antipasti. The quality of the bread, as well as the olive oil, makes all the difference, so make sure the crust is crisp and the middle is soft and chewy. Buy it fresh from a good bakery.

serves 4

Four ½-inch-thick slices sourdough or any Italian country-style bread
¼ cup olive oil
Kosher salt and freshly ground black pepper
1 garlic clove, peeled
1 tablespoon freshly grated Parmigiano-Reggiano cheese

1 Prepare a charcoal or gas grill by spraying the grilling rack with nonstick vegetable spray, or preheat the broiler or panini press. Heat the grill, broiler, or press until medium-hot.

2 Cut the bread slices in half and brush both sides with a generous amount of olive oil. Season both sides to taste with salt and pepper.

3 Grill or broil the bread, turning once, until lightly browned on both sides.

4 Gently rub one side of each slice with the garlic clove to give it mild garlic flavor, sprinkle with the grated cheese, and serve.

semolina-crusted calamari with lemon–black pepper aioli

calamari in semolina con aioli di limone

aioli

1 cup homemade or high-quality store-bought mayonnaise

¼ cup sour cream

2 tablespoons fresh lemon juice

1 tablespoon grated lemon zest

1 tablespoon chopped fresh flat-leaf parsley

1 teaspoon minced garlic

Kosher salt and lots of freshly ground black pepper

calamari

1 pound calamari, tubes and tentacles, cleaned and rinsed

2 cups whole milk

Peanut oil or corn oil

½ cup semolina or cornmeal

2 large eggs, slightly beaten

2 garlic cloves, mashed

1 cup panko

1 tablespoon freshly grated Parmigiano-Reggiano cheese

1 teaspoon kosher salt

1 teaspoon freshly ground black pepper

½ teaspoon cayenne

to serve

4 lemon wedges

Fried calamari is about as Italian as it gets, but I have taken this to a new level by coating the squid with a cornmeal crust and serving it with aioli instead of tomato sauce. I have eaten fried calamari countless times both in Italy and in the United States, and though some has been great, I always wanted a little more crunch than I got. The cornmeal solves that problem very nicely. I use Point Judith calamari, which are cleaned and ready to go.

serves 4

1 To prepare the aioli, in a mixing bowl, whisk the mayonnaise, sour cream, lemon juice, lemon zest, parsley, and garlic. Season to taste with salt and lots of pepper. Refrigerate until needed.

2 To prepare the calamari, cut the tubes into ¼-inch-thick rings. Transfer to a bowl and pour the milk over them. Set aside to soak for 30 minutes. Drain and pat dry with paper towels.

3 Pour enough oil into a deep, heavy pot or Dutch oven to reach a depth of 4 inches. Heat the oil to 250°F over high heat. Use a deep-fat thermometer to determine the oil's temperature.

4 Moderate the heat to maintain the temperature. Spread the semolina in a shallow bowl. In another shallow bowl, mix the eggs and mashed garlic. In a third shallow bowl, mix the panko, cheese, salt, pepper, and cayenne. Line up the bowls on the counter next to each other and near the stove.

5 Dredge the calamari rings in the semolina and shake off any excess. Dip next in the egg and then the panko mixture. Shake off any excess crumbs.

6 Fry a few of the calamari rings for about 1 minute, or until crispy and golden brown. Using a metal slotted spoon, lift the fried rings from the oil and drain on paper towels. Let the oil regain its temperature before frying the next batch.

7 Season the warm calamari with salt to taste. Divide them among 4 plates and garnish each with a lemon wedge. Serve with the aioli on the side for dipping.

fregula with clams
fregola con vongole

2 to 3 tablespoons kosher salt
1 pound fregula or Israeli couscous (see Note)
2 tablespoons extra virgin olive oil
2 cups bottled clam juice, or 1 cup clam juice and
    1 cup chicken stock
24 littleneck clams
¾ cup Herb Compote (recipe follows)

1 In a large pot, bring 1 gallon of water to a boil over high heat. Salt the water and then add the pasta. Bring the water back to a boil and cook for about 10 minutes, or until parcooked, or about half done. Drain.

2 Transfer the hot pasta to a bowl and toss with the olive oil.

3 Meanwhile, in a small saucepan, heat the clam juice (or juice and stock) over medium heat. When the liquid is simmering, add the clams, cover the pan, and cook for about 4 minutes, or until the clams open. Drain the clams and discard any that do not open.

4 Return the opened clams to the pan and spoon the Herb Compote over the hot clams. Stir gently to distribute the herbs among the clams. There will be some residual broth from the clams in the pan, which is as it should be. Add the pasta and cook over medium heat for about 2 minutes, or until the pasta is al dente and heated through. Serve immediately.

note Fregula is semolina pasta that is rolled into small balls and then baked. It resembles Israeli couscous, but it requires slightly longer cooking and its flavor is a little toastier, which is why I urge you to find it for this recipe. It is a Sardinian specialty, particularly when cooked with clams, with culinary roots in North Africa.

herb compote
makes about ¾ cup

Stems from ½ bunch flat-leaf parsley
1 tablespoon fresh tarragon leaves
1 cup chopped fennel fronds
2 ice cubes, plus water if needed

1 In a large pot filled with boiling water, blanch the parsley, tarragon, and fennel fronds for 30 to 60 seconds, or until bright green. Drain and plunge in a bowl of ice water to shock. Drain again and shake off as much excess water as possible.

2 Transfer the herbs to a blender and add the ice cubes. Blend until smooth, adding a little water if needed. Set aside until needed, or cover and refrigerate for up to 24 hours.

This is a great antipasto, although I came up with it when I was looking for a starch to go with whole roasted fish. It's wonderful with fish or just as it is as a first course. I added the clams as another layer of flavor and it was dynamite. If you haven't tasted fregula, which is similar to but not exactly like Israeli couscous, you will fall in love with it, as I did. Look for it at Italian delis if your local market doesn't carry it. *serves 4*

peperonata with white anchovies

peperonata con acciughe bianche

2 cups sliced roasted red and yellow bell peppers
    (see page 11)
½ cup extra virgin olive oil
½ cup pitted and crushed green olives
½ cup chopped fresh flat-leaf parsley, plus more
    for garnish
¼ cup drained capers, smashed
2 garlic cloves, minced
2 tablespoons chopped fresh oregano
2 tablespoons red wine vinegar
Pinch of crushed red pepper flakes
Kosher salt and freshly ground black pepper
2 white anchovies drained, halved

1 In a small bowl, mix the bell peppers, olive oil, olives, parsley, capers, garlic, oregano, and vinegar. Season to taste with red pepper and salt and pepper.

2 Divide the peperonata among 4 serving plates. Lay half an anchovy on top of each portion, garnish with parsley, and serve. The peperonata, without the parsley and anchovy garnish, keeps for up to 6 days if covered and refrigerated.

If you are looking for something bright and colorful to start a meal—as well as boldly flavorful—look no further. Yellow and red bell peppers make a stunning combination, but you could also try orange and purple peppers, too. I toss in some green olives for a little extra flavor, but you might want to use more or less or none at all. And finally, I prefer white anchovies, which tend to be less salty and a little meatier than others. Serve the peperonata on great bread or crostini.

serves 4; makes about 1 cup

veal carpaccio
carpaccio di vitello

½ pound veal tenderloin
½ cup Rick's Homemade Aioli (page 39)
1 tablespoon whole-grain mustard
1 tablespoon fresh lemon juice
1 anchovy, slightly mashed
½ cup extra virgin olive oil
½ cup sliced radishes
¼ cup sliced caper berries
¼ cup minced red onion
½ cup celery leaves
¼ cup shaved Pecorino-Romano cheese
Sea salt and freshly ground black pepper

1 Wrap the veal tenderloin in plastic wrap and freeze just until firm. Do not let it freeze solid.

2 In a small bowl, mix the aioli, mustard, lemon juice, and anchovy.

3 Once the veal is semifrozen, slice it into extremely thin pieces. If they are not thin enough, put them between plastic wrap and pound lightly until thin.

4 Arrange the pieces of veal on 4 serving plates. Drizzle with olive oil and then a tablespoon of aioli.

5 Arrange the radishes, caper berries, onion, and celery leaves around the carpaccio. Top the carpaccio with the shaved cheese. Season to taste with salt and pepper and serve immediately.

This is a recipe that calls for raw meat; in this case, veal. Like beef, veal is sold as prime meat and I suggest you seek it out (for more on prime meat, refer to the recipe for Beef Tartare on page 94). Carpaccio is an Italian specialty made from beef, veal, lamb, or fish, depending on the part of Italy. It's usually a first course but can also be a light meal, as the flavors that accompany it—capers, onions, and radishes—are strong and satisfying.

serves 4

prosciutto with "dirty pears" and chestnut honey

prosciutto con pere e miele di castagne

4 firm, ripe pears, such as Anjou, Bosc, or Bartlett

4 ounces prosciutto, thinly sliced

2 tablespoons chestnut or another high-quality honey

This simple dish is all about the flavor profile of the ripe pears, the ham, and the honey. When you get some black char on the pears, they turn sweeter than ever, with a subtle smokiness that infuses the fruit. Match the fruit with the fat and saltiness of the ham and the sweetness of the honey and your palate will sing with joy. I have made this with charred peaches and figs, too, and both are magnificent with the prosciutto and honey.

serves 4

1 Heat a charcoal or gas grill or broiler until medium-hot.

2 Set the washed pears on the grill or under the broiler and cook, turning, for 10 to 12 minutes, or until charred on all sides.

3 When the pears are cool enough to handle, scrape away the charred exterior to expose the caramelized fruit. Cut the pears in half and, using a small knife, slice out the core and any seeds. Cut the halves into quarters and then into wedges.

4 Divide the sliced prosciutto among 4 serving plates and divide the pears evenly among the plates, scattering them over the prosciutto. You could also arrange this on a single serving platter. Drizzle with the honey and serve.

asparagus with fried egg and pecorino

asparagi con uova fritte e pecorino

1½ bunches thick asparagus

1 tablespoon extra virgin olive oil, plus more for
   drizzling

Kosher salt and freshly ground black pepper

1 tablespoon unsalted butter

4 large eggs

2 ounces Pecorino-Romano cheese, shaved (about
   2 tablespoons)

1 Snap the asparagus spears to break off the
   woody, white ends.

2 In a large sauté pan, heat 1 tablespoon of
   olive oil over medium-high heat. When the
   olive oil is hot, gently lay the asparagus in
   the pan and season with salt and pepper.
   Cook, rolling the asparagus spears in the
   pan, for about 4 minutes, or until lightly
   caramelized on all sides.

3 Meanwhile, in another large sauté pan,
   melt the butter over medium-high heat.
   When the butter is melted, crack the eggs
   into the pan and cook for 2 to 3 minutes, or
   until cooked sunny side up. Season to taste
   with salt and pepper.

4 Lay 5 or 6 asparagus spears on each of
   4 serving plates and put 1 fried egg on top
   of each portion. Garnish with shaved
   cheese and season to taste with pepper and
   a drizzle of olive oil.

There's nothing complicated about this classic
Milanese dish with very few ingredients, so go
for the best. I like the pencil asparagus that
come into the markets in the early spring, but
you could use thicker spears or even white
asparagus and grill, blanch, or roast them
instead of pan-cooking them. When this is
served, the egg yolks spill over the asparagus
and mingle deliciously with the sharp, salty
cheese. Heaven! *serves 4*

heirloom beets with mascarpone and poppy seeds

barbabietole con mascarpone e semi di papavero

4 large heirloom beets, stems removed, beets left
    whole (about 2½ pounds)
½ cup extra virgin olive oil
Sea salt and freshly ground black pepper
3 tablespoons fresh lemon juice
4 ounces mascarpone cheese
1 teaspoon grated lemon zest
1 tablespoon poppy seeds

1 Preheat the oven to 400°F.

2 Toss the beets with a tablespoon or so of
olive oil, salt, and pepper. Wrap the beets in
aluminum foil, put them on a baking sheet,
and bake for about 45 minutes, or until fork
tender. Let the beets cool, still wrapped in
the foil, to room temperature.

3 Use a kitchen towel (preferably one you are
not attached to because it will get stained)
to peel the beets by rubbing them gently.
The skin will come right off.

4 Dice the beets into 1-inch cubes and toss
with the remaining olive oil and the lemon
juice. Season to taste with salt and pepper.

5 In a small bowl, mix the cheese with the
lemon zest and season to taste with salt and
pepper.

6 Arrange equal amounts of the beets on
4 plates and put a dollop of cheese on each
plate. Sprinkle with the poppy seeds and
serve.

Happily, beets have not escaped the heirloom
vegetable and fruit movement, which seeks to
reclaim varieties that were grown before mass-
market farming homogenized everything. Any
freshly dug beets taste wonderful, but if you
are fortunate enough to have a farmers'
market or local grower who offers heirlooms,
try them for a lovely surprise. They are sure to
taste sweet and rich with an undercurrent of
earthiness, as befits a great beet. Heirloom
beets may be red, pink, yellow, or white, and
some are striped when cut open. They can be
round or more cylindrical and have names
such as Butter Slicer, Bull's Blood, Golden,
Chioggia, Albino, and Crosby's Egyptian, to
name just a few. *serves 4*

poached fingerling potatoes and green beans with bagna cauda

patate e fagiolini alla bagna cauda

1 pound fingerling potatoes

2 tablespoons kosher salt, plus more for seasoning

1 teaspoon coriander seeds

1 bay leaf

6 ounces green beans

1 cup Bagna Cauda (recipe follows)

1 tablespoon chopped fresh flat-leaf parsley

1 Put about 2 gallons of water in a large pot. Add the potatoes, salt, coriander seeds, and bay leaf, and bring to a boil over medium-high heat. Reduce the heat to medium and simmer briskly for about 20 minutes, or until fork tender.

2 Meanwhile, cook the green beans in a few inches of boiling water for 2 to 3 minutes, or until bright green and slightly softened. Drain and cool. Cut the green beans in half crosswise.

3 Drain the potatoes and set them aside to cool to room temperature. Slice in half lengthwise and transfer to a bowl. Add the green beans.

4 In a small saucepan, warm the bagna cauda over low heat. Add to the potatoes and green beans and toss gently until they are coated. Season to taste with salt. Add the parsley and toss to mix. Serve while still warm.

bagna cauda
makes about 3 cups

4 whole garlic heads

1 pound (4 sticks) unsalted butter, cut into small cubes

1 cup extra virgin olive oil

8 anchovy fillets, drained

Juice of ½ lemon

Kosher salt and freshly ground black pepper

1 Remove the loose skin from the garlic heads and slice the tops off them, but do not let the cloves separate.

2 In a heavy saucepan, heat the garlic heads, butter, olive oil, and anchovies over very low heat until the butter melts. Cook for 1 hour longer, until the garlic softens and cooks through, the anchovies dissolve, and the butter begins to foam.

3 Remove the garlic from the bagna cauda, as well as any skins that have fallen loose during cooking.

4 Squeeze the garlic through a strainer back into the pan. Add the lemon juice and season to taste with salt and pepper. Using a handheld mixer, blend the bagna cauda until well mixed. Cool and set aside until needed. The bagna cauda will keep in the refrigerator for up to 7 days.

The centerpiece of this dish is the bagna cauda, which is a buttery, garlicky sauce spiked with anchovies and often served as a warm dip, set over a flame like fondue. I like to dress tender fingerlings and barely cooked green beans with it and serve it as an antipasto, but you could try it as a dip. It's great either way.

serves 4

pecorino cheese custard with tomato sauce

budino di pomodoro

1 quart whole milk

3 cups heavy cream

10 large egg yolks

5½ ounces ciabatta bread (about 5 slices), crust removed, diced, plus 12 slices ½-inch-thick ciabatta bread

1¾ pounds young Pecorino-Romano cheese, shredded

½ cup extra virgin olive oil, plus more for drizzling

1 cup Pomodoro Sauce (page 16)

Freshly ground black pepper

Don't think of puddings as being only sweet. This one, made with cream, egg yolks, and several slices of bread, is a divine custard with the texture and flavor to stand up to the tomato sauce. The bread gives the *budino* its substantial texture. If you can, try to get young pecorino cheese—some that is not too firm—so that it doesn't turn gritty when it melts. ❀ *serves 4*

1 Preheat the oven to 300°F.

2 In a heavy saucepan, warm the milk and cream over medium-high heat until heated through but not boiling.

3 In a large mixing bowl, whisk the egg yolks. When they are blended, slowly add about ½ cup of the hot cream mixture to temper the eggs, whisking continuously. Slowly add the tempered eggs to the hot cream in the pan, as you continue to whisk the mixture.

4 Spread the diced bread on a baking sheet and dry in the oven for 1 minute.

5 Increase the oven temperature to 325°F.

6 Transfer the diced bread to a mixing bowl and pour the egg-cream mixture over it to soak the bread. Using a handheld mixer, purée until smooth. Stir in the cheese.

7 Divide the mixture evenly among four 6-ounce ramekins. Put the ramekins in a roasting pan and add enough water to come ½ inch up the sides of the pan. Cover the pan with aluminum foil.

8 Very carefully, transfer the pan to the oven and bake for 15 to 20 minutes, or until the custard is heated through and a toothpick inserted in the center comes out clean.

9 Lay the bread slices on a baking sheet and brush with olive oil. Toast in the oven, turning once, for 2 to 3 minutes, or until golden brown.

10 Meanwhile, heat the Pomodoro Sauce in a small saucepan over medium-high heat until hot and bubbling.

11 Put 1 ramekin on each of 4 serving plates and top each with about ¼ cup of Pomodoro Sauce. Drizzle each ramekin with olive oil and pepper. Put 3 slices of toast on each plate and serve.

chilled globe artichokes
carciofi marinati

2 globe artichokes
1 cup olive oil
1 cup peeled and chopped carrot
1 cup peeled and chopped onions
1 cup white wine
1 lemon, halved, plus juice of ½ lemon
4 sprigs fresh flat-leaf parsley
Sea salt and freshly ground black pepper
¼ cup balsamic vinegar
3 tablespoons Rick's Homemade Aioli (page 39)
2 ounces Parmigiano-Reggiano cheese, shaved
   (about 2 tablespoons)

I love the ritual of eating a big, beautiful globe artichoke—pulling off the leaves and dipping them in a rich aioli. Artichokes are at their very best from March through May, and during those months I eat as many as I possibly can. When you buy artichokes, look for those that are evenly olive-green or with some purple and that have tightly closed leaves that squeak when you rub them together. Cook them in plenty of water and then strain the cooking water to add to chicken or vegetable stock for a sweet vegetal flavor. Eat the artichokes soon after buying—the fresher the better.

serves 4

1. Clean the artichokes by removing the tips of the leaves and peeling the stem. Otherwise, leave the stem and outer leaves intact.

2. In a saucepan large enough to hold both artichokes, heat 2 tablespoons of olive oil over medium heat and cook the carrot and onions for about 5 minutes, or until softened. Add the wine, raise the heat, and bring to a boil.

3. Add 3 cups of water and then squeeze the lemon halves into the pan. Drop the squeezed lemon halves into the pan, add the parsley, and season generously with salt and pepper. Return the mixture to a boil.

4. Submerge the artichokes in the liquid, adjust the heat to maintain a low simmer, and cook for 15 minutes, or until the outer leaves are soft enough to puncture. If there is not enough liquid to cover the artichokes, add more water.

5. Let the artichokes cool in the cooking liquid. When they are cool, remove and refrigerate until well chilled.

6. Transfer the artichokes to a work surface. Using a large knife, split them in half and remove the choke with a spoon. Cut each artichoke in half again and put 2 pieces on each of 4 serving plates.

7. Sprinkle with salt and pepper and drizzle with the remaining olive oil, the vinegar, the aioli, and a squeeze of lemon juice. Shave the cheese over the artichokes and serve.

roasted zucchini and mint salad

zucchini arrostiti con menta

8 zucchini, halved lengthwise
4 sprigs fresh mint
About ⅔ cup croutons
About ½ cup toasted almonds
½ cup extra virgin olive oil
Juice of 3 lemons
Kosher salt and freshly ground black pepper
Fresh mint leaves

1 Preheat the oven to 500°F.

2 Lay the zucchini on a baking sheet, skin side up, and bake for about 8 minutes, or until the zucchini are golden brown on the flat, fleshy side. Let the zucchini cool slightly and then slice into half moons.

3 In a bowl, mix the zucchini, mint sprigs, croutons, and almonds. Drizzle with olive oil and lemon juice, toss, and then season to taste with salt and pepper.

4 Arrange on a serving platter and garnish with fresh mint leaves.

This summer salad is light and refreshing with the crunch of almonds and croutons and the brightness of mint and lemon juice. Try it—you'll love it as much as our customers do. It's a perfect antipasto, but also can be a side salad. Your choice. *serves 4*

beef tartare with cerignola olives, capers, and parmigiano-reggiano

manzo alla tartara con olive, capperi e parmigiano-reggiano

beef tartare
1¼ pounds prime sirloin
1 large egg yolk
½ cup extra virgin olive oil
2 tablespoons minced shallot
2 tablespoons finely diced Cerignola olives

1 tablespoon capers, chopped
4 teaspoons kosher salt
2 teaspoons freshly ground black pepper
2 tablespoons whole-grain mustard
1 anchovy, minced to a paste
Juice of 1 lemon

assembly
Eight ½-inch-thick slices ciabatta or Italian
    country-style bread
¼ cup extra virgin olive oil, plus more for
    drizzling
½ cup fresh flat-leaf parsley leaves
½ cup celery leaves
1½ ounces Parmigiano-Reggiano cheese, shaved
    (about 1½ tablespoons)
Kosher salt and freshly ground black pepper
Grated zest of 1 lemon

Some people are put off by beef tartare. I completely understand the hesitation, but if you buy prime beef from a butcher you trust and grind it yourself, you shouldn't have a problem.

Prime beef accounts for less than 2 percent of the beef produced in the United States and consequently it's expensive and relatively rare. Butchers and chefs who know choose the best prime at the wholesalers based on the marbling and cherry-red color of the beef. Without question, prime beef, which is webbed with veins of fat, tastes amazing, and it's the only beef I use for tartare. I like the flavorful prime sirloin more than the more tender beef tenderloin, although you may not agree.

Whatever beef you select, chop it by hand, never in the food processor, which will turn it mushy. I was served tartare in Paris that was diced pretty large, so it's really up to you how to cut it. Keep everything cold, work with good meat and farm-fresh, organic eggs, and enjoy a rare treat! *serves 4*

1 Preheat the oven to 400°F.

2 To prepare the beef tartare, remove as much fat and silver skin as possible from the sirloin and finely dice with a sharp knife. Transfer to a chilled stainless steel bowl.

3 Add the egg yolk, olive oil, shallot, olives, capers, salt, pepper, mustard, anchovy, and lemon juice and mix thoroughly. Set aside for about 10 minutes to blend the flavors.

4 Brush the bread slices with oil and lay on a baking sheet. Toast for 4 to 5 minutes on each side, or until lightly browned.

5 Mound a quarter of the beef tartare onto each of 4 serving plates. Garnish each plate with the parsley and celery leaves and sprinkle with the shaved cheese. Put 2 slices of the toast on each plate. Drizzle with olive oil, season to taste with salt and pepper, garnish with lemon zest, and serve.

roasted olives with grilled citrus

olive arrostite al forno con agrumi

1 orange, sliced
1 lemon, sliced
1 fennel bulb, sliced
1 red onion, peeled and sliced
2 cups extra virgin olive oil
1 tablespoon kosher salt
Freshly ground black pepper
½ cup Cerignola olives
½ cup Gaeta olives

½ cup Ligurian olives
⅓ cup Castelvetrano olives
8 garlic cloves
1 bird chile or other small hot chile

In Tuscany, as well as other parts of Italy, cured olives are put in wood ovens to get some heat through them all the way to the pit. They aren't actually cooked but instead are warmed. I do the same here, but in a hot oven with the olives and other ingredients placed together in an earthenware dish to ensure that they flavor each other as they heat up. Grilling the citrus intensifies the flavor. These olives are a dramatic change of pace. *serves 4*

1 Preheat the oven to 400°F.

2 Prepare a charcoal or gas grill by spraying the grilling rack with nonstick vegetable spray. Heat the grill until hot.

3 In a mixing bowl, toss the orange, lemon, fennel, and onion slices with the olive oil and season with salt and pepper. Lay the fruit and vegetables on the grill, using a grill basket, if necessary. Reserve the oil in the bowl. Cook for 2 to 3 minutes on each side, or until softened. Transfer to an ovenproof earthenware dish and add the reserved oil.

4 Add the olives, garlic, and chile to the dish and gently toss all of the ingredients together. Bake, uncovered, for 12 to 15 minutes, or until the oil is bubbling but not boiling.

5 Remove the dish from the oven, set aside until cooled to room temperature, and serve.

olives

Whether brined, salt-cured, or oil-cured, olives are one of the finest foods to grace our tables. Who knows who first decided to cure the inedible raw fruit from the gnarled, long-lived olive trees that grew in ancient lands? But we can all be grateful someone did!

We have been eating and enjoying olives for centuries, just as we've been benefiting from the oil squeezed from the small fruit. It's hard to imagine Italian food without either. Luckily, in the past few decades Americans have come to appreciate good olives. We love the flavor of giant green olives such as the jade-green

Cerignolas and the smaller, rounder, bright green Castelvetranos—both from Italy, both meaty, mild, and salty.

All olives are cured somehow. They cannot be eaten otherwise, and so even if a recipe calls for you to make your own marinade for olives, the olives you use will already be cured. You can rinse them under cool water before adding them to the marinade, if you like, but you don't have to. Those cured in brine retain a smooth texture; those cured with salt or in oil wrinkle and shrivel. Salt- and oil-cured olives don't appeal to everyone at first because they tend to be bitter.

charred squash with balsamic vinegar and parmigiano-reggiano

zucca arrostita con balsamico e parmigiano-reggiano

2 delicata squash (about 1½ pounds total) or other
    fall squash such as butternut, acorn, or kabocha
Sea salt and freshly ground black pepper
½ cup olive oil
3 tablespoons unsalted butter
2 fresh sage leaves
2 sprigs fresh rosemary
6 tablespoons balsamic vinegar
½ ounce Parmigiano-Reggiano cheese, shaved
    (about 1 teaspoon)

I like family-style platters, and this is one of those platters that I put together in the fall when squash is at its best. You can char-grill or roast the squash and then finish it simply with balsamic and cheese, both of which mix lusciously with the butter. There are very few ingredients here, so don't skimp; make sure they are the real deal. *serves 4*

1 Preheat the oven to 450°F.

2 Split the squash in half but do not peel them. Using a spoon, scoop out the seeds and discard. Slice the squash halves lengthwise into 4 pieces each and sprinkle with salt and pepper. Depending on the size of the squash, you may want to cut more slices. Each should be between ¼ and ½ inch thick.

3 Heat a large ovenproof sauté pan over medium-high heat until it is very hot. Put the olive oil in the pan. Arrange the squash in the pan and then add 1 tablespoon of butter to the hot pan. Remove from the heat. Top with the sage and rosemary.

4 Return the pan to the heat and cook over high heat for about 2 minutes, or until the butter foams and begins to brown. Transfer the pan to the oven and cook for 10 to 12 minutes. Do not turn the squash while it roasts. When the squash is fork tender and the underside is darkly caramelized but not burned, remove from the oven.

5 Put 4 slices of squash on each of 4 serving plates and set aside. Leave the herbs in the pan.

6 Return the pan to the heat, add 2 tablespoons of butter, and let it foam and brown lightly. Add the vinegar and stir with a wooden spoon, scraping up any browned bits. Spoon all of this sauce over the squash. Shave the cheese over the squash and serve warm.

mushroom rice balls stuffed with mozzarella
arancini alla siciliana

mushrooms
2 tablespoons vegetable oil

3 ounces fresh wild mushrooms, such as shiitake, morel, or forest, sliced (about 1¼ cups)

Kosher salt and freshly ground black pepper

1 tablespoon unsalted butter

1½ teaspoons minced shallot

1 sprig fresh thyme

rice balls
4 cups cooked and cooled Arborio rice

¼ cup frozen peas, rinsed

1 generous cup freshly grated Parmigiano-Reggiano cheese

Kosher salt and freshly ground black pepper

1½ pounds fresh mozzarella cheese, cut into 16 small cubes

About 4 cups all-purpose flour

2 large eggs

4 cups seasoned dried bread crumbs (see page 67)

Olive oil for deep-frying

assembly
1½ cups Pomodoro Sauce (page 16)

8 ounces ricotta cheese

2 ounces goat cheese, slightly softened

½ cup chopped fresh flat-leaf parsley

Rice balls, stuffed with a savory mixture and often served with tomato sauce, are popular in much of Italy. In Rome they are called *suppli*, which means "telephone cords"; in other parts of the country they are referred to as *arancini*, which means "oranges" and refers to their size, which is approximately that of the small oranges grown in Sicily.

Mine are stuffed with a mixture of wild mushrooms and shallots and then breaded and fried for a celebration of tastes and textures possible only with deep-fried foods. This recipe is similar to one my mother and grandmother made when I was a boy, and so I am attached to it. *serves 4*

1 To prepare the mushrooms, heat a sauté pan on high heat. Put the vegetable oil in the pan; when it is hot, add the mushrooms and season with salt and pepper. Cook for 3 to 4 minutes, or until the mushrooms release their liquid.

2 Add the butter, shallot, and thyme. Stir the mushrooms into the melting butter and let them caramelize in the pan. When the mushrooms are golden brown, drain the excess fat from the pan and let the mushrooms cool. When they are cool, chop into small pieces and set aside.

3 To prepare the rice balls, in a large mixing bowl, mix the rice, mushrooms, peas, and the Parmigiano-Reggiano. Season to taste with salt and pepper.

4   With dampened hands, roll the mixture into 16 balls. Each ball should weigh about 1½ ounces. Using your thumb, make an indentation in each ball.

5   Put a piece of mozzarella into the indentation in each ball and work the rice over the top of it so that it's completely covered.

6   Put the flour in a shallow bowl. Whisk the eggs with ½ cup of water in a second bowl. Put the bread crumbs in a third bowl.

7   One at a time, dredge the balls in the flour, dip them in the egg wash, and then coat with the bread crumbs.

8   Pour enough olive oil into a large, deep skillet to a depth of 4 inches (leaving at least 2 inces from the oil to the top of the pan). Heat the olive oil to 325°F. Use a deep-fat thermometer to determine the oil's temperature. Carefully lower the rice balls into the hot oil and fry for 5 to 6 minutes, or until golden brown and cooked all the way through. Lift from the oil with a slotted spoon and drain on paper towels. Cook only a few rice balls at a time so as not to crowd the pan.

9   Meanwhile, heat the Pomodoro Sauce in a small saucepan over medium-high heat until hot and bubbling.

10   In a small bowl, whisk the ricotta and goat cheeses until blended.

11   Put 4 rice balls on each of 4 serving plates. Divide the sauce evenly among small bowls and set a bowl on each plate, too. Garnish with the parsley and cheese mixture and serve.

roman-style yellow polenta with fontina fonduta
polenta alla romana con fonduta di fontina

2 quarts chicken stock
1 quart heavy cream
Kosher salt
4 cups yellow polenta
1 cup freshly grated Parmigiano-Reggiano cheese
¼ cup extra virgin olive oil
2 tablespoons unsalted butter

Freshly ground black pepper
1½ cups Fontina Fonduta (recipe follows)
½ cup shaved Parmigiano-Reggiano cheese

Polenta has been part of the Roman culture since traders from the New World brought native-grown corn back to Europe. The Italians took to it as readily as they took to tomatoes and quickly made both their own. What good luck for the rest of us!

For this dish, I make traditional polenta and pour it over a platter—or, better yet, a slab of marble—and then top it with a tasty sauce and generous shavings of aged Parmigiano-Reggiano cheese. I serve this with Fontina Fonduta, but you could substitute bolognese sauce, Pomodoro Sauce (page 16), or even a mixture of sausage, peppers, mushrooms, and garlic and great olive oil.

Wow your guests by placing a large piece of marble in the center of the table, about 12 inches square or a similarly sized rectangle, pour the hot polenta over it, spread it on the slab, and then while it's setting up for a minute or two, return to the kitchen and bring out the hot sauce and cheese. Finish the dish at the table and let everyone dig in. ❧ *serves 4*

1 In a large, heavy pot, bring the stock and heavy cream and 1 quart of water to a boil over high heat. Season to taste with salt and let the liquid return to a boil. Add the polenta, reduce the heat to medium, and cook gently for about 10 minutes, or until the cornmeal has absorbed all of the liquid and begins to resemble wet sand. At this point, the grittiness will subside as the polenta cooks, and it will be thick and smooth all the way through.

2 Stir in the grated cheese, olive oil, butter, and pepper to taste.

3 At this point the polenta is done. Warm the Fontina Fonduta over low heat. Lay a marble slab on the table and pour a generous amount of polenta onto the slab, spreading it out with a spoon so that it is ½ to ¾ inch thick.

4 Gently pour the Fontina Fonduta in the center of the polenta and spread it over the polenta with a large spoon or spatula. Top with the shaved cheese and let it melt into the hot polenta and fonduta as you serve it.

fontina fonduta

I had eaten fonduta many times before but had never appreciated it until I traveled to Italy. Similar to the fondue served in Switzerland, fonduta is lovely served with bread or crostini, and also good with raw vegetables such as carrot and celery sticks, but I like using it to top polenta perhaps best of all.

Fontina cheese has been produced in

polenta and cornmeal

Polenta is a great favorite in Italy and has gained a foothold here, too. The little secret about polenta is that it is nothing more exotic than cornmeal—a product Americans have been eating forever. For polenta, the cornmeal is cooked in water or stock until it becomes soft and thick; American cornmeal is found mainly in baked goods such as cornbread and muffins. (Our version of porridge-like cornmeal is grits, a staple of Southern cooking.)

You can buy imported Italian cornmeal, which is labeled "polenta," in many markets. You can also buy it already made and sold in bricks that need only to be sliced and heated. Because it's so easy to make yourself, I recommend starting with cornmeal.

When you make polenta, look for cornmeal—American grown and ground, or imported from Italy—that has been minimally processed. This generally means it's stone-ground, a process that relies on large stones for grinding, often powered the old-fashioned way, by water. This cornmeal contains the germ of the grain and therefore is not only more nutritious, but also grittier than steel-ground cornmeal and has a slightly nutty flavor. It's more fragile, too, so once you open the package, refrigerate it and try to use it within a month or so of purchase.

Cornmeal can be white, yellow, or blue. Blue, a staple of the American Southwest, is not as common, but white and yellow are easy to find and there is no difference between them other than color. One is ground from yellow corn, the other from white. The choice is a matter of personal preference, and both make superb polenta!

Italy's Val d'Aosta since the Middle Ages and perhaps longer. Not all cheeses called "fontina" are produced in the Aosta Valley, and those imitations range from very good to rather poor. Choose your fontina carefully and prepare yourself a glorious treat. *serves 4; makes about 4½ cups*

14 ounces young fontina cheese without rind, such as Fontina Val d'Aosta
1 cup heavy cream
2 tablespoons unsalted butter
4 large egg yolks
1 tablespoon white truffle oil
Kosher salt and freshly ground black pepper
Black or white truffles, shaved, as many as you can afford, optional

1 Cut the fontina into thin slices and lay them in a shallow bowl. Add the cream and refrigerate for 4 to 6 hours.

2 Lift the fontina slices from the cream. Reserve the cream.

3 In the top of a double boiler, fondue pot, or other saucepan, combine the butter and fontina slices and 3 tablespoons of the cream. Set over simmering water (do not let it boil) and stir just until the cheese melts and can be pulled into strings.

4 In a mixing bowl, whisk the egg yolks with the remaining cream. Add to the cheese mixture, still over simmering water, and stir until thick and smooth. Stir in the truffle oil and season to taste with salt and pepper.

5 Divide the fonduta among 4 small bowls and garnish with truffle shavings, if desired. Serve with desired accompaniments.

pizza

To some, pizza is a religion. I know chefs who have left their restaurants and turned their attention solely to making pizzas. Although I may not be a fanatic, I am passionate about pizza and I make it at least once a week for my wife and kids.

My grandparents and parents made pizzas in old black sheet pans that must have come from Italy with my grandparents and then were passed down to my parents. They were beat-up pans, about 2 inches deep, with a heavy coating of baked-on grease. The pizzas that came out of them were awesome. The crusts were thin and tender and the fillings started with our homemade sauce. I remember my friends were fascinated by the pizzas because they weren't round—and because my mom cut them with a pair of scissors, not a pizza wheel or knife.

I grew up in the East, and so I am inclined to prefer thin-crusted, hand-rolled crusts, topped with skinny layers of fresh tomato sauce and then any number of judiciously applied toppings, such as salami, mushrooms, and arugula. When I moved to Chicago, I was surprised by the thick-crusted, deep-dish pizza so beloved here; though I appreciate it, I prefer the sort of thin-crust pizza I grew up with.

Any pizza tastes best when cooked in a wood-burning pizza oven but not everyone has access to one. If you use a pizza stone in a very hot oven, the crust should crisp up nicely. This is how I cook pizza at home for my family. I don't have a wood-burning oven (although someday I would like to build one in the backyard), and so I bake the pizza in my regular oven or sometimes on a charcoal grill. And always it's great!

notes from the sommelier
wines for daily drinking

While best known for their ultraluxury cuvées and high-scoring prestige wines, many of the remarkable producers represented on the Osteria di Tramonto wine lists also take great pride in the wines they produce for everyday drinking. Winemakers that have been awarded perfect 100-point scores for their creations and Tre Bicchieri, the top awards from Gambero Rosso (Italy's high authority on wine), also make wines that don't make credit cards scream for mercy.

These are the gems we love to stock in our home cellars and the wines we drink during simple family dinners. Although we all love to dream of nightly sipping magnums of Masseto, that rare and amazing Tuscan Merlot, for the less decadent there is Le Serre Nuove, which is also produced by Tenuta Ornellaia. For Sassicaia devotees there are Guidalberto and Barrua from Tenuta San Guido at more down-to-earth prices. Many of these second and third wines are found in less-established regions; Barrua is from Sardegna, for example. From our cellars, we delight in revealing the hidden treasures. Our favorite producers include Cusumano in Sicily (single-varietal whites and reds offer great bang for the buck), Villa del Borgo in Friuli (try their Refosco), Terragens in Emilia-Romagna (excellent reds for nightly drinking), and Caldora in Abruzzo (Trebbiano and Montepulciano are specialties). If it's a Tramonto's Signature Pizza night, open one of these excellent wines.

breakfast pizza with potato, leek, prosciutto, and egg

pizza con patate, porro, prosciutto, e uovo

1 small Red Bliss potato, sliced
½ leek
3 tablespoons extra virgin olive oil
1 teaspoon unsalted butter
½ recipe Pizza Dough (page 115)
1 ounce sliced mozzarella cheese (about ¼ cup)
1 large egg
½ ounce prosciutto, sliced (4 to 5 paper-thin slices)
1 teaspoon Garlic Oil (recipe follows)
Kosher salt and freshly ground black pepper

1 Position the oven rack in the middle of the oven. If you have a pizza stone, put it on the rack to heat up. Preheat the oven to 450°F.

2 Put the potato slices in a saucepan of cold water and bring to a boil over high heat. Immediately remove from the heat, drain, and set aside to cool.

3 Slice and wash the leek. In a skillet, heat the olive oil and butter over medium heat until the butter melts. Add the leeks and cook over medium-low heat for about 10 minutes, or until the leeks are very soft. Set aside to cool.

4 Roll out the dough to a circle 12 inches in diameter and ¼ to ½ inch thick. Work on a lightly floured cutting board so you can slide the pizza onto a baking sheet or the pizza stone.

5 Cover the crust with the potato slices, leeks, and cheese.

6 Transfer the pizza to the oven and bake for about 5 minutes, or until the cheese bubbles. Pull the oven rack out and, without removing the pizza, crack the egg on top of the pizza. Return to the oven for about 10 minutes, or until the egg is cooked and the pizza crust is golden brown. Gently lift the pizza up and peek at the bottom. If it is golden brown and solid, it's done. If it's still pale and a little soft looking, let it cook for a few minutes longer.

7 Drape the prosciutto over the pizza. Drizzle with Garlic Oil, season to taste with salt and pepper, cut into 4 wedges, and serve hot.

When I sat down to write about this recipe, I was tempted to put it in the breakfast chapter, but reason prevailed and so it's here in the pizza chapter. This does not mean it wouldn't make a superb breakfast or brunch dish—and I have made this countless times for my three boys for breakfast—but it's also great for supper. And who doesn't like breakfast for dinner? *serves 4*

garlic oil
makes about 1¼ cups

2 cups extra virgin olive oil
6 garlic cloves, minced

1 In a glass jar or similar container, combine the olive oil and garlic. Cover and refrigerate for at least 24 hours to give the oil time to steep.

2 The oil will keep for 4 days if stored in a cool, dark place, and for up to 3 weeks refrigerated. If you refrigerate it, take it out of the refrigerator for about 15 minutes before using to allow it to warm up.

pepperoni pizza

pizza con salumi

½ recipe Pizza Dough (page 115)
1 teaspoon Garlic Oil (page 104)
½ cup Pizza Sauce (page 115)
2 ounces diced mozzarella cheese (about ½ cup)
1 ounce imported Calabrese salami, thinly sliced
     (4 to 5 slices)
½ ounce freshly grated Parmigiano-Reggiano
     cheese (about 1 teaspoon)
2 tablespoons extra virgin olive oil
Kosher salt and freshly ground black pepper

If you canvass any group of pizza lovers, pepperoni often ranks as their preferred topping. It's one of my favorites, too, and when I was in Florence I was able to satisfy my craving for really good pepperoni pies. Back in Chicago, I buy fantastic imported and local pepperoni and salami from the Italian markets, and I have to say my pizza rivals those I've had in Italy.

It's all about the ingredients. If you expect this to taste like the pepperoni pizza you get from the corner pizzeria, you will be surprised how much better it is made with Calabrese salami, sliced very thin. From Calabria in southern Italy, Calabrese salami is air-dried salami flavored with hot peppers, garlic, and salt and pepper. Usually it's made from pork only, although in some cases a little beef is added, too. Buy the best you can find.

serves 4

1 Position the oven rack in the middle of the oven. If you have a pizza stone, put it on the rack to heat up. Preheat the oven to 450°F.

2 Roll out the dough to a circle 12 inches in diameter and ¼ to ½ inch thick. Work on a lightly floured cutting board so you can slide the pizza onto a baking sheet or the pizza stone.

3 Brush the crust with the Garlic Oil and spread the pizza sauce over the crust to the edges.

4 Evenly arrange the mozzarella over the pizza, layer the salami on top of the cheese, and sprinkle with the Parmigiano-Reggiano.

5 Transfer the pizza to the oven and bake for about 15 minutes, or until the sauce bubbles. Gently lift the pizza up and peek at the bottom. If it is golden brown and solid, it's done. If it's still pale and a little soft looking, let it cook for a few minutes longer.

6 Drizzle with the olive oil and season to taste with salt and pepper. Cut into 4 wedges and serve hot.

tuscan lardo and onion pizza
pizza con lardo e cipolle

½ recipe Pizza Dough (page 115)
1 teaspoon Garlic Oil (page 104)
2 ounces mascarpone cheese (about 2 teaspoons)
2 tablespoons Caramelized Onions (recipe follows)
1 ounce lardo, thinly sliced (see page 28)
1 tablespoon extra virgin olive oil
Leaves from 4 sprigs fresh thyme

1 Position the oven rack in the middle of the oven. If you have a pizza stone, put it on the rack to heat up. Preheat the oven to 450°F.

When I travel through the regions of Piedmont and Tuscany in Italy, I visit wineries with wood-burning ovens where cooks pull out one pizza after another to taste with the wine. Many of these just-baked pizzas are topped with thinly sliced, handmade lardo, as well as other ingredients, which means the topping melts in the mouth with the first bite. Lardo does not play too well with Americans—could it be the name?—but one taste and you'll agree that it's delicious. I added onions and mascarpone to the lardo topping, and it's become a very popular pizza with our customers. Once you try it, it will be popular with you, too.

serves 4

2 Roll out the dough to a circle 12 inches in diameter and ¼ to ½ inch thick. Work on a lightly floured cutting board so you can slide the pizza onto a baking sheet or the pizza stone.

3 Brush the crust with the Garlic Oil and spread the cheese and onions evenly over the crust.

4 Transfer the pizza to the oven and bake for about 15 minutes, or until the cheese bubbles. Gently lift the pizza up and peek at the bottom. If it is golden brown and solid, it's done. If it's still pale and a little soft looking, let it cook for a few minutes longer.

5 Remove the pizza from the oven and lay the sliced lardo over the hot pizza so that it melts.

6 Drizzle with the olive oil and garnish with the thyme leaves. Cut into 4 wedges and serve hot.

caramelized onions
makes about 1 cup

1 tablespoon unsalted butter
2 large Spanish onions, thinly sliced
Kosher salt

1 Over medium heat, melt the butter in a sauté pan. Add the onions and cook over medium heat for about 40 minutes, stirring every 5 minutes with a wooden spoon and scraping up any browned bits.

2 The onions are done when they have darkened to a medium brown and are very soft. Season lightly with salt and use as needed.

sausage, broccoli rabe, and calabrian chile pizza

pizza con salsiccia, rapini, e peperoncino

1 small bunch broccoli rabe, stems removed
3 tablespoons extra virgin olive oil
Pinch of chopped Calabrian chiles
Kosher salt and freshly ground black pepper
½ recipe Pizza Dough (page 115)
1 teaspoon Garlic Oil (page 104)
½ cup cooked crumbled Italian sausage
3 ounces diced mozzarella cheese (about ¾ cup)
Freshly grated Parmigiano-Reggiano cheese
Crushed red pepper flakes, more chopped
    Calabrian chiles, or a little Calabrian chile oil,
    optional

Calabrian chiles are among my favorites. Any number of chiles grow well in the sunny, southern reaches of Italy called Calabria, and therefore you can argue that it's hard to label any one kind as Calabrian. When I call for Calabrian chiles, I mean round, red spicy peppers packed in oil. Don't use more than one here, and even that may be strong enough to explode with too much heat. Use them sparingly but remember: a little goes a long way and makes this pizza sing. I combine them with broccoli rabe—also called rapini—and sausages for a magical meal. ❦ *serves 4*

1 In a pan filled with lightly salted boiling water, blanch the broccoli rabe for 2 to 3 minutes, or until bright green. Drain and set aside to cool.

2 Chop the broccoli rabe and transfer to a bowl. You should have about 1 cup of chopped broccoli rabe. Add 2 tablespoons of olive oil and the chiles.

3 In a small sauté pan, sauté the broccoli rabe mixture over medium-high heat for 2 to 3 minutes, or until the flavors blend. Season to taste with salt and pepper and set aside.

4 Position the oven rack in the middle of the oven. If you have a pizza stone, put it on the rack to heat up. Preheat the oven to 450°F.

5 Roll out the dough to a circle 12 inches in diameter and ¼ to ½ inch thick. Work on a lightly floured cutting board so you can slide the pizza onto a baking sheet or the pizza stone.

6 Brush the crust with the Garlic Oil and scatter the sausage over the crust, followed by the broccoli rabe and the mozzarella.

7 Transfer the pizza to the oven and bake for about 15 minutes, or until the cheese bubbles. Gently lift the pizza up and peek at the bottom. If it is golden brown and solid, it's done. If it's still pale and a little soft looking, let it cook for a few minutes longer.

8 Drizzle with 1 tablespoon of olive oil and sprinkle with grated Parmigiano-Reggiano and, if you want some heat, red pepper flakes, chopped chiles, or chile oil. Cut into 4 wedges and serve hot.

four-cheese pizza

pizza ai quattro formaggi

½ recipe Pizza Dough (page 115)
1 teaspoon Garlic Oil (page 104)
1 garlic clove, minced
¼ cup Pizza Sauce (page 115)
1 ounce soft goat cheese, broken into pieces (about 1 tablespoon)
1 ounce diced mozzarella cheese (about ¼ cup)
¼ cup freshly grated Pecorino-Romano cheese
¼ cup freshly grated Parmigiano-Reggiano cheese
1 tablespoon extra virgin olive oil
Kosher salt and freshly ground black pepper
1 tablespoon dried oregano

It's no surprise that I love cheese, and these four are among my favorites. I think anyone who appreciates pizza will like the way the cheese melts over the topping and adds to the flavor and mouthfeel of the finished dish. For this pizza, I chose these cheeses because of how they subtly relate to each other when they mingle and melt together. I like the way the pizza looks when the cheeses are segregated except along their borders, but if you prefer, mix the cheeses together and let them play with each other in a more obvious, but equally tasty, way. Choose the best cheeses you can find. *serves 4*

1 Position the oven rack in the middle of the oven. If you have a pizza stone, put it on the rack to heat up. Preheat the oven to 450°F.

2 Roll out the dough to a circle 12 inches in diameter and ¼ to ½ inch thick. Work on a lightly floured cutting board so you can slide the pizza onto a baking sheet or the pizza stone.

3 Brush the crust with the Garlic Oil and scatter the minced garlic over the crust. Spread the pizza sauce over the crust to the edges.

4 Put each cheese on top of the pizza, arranging the goat cheese on one quarter, pinching pieces from the softened log; the mozzarella on another quarter; the Pecorino-Romano on the third quarter; and the Parmigiano-Reggiano on the fourth quarter.

5 Transfer the pizza to the oven and bake for about 15 minutes, or until the sauce bubbles. Gently lift the pizza up and peek at the bottom. If it is golden brown and solid, it's done. If it's still pale and a little soft looking, let it cook for a few minutes longer.

6 Drizzle with the olive oil and season to taste with salt and pepper. Sprinkle with oregano, cut into 4 wedges, and serve hot.

tomato and mozzarella pizza

pizza margherita

½ recipe Pizza Dough (page 115)

1 teaspoon Garlic Oil (page 104)

½ cup plus 2 tablespoons Pizza Sauce (page 115)

2 ounces diced mozzarella cheese (about ½ cup; preferably buffalo, see Note)

1 tablespoon freshly grated Parmigiano-Reggiano cheese

2 tablespoons fresh basil leaves, torn

2 tablespoons extra virgin olive oil

Kosher salt and freshly ground black pepper

This might be one of the most classic of all pizzas, and so it pays to use fresh buffalo mozzarella, great Parmigiano-Reggiano, rich fruity olive oil, fresh-picked basil, kosher salt, and freshly ground pepper. Sounds obvious, doesn't it? But for this pizza, the best ingredients make all the difference!

serves 4

1 Position the oven rack in the middle of the oven. If you have a pizza stone, put it on the rack to heat up. Preheat the oven to 450°F.

2 Roll out the dough to a circle 12 inches in diameter and ¼ to ½ inch thick. Work on a lightly floured cutting board so you can slide the pizza onto a baking sheet or the pizza stone.

3 Brush the crust with the Garlic Oil and spread the pizza sauce over the crust to the edges.

4 Arrange the mozzarella evenly over the pizza and sprinkle with the Parmigiano-Reggiano.

5 Transfer the pizza to the oven and bake for about 15 minutes, or until the sauce bubbles. Gently lift the pizza up and peek at the bottom. If it is golden brown and solid, it's done. If it's still pale and a little soft looking, let it cook for a few minutes longer.

6 Sprinkle with the basil, drizzle with the olive oil, and season to taste with salt and pepper. Cut into 4 wedges and serve hot.

note If you use buffalo mozzarella, drain it first in a sieve set over a bowl to extract excess moisture. Let it sit in the refrigerator for 3 to 4 hours to drain. This may not be necessary, depending on the cheese, because some buffalo mozzarellas are wetter than others.

roasted pepper and goat cheese pizza

pizza con peperoni arrostiti e formaggio caprino

½ recipe Pizza Dough (page 115)
1 teaspoon Garlic Oil (page 104)
2 tablespoons Pizza Sauce (page 115)
3 tablespoons chopped roasted pepper (see page 11)
1½ ounces crumbled goat cheese (about 1½ tablespoons)
¼ ounce sliced coppa (2 to 3 slices) or prosciutto (4 to 5 slices)
Large pinch of chopped fresh rosemary
1 tablespoon extra virgin olive oil
Kosher salt and freshly ground black pepper

When red and yellow peppers are fresh from the garden or farmers' market and sweet as can be, this pizza is a sure winner. It's good any other time, of course, and I highly recommend that you roast your own peppers rather than buy roasted peppers. This brings out all of their succulent flavor. You can eliminate the salami for a vegetarian pizza and have a terrific meal; I include it for the fat and salt! ❦ *serves 4*

1 Position the oven rack in the middle of the oven. If you have a pizza stone, put it on the rack to heat up. Preheat the oven to 450°F.

2 Roll out the dough to a circle 12 inches in diameter and ¼ to ½ inch thick. Work on a lightly floured cutting board so that you can slide the pizza onto a baking sheet or the pizza stone.

3 Brush the crust with the Garlic Oil and spread the pizza sauce over the crust to the edges.

4 Sprinkle the roasted pepper and cheese over the pizza. Layer the coppa over the cheese and sprinkle with the rosemary.

5 Transfer the pizza to the oven and bake for about 15 minutes, or until the sauce bubbles. Gently lift the pizza up and peek at the bottom. If it is golden brown and solid, it's done. If it's still pale and a little soft looking, let it cook for a few minutes longer.

6 Drizzle with the olive oil and season to taste with salt and pepper. Cut into 4 wedges and serve hot.

tramonto's signature pizza

pizza tramonto

½ recipe Pizza Dough (page 115)
2 tablespoons Garlic Oil (page 104)
1 tablespoon Roasted Garlic Purée (recipe follows)
2 ounces sliced mozzarella cheese (4 to 5 slices)
1½ teaspoons red wine vinegar
1 teaspoon truffle oil
⅓ cup arugula
¼ cup seeded and diced Roma tomatoes
¼ ounce pitted Gaeta olives
Kosher salt and freshly ground black pepper
1 lemon, quartered

1 Position the oven rack in the middle of the oven. If you have a pizza stone, put it on the rack to heat up. Preheat the oven to 450°F.

2 Roll out the dough to a circle 12 inches in diameter and ¼ to ½ inch thick. Work on a lightly floured cutting board so you can slide the pizza onto a baking sheet or the pizza stone.

3 Brush the crust with 1 tablespoon of Garlic Oil and spread the Roasted Garlic Purée over the crust to cover it generously. Top with the cheese.

4 Transfer the pizza to the oven and bake for about 15 minutes, or until the cheese bubbles. Gently lift the pizza up and peek at the bottom. If it is golden brown and solid, it's done. If it's still pale and a little soft looking, let it cook for a few minutes longer.

5 Meanwhile, in a small bowl, stir together the vinegar, truffle oil, and 1 tablespoon of Garlic Oil. Add the arugula, tomatoes, and olives and toss lightly to make a small salad. Season to taste with salt and pepper.

6 Cut the pizza into 4 wedges, top each wedge with some salad and a lemon quarter, and serve.

roasted garlic purée
makes about 1½ tablespoons

12 unpeeled garlic cloves, lightly crushed and top ends cut off
½ cup extra virgin olive oil
1 teaspoon kosher salt

1 Preheat the oven to 300°F.

2 Lay a large sheet of aluminum foil on the countertop and put the garlic cloves in the center. Drizzle with the olive oil and sprinkle with the salt. Fold the foil into a sealed package. Set in a small baking pan and bake for about 35 minutes, or until tender.

3 Open the package and let the garlic cloves cool a little. When they are cool enough to handle, squeeze the soft garlic pulp from the skins into a small bowl. Discard the skins.

4 Mash the garlic pulp with a fork to make a purée. Use immediately or cool to room temperature. Put the pulp in a small dish, cover with olive oil, cover the dish with plastic wrap, and refrigerate for up to 5 days.

Since my days at Brasserie T back in the 1990s, this has been my signature pizza. I love salad pizzas and this one is the ultimate, as far as I am concerned, topped as it is with a tasty arugula, tomato, and olive salad dressed with truffle vinaigrette. If you don't have truffle oil, dress the salad with olive oil and lemon juice— it will be just as good. I like to mingle salad, cheese, and bread and here they are, all in one glorious pizza. ❁ *serves 4*

mushroom pizza
pizza con funghi

¼ cup olive oil

½ pound mushrooms, such as cremini, shiitake, or white button, sliced (about 1⅔ cups)

½ teaspoon chopped garlic

½ teaspoon chopped shallot

Kosher salt and freshly ground black pepper

1 to 2 teaspoons sherry vinegar

1 teaspoon unsalted butter

½ recipe Pizza Dough (page 115)

1 teaspoon Garlic Oil (page 104)

2 ounces sliced mozzarella cheese (4 to 5 slices)

15 to 20 pitted Castelvetrano Sicilian olives or other large green olives, crushed

¾ ounce Piave cheese, shaved (about 3 tablespoons)

1½ teaspoons extra virgin olive oil

If you are a mushroom lover, here is the pizza for you! I suggest you plan to make it when the spring and fall mushrooms show up in the markets in all their rich, earthy deliciousness. You can use ordinary white button mushrooms, if you can't find any others, and still have a mushroom feast, but if you can, try different kinds. Be sure the mushrooms are of the highest quality and are wiped clean of grit and dirt. *serves 4*

1. Position the oven rack in the middle of the oven. If you have a pizza stone, put it on the rack to heat up. Preheat the oven to 450°F.

2. Set an ovenproof skillet over high heat. When it is hot, put in ¼ cup of olive oil and heat until hot. Add the mushrooms and sauté for 3 to 5 minutes, or until they release their moisture.

3. Add the garlic and shallot and season to taste with salt and pepper. Add 1 teaspoon of vinegar and the butter to the pan, stirring with a wooden spoon and scraping up any browned bits. Add more vinegar if needed. Transfer the pan to the oven and cook for 8 to 10 minutes, or until the juices evaporate and the mushrooms start to brown and caramelize.

4. Roll out the dough to a circle 12 inches in diameter and ¼ to ½ inch thick. Work on a lightly floured cutting board so you can slide the pizza onto a baking sheet or the pizza stone.

5. Brush the crust with the Garlic Oil. Arrange the mushrooms, mozzarella, and olives evenly on the crust.

6. Transfer the pizza to the oven and bake for about 15 minutes, or until the cheese bubbles. Gently lift the pizza up and peek at the bottom. If it is golden brown and solid, it's done. If it's still pale and a little soft looking, let it cook for a few minutes longer.

7. Top with the shaved Piave, drizzle with the extra virgin olive oil, and season to taste with salt and pepper. Cut into 4 wedges and serve hot.

pizza dough

This is a great, authentic Italian pizza dough that will perform beautifully for you if you treat it right. Make it with really good olive oil and don't overwork the dough, which toughens it. Otherwise, there is nothing complex about this forgiving dough. Roll it as thinly or as thickly as you like, depending on your personal preference. As I've said, I like thin-crust pizzas and so I instruct you to roll the pizza dough so that it's ¼ to ½ inch thick. You could go thicker (and increase the baking time a little). Although the crust may not taste exactly like those that have been cooked in a hot, wood-fired oven, it's a terrific dough that results in an amazing crust!

makes 2 crusts

¼ ounce (1 package) active dry yeast
2 cups all-purpose flour
2 teaspoons kosher salt
1 teaspoon sugar
1 teaspoon extra virgin olive oil

1   In the large bowl of an electric mixer fitted with the paddle attachment, gently stir the yeast (by hand) into ¾ cup of room-temperature water and set aside for about 10 minutes. The mixture will bubble and foam.

2   Add the flour, salt, and sugar and mix on low speed for about 3 minutes, or until the dough comes together in a cohesive mass. Increase the speed to medium and mix for about 10 minutes, or until the dough is smooth and elastic.

3   Transfer the dough to a lightly oiled bowl. Cover the bowl with a well-wrung, damp kitchen towel and set aside in a warm, draft-free place for 30 minutes, or until the dough rises and doubles in size.

4   Turn the dough out onto a lightly floured surface and knead a few times to expel the air from the dough. Divide the dough into 2 balls. Brush each with olive oil and set on a baking sheet. Cover with plastic wrap and set aside for 2 to 12 hours. Roll out as desired.

pizza sauce

This is an uncooked sauce, perfect for spreading over the pizza dough before it's baked. It's so easy to make, particularly if you keep cans of good Italian plum tomatoes, such as San Marzano and Paradiso, in your pantry.

makes about 1 ¼ cups

One 10-ounce can peeled tomatoes, drained
2 tablespoons extra virgin olive oil
1½ teaspoons chopped fresh oregano
1½ teaspoons minced garlic
1 teaspoon kosher salt

In a large mixing bowl, crush the tomatoes with the back of a wooden spoon or a fork. Add the olive oil, oregano, garlic, and salt and mix well. Taste and adjust the seasoning with salt. This is now ready to spoon over a pizza crust and bake.

pasta

When I visited the Tenuta Vitanza winery in Montalcino, Tuscany, Rosalba Andretta, the winemaker, invited me to eat with her; her husband, Guido; and her daughter, Emma. It was about eleven in the morning, and as soon as we sat down at the table in the kitchen of the old stone farmhouse, Rosalba took out three wooden boards. She handed one to me and one to Emma and said, "Let's make *pici.*" She took out the flour and Guido went to the henhouse for eggs. We sat there for four hours making pasta. I felt like I was in an amazing dream, but it was also bittersweet. The afternoon reminded me so much of spending time with my mother, who died twelve years ago. We used to make pasta together as a natural preparation for dinner and would sit in the kitchen and talk about anything and every-thing as we formed the dough, rolled it, and cut the pasta. Rosalba will never know how much the time I spent with her and her family meant to me, and so I dedicate this chapter to her.

Homemade pasta is wonderful, but I think dried pasta is excellent, too, and far easier. Think about how you are using the pasta. If you want it to be simply a vehicle for the flavors of the sauce, dried pasta is more than fine, but if you have some ingredients that you want to make into ravioli, consider making the pasta yourself.

Think, too, about the sauce when you select the pasta. Textured sauces do best with chunky, ridged pastas; thin, smooth sauces are better with strand pasta. Cook the pasta to the right consistency. Because you don't want it to soften too much in the sauce but to stand up to it, take great care not to overcook pasta. In the end, nothing is more satisfying than a dish of pasta.

notes from the sommelier
the sunday fiasco

A *fiasco* is a jug or a flask. Since the fourteenth century, the term has referred to the round-bottomed, straw-covered bottles used for Chianti, celebrated in paintings by artists such as Botticelli and Ghirlandaio. For Chef Tramonto and me, though, a "fiasco" is a gathering of foodies, wine geeks, and wine-geeks-to-be. It's our dinner party! On the third Sunday of every month, we invite all of our favorite friends of the osteria to participate in a dinner party during which everyone sits at a long communal table to enjoy a feast celebrating the wines and the cuisine of a particular region of Italy. Our chefs expound on the products and culinary techniques of the region, such as Le Marche, Piedmont, or Sicily, and I speak about the area's wine scene. The wines of each region always prove to be the perfect match or foil for the regional meal.

During our celebration of Le Marche, for example, the wine lineup included that central Italian region's finest—floral, perfumed white Verdicchio dei Castelli Jesi, and a venerable lineup of reds from that region's classic appellations that deal in the Montepulciano grape: Rosso Piceno, Rosso Conero, and even "Super Marche" reds from tireless Le Marche promoter Antonio Terni of Fattoria Le Terrazze. Likewise, each of the other twenty regions of Italy provides a full complement of white and red wines to pair with its proper meal.

In the spirit of the many wonderful dinners that we have enjoyed at our favorite Italian winemakers' homes, everything for the evening's menu comes from the local market, the dishes are served with the wines for which they were designed, and everything, including the copious bowls of steaming ricotta gnocchi or pappardelle with meat ragù, is served family style. Make your Sunday dinners special by cooking one of Rick's pasta dishes and opening a wine from sunny southern Italy.

tagliatelle with octopus puttanesca
tagliatelle con polipo "puttanesca"

octopus sauce
5 pounds baby octopus
½ cup extra virgin olive oil
1 white onion, sliced
1 fennel bulb, sliced
2 cups pitted black Ligurian olives
1 cup drained capers, rinsed
1½ teaspoons crushed red pepper flakes
1½ teaspoons dried oregano
1 sprig fresh oregano
One 750-ml bottle red wine
One 14-ounce can tomatoes, drained
¼ cup red wine vinegar
1 anchovy fillet
1½ tablespoons kosher salt

1 pound tagliatelle

assembly
2 tablespoons unsalted butter
2 tablespoons extra virgin olive oil
Kosher salt and freshly ground black pepper
½ cup chopped fresh flat-leaf parsley
½ cup chopped fresh basil

I open this chapter with a recipe that some might find exotic: pasta with octopus. I am a fan of the creature from the briny deep, and once we persuade our customers to try octopus, they are hooked. I suspect you will be, too. The trick is to buy high-quality octopus from a fishmonger you trust and cook it slowly, as described here, so that it becomes as tender as can be. It goes extremely well with other seafood, too. ❁ *serves 4*

1 Preheat the oven to 300°F.

2 To prepare the octopus sauce, clean the octopuses by removing and discarding the beaks and the heads. You need to make only one cut to separate these from the legs.

3 In a large ovenproof saucepan, heat the olive oil over medium-high heat. Add the onion, fennel, olives, capers, red pepper, dried oregano, and oregano sprig. Cook over medium heat for about 4 minutes, or just until the onion softens.

4 Add the wine and boil over high heat for about 6 minutes, or until reduced by half.

5 Add the octopus, tomatoes, vinegar, anchovy, and salt to the pan and bring to a boil. Cover the pan with parchment paper, transfer to the oven, and cook for 1 to 1½ hours, until the octopus is tender.

6 Allow the octopus to cool in the sauce. Remove the octopus and cut into 1-inch pieces. Set the octopus aside and reserve the sauce.

7 To prepare the tagliatelle, cook the pasta according to the package instructions until firm but not yet al dente. Drain.

8 Meanwhile, heat the octopus and sauce over medium-high heat. Add the drained pasta to the sauce and cook for a few minutes until al dente. Add the butter and olive oil and stir until incorporated. Season to taste with salt and pepper. Sprinkle with parsley and basil, divide evenly among 4 plates, and serve.

the sommelier recommends
This zesty, full-flavored pasta sings with a likewise zesty, full-flavored red from Calabria. The Gaglioppo and Maglioppo grapes make spicy, mouth-filling reds, and we love the Terre di Balbia label.

gloria's lasagna
rick's mom's recipe

meat sauce

3 tablespoons olive oil

½ large yellow onion, finely diced

2 tablespoons minced garlic

1 pound ground spicy Italian sausage

1 pound ground beef

½ cup white wine

Two 14-ounce cans plum tomatoes

1 tablespoon ground fennel seeds

2 teaspoons crushed red pepper flakes

1 tablespoon chopped fresh basil

1 teaspoon chopped fresh oregano

cheese filling

1 pound ricotta cheese

1 large egg

½ cup freshly grated Parmigiano-Reggiano cheese

Kosher salt and freshly ground black pepper

lasagna

1 pound lasagna sheets

Olive oil

1 cup freshly grated Parmigiano-Reggiano cheese

Because my mom made a big pan of this lasagna at least once a week when I was growing up, it's near and dear to my heart. There is nothing fancy or "restauranty" about the recipe; instead it's about as down-to-earth and satisfying a dish as you will ever find. My mother insisted on high-quality ricotta cheese and always mixed Italian sausage with ground beef. I remember eating it for breakfast the next day. *serves 8; makes 1 lasagna*

1   Preheat the oven to 400°F.

2   To prepare the meat sauce, heat the olive oil in a large sauté pan over medium-high heat. Add the onion and garlic and cook for 3 to 4 minutes, or until softened but not colored. Add the sausage and beef and cook, stirring, for 10 to 12 minutes, or until cooked through and no pink beef remains. Using a slotted spoon, remove the meat and vegetables from the pan. Drain and discard the fat left in the pan.

3   Add the wine and cook over medium-high heat, stirring with a wooden spoon and scraping up any browned bits. Let the wine simmer briskly for about 2 minutes, or until the pan is dry. Add the tomatoes, fennel seeds, and red pepper to the pan along with the meat mixture. Cook over medium heat until hot. Stir in the basil and oregano, remove from the heat, and set aside until needed.

4   To make the cheese filling, in a large mixing bowl, stir the ricotta, the egg, and ½ cup of Parmigiano-Reggiano. Season to taste with salt and pepper.

5   Using a handheld mixer, beat the cheese mixture for about 4 minutes, or until smooth. Set aside until needed.

6   To prepare the lasagna, bring about 1½ gallons of salted water to a boil in a large pot over high heat. Add the lasagna sheets one by one, stirring the water as each one enters the pot. Cook for about 8 minutes, or until the lasagna sheets are cooked about three-quarters of the way through. They should be tender, but not ready to fall apart.

7 Drain the lasagna sheets and toss lightly with a touch of olive oil so they do not stick together. Lay them out on a kitchen towel until you are ready to assemble the lasagna. (This can be done 24 hours in advance.)

8 To assemble the lasagna, ladle about ½ cup of the meat sauce into the bottom of a rectangular baking dish measuring about 9 × 13 × 2 inches. Spread the sauce over the bottom of the pan.

9 Lay pasta sheets on top of the sauce and then top with half of the cheese filling, spreading it evenly over the pasta. Spoon a third of the remaining sauce over the cheese and top with a third of the Parmigiano-Reggiano.

10 Add more sheets of pasta and repeat the layering. Finally, finish with pasta and the remaining ingredients, ending with the Parmigiano-Reggiano.

11 Bake for about 1 hour, or until heated through and bubbling around the edges. Let the lasagna sit for 15 minutes before cutting into squares for serving.

the sommelier recommends
The spicy Italian sausage in this rendition of lasagna gears it up for a red wine with some spunk. A simple, straightforward Barbera from Castello del Poggio or the Barbera and Pinot Nero blend "Le Grive" from Forteto della Luja will add a nice dash of bright red fruit.

pappardelle with meat ragù
pappardelle con ragù di carne

ragù
1 ounce dried porcini mushrooms (about 1 cup)
¾ cup dry white wine
1 pound pork butt
1 pound beef chuck
3 tablespoons olive oil
1 pound ground hot Italian sausage
2 cups diced Spanish onions (about 3 onions)
3 to 4 garlic cloves, minced
Kosher salt and freshly ground black pepper
2 cups drained canned plum tomatoes, crushed
About 8 cups Pomodoro Sauce (page 16)
1 quart veal stock or chicken stock
1 quart chicken stock
1 teaspoon finely ground fennel seeds

1 bay leaf
Pinch of dried oregano
¾ cup chopped fresh basil

pappardelle
1 pound dried pappardelle

assembly
2 tablespoons unsalted butter
2 tablespoons olive oil
Kosher salt and freshly ground black pepper
¼ cup chopped fresh basil
1 ounce Parmigiano-Reggiano cheese, shaved

This dish changed my life, or, at any rate, made a lasting impression on my taste buds. After visiting the Colosseum in Rome, I sat down to a big bowl of handmade pappardelle pasta with a thick, rich meat ragù. The sauce was as spectacular as the ancient monument, and both made for a memorable day.

The old-world ragù is not unlike bolognese sauce, but it's a little chunkier and more rustic and flavorful. I've tasted similar ragùs throughout Italy, but the one from Rome was the most inspirational; when I created this recipe, my goal was to reproduce the Roman sauce while making it even more intensely flavored. There are other variations, and I have had it made with wild boar and venison, but I like the mixture of pork butt, chuck, and good, hot Italian sausage. ❧ *serves 4*

1 To prepare the ragù, soak the porcini mushrooms in the white wine in a nonreactive glass or ceramic bowl for 30 minutes. Lift the mushrooms from the wine and then strain the wine through a fine-mesh sieve or chinois. Roughly chop the hydrated mushrooms.

2 Trim the excess fat from the pork and beef and cut the meat into ½-inch cubes.

3 In a large saucepan, heat the olive oil over medium heat. When the olive oil is hot, cook the sausage, breaking it into chunks as you do, for 6 to 8 minutes, or until nicely browned. Using a slotted spoon, lift the sausage from the pan and set aside. Leave the fat in the pan. Add the beef and pork to the pan and cook, turning, for about 5 minutes, or until well browned. Lift the beef and pork from the pan and add to the sausage.

4 Add the onions to the pan and cook for about 5 minutes, or until lightly browned. Add the garlic and strained wine. Bring to a boil over medium-high heat and cook for about 4 minutes, or until reduced by half.

5 Return the meat to the pan and season to taste with salt and pepper. Stir in the mushrooms, tomatoes, Pomodoro Sauce, stocks, fennel seeds, bay leaf, and oregano. Bring to a simmer over medium heat and then reduce the heat so that the mixture simmers gently, uncovered.

6 Cook at a gentle simmer, frequently skimming off any fat that rises to the top, for 3 hours, until the meat is very tender. Stir in the basil at the end of cooking and remove from the heat. Serve or let the sauce cool to room temperature and refrigerate, covered, for up to 5 days. The sauce freezes very well for up to 1 month.

7 To prepare the pappardelle, cook the pasta according to the package instructions until almost al dente. Drain the pasta and add it to the saucepan with the ragù. Set over medium heat and cook for a few more minutes until the pasta is al dente.

8 Stir the butter and olive oil into the sauce to emulsify it and season to taste with salt and pepper. Serve the pasta garnished with the chopped basil and shaved cheese.

the sommelier recommends

Sangiovese is the root of all things Tuscan, but there are great examples of Sangiovese-based red wines to be found throughout Italy. Celebrity winemaker Riccardo Cotarella owns the La Carraia winery in Umbria, and its 100 percent stainless steel–fermented Sangiovese gets just a kiss of oak right before bottling.

how to cook pasta

Whether you are cooking dried or fresh pasta, the concept is the same: pasta needs time in boiling water to soften and become tender. Dried pasta requires longer in the water than fresh pasta, which is moister by definition. Depending on the type of pasta, dried pastas can take from 8 to 15 minutes to cook; fresh pastas need only a few short minutes. The goal for all pasta is to cook it just until al dente, which, as most people know, means "to the tooth." There should be a little bite in the center of the pasta at this point; it should not be mushy. When I don't make my own pasta, I buy high-quality dried pasta; the brands I like best are De Cecco, Guisseppe Coco, and Barilla.

Pasta needs lots of water—6 to 8 quarts for every pound—and you should always salt it lightly before submerging the pasta in it. This is the most effective way to salt pasta, rather than relying on seasoning it after it's cooked. Stir the pasta after you add it to the boiling water to ensure that it cooks evenly.

In nearly every recipe, I suggest that you save some of the pasta water to thin sauces. This is a great trick. The water is rich with starch and salt, and so it adds good flavor and even some texture to the sauce. You may not need it every time, but wait before you pour all that good cooking water down the drain. I also urge you to toss the sauce and the pasta together and let them cook for a very brief time. This allows the pasta to absorb some of the flavor from the sauce—and flavor is what it's all about!

gemelli with chicken and spring herb sauce

gemelli con salsa di erbe e pollo

12 ounces asparagus tips (usually 1 bunch)
3 cups Parmesan Broth (page 57)
1 cup shredded roast chicken
2 tablespoons unsalted butter
1 pound gemelli pasta
16 Oven-Dried Cherry Tomatoes (page 12)
¾ cup Spring Herb Sauce (recipe follows)
Kosher salt and freshly ground black pepper
4 ounces Parmigiano-Reggiano cheese

1 Fill a saucepan with water to a depth of about 6 inches and bring to a simmer over medium-high heat. Add the asparagus tips and cook for about 1 minute, or just until bright green. Place the tips in ice water to stop the cooking. Drain the asparagus tips.

2 In a separate saucepan, bring the Parmesan Broth to a boil over medium-high heat. Add the chicken, asparagus, and butter. Return to a simmer and cook for about 5 minutes. Cover to keep warm.

3 Meanwhile, cook the pasta according to the package instructions until nearly al dente. Drain, reserving about ¼ cup of the pasta water.

When you run a restaurant, you soon learn that chicken and pasta dishes sell very well; when they are as fantastic as this one, they sell like crazy! I think of this as a wonderful spring or summer dish, with tender asparagus and an herb sauce that shouts "fresh!" I suggest using gemelli pasta, which refers to the astrological Gemini twins, because it's made of two short strands of pasta twisted together, but you could use any short, thick dried pasta.

❧ *serves 4*

4 Add the pasta, tomatoes, and Spring Herb Sauce to the saucepan with the chicken and season to taste with salt and pepper. Bring to a brisk simmer over medium-high heat and cook for 2 minutes, or until the pasta is al dente. Add a little pasta water, if needed, to thin or loosen the sauce.

5 Ladle into bowls and shave the cheese over the servings.

the sommelier recommends
Asparagus is many sommeliers' food-and-wine pairing Achilles' heel, but in Italy, Rosato comes to the rescue. Lively, fleshy pink wines with their bright acidity and body handle the green troublemakers beautifully. Look for a dry style like the Bastianich bottling from Friuli, which is made from Refosco grapes.

spring herb sauce
makes about 3 cups

1 cup extra virgin olive oil
3 bunches flat-leaf parsley, stems removed
2 cups fresh basil leaves
½ cup fresh tarragon leaves
½ cup fresh chervil leaves
1 tablespoon chopped garlic
6 ice cubes
1 cup freshly grated Parmigiano-Reggiano cheese

1 Put the olive oil, parsley, basil, tarragon, chervil, and garlic in the jar of a blender and process until smooth.

2 Add the ice cubes and blend for 30 seconds until the ice is crushed.

3 Add the cheese and purée until incorporated. Cover and refrigerate for up to 2 days.

spaghetti carbonara
spaghetti alla carbonara

¾ pound fresh or frozen English peas
½ pound bacon or pancetta, diced
1 yellow onion, sliced
2 cups Parmesan Broth (page 57)
1 cup heavy cream
1 pound spaghetti
4 large egg yolks
½ cup freshly grated Pecorino-Romano cheese
Kosher salt and coarsely ground black pepper

Here is another dish with origins in the Eternal City. It is a simple meal finished by breaking raw eggs over hot pasta and letting the residual heat cook the eggs so that the peas, bacon, cream, and cheese are bound by them. Remember to reserve some of the starchy, salty pasta cooking water to thin the sauce, if necessary.

For added richness, I use only egg yolks, rather than whole eggs, and suggest you use the best organic eggs for this dish. It's almost always made with spaghetti, but use another strand pasta if you have it on hand. The finishing grind of black pepper may explain its name, as *carbonara* refers to "carbon" or coal.

serves 4

1 Pour water into a saucepan to a depth of about 2 inches and bring to a simmer over medium-high heat. Add the peas and cook for about 1 minute, or just until bright green and heated through. Chill in ice water so they do not overcook.

2 In a saucepan, cook the bacon over medium-low heat until crispy and all the fat is rendered. Lift the bacon from the skillet and drain on paper towels. Leave the fat in the pan.

3 Add the onion to the pan and cook over medium heat for about 6 minutes, or until nicely browned and caramelized.

4 Put the Parmesan Broth, cream, and cooked bacon in the saucepan and bring to a simmer over medium-high heat. Cook for about 3 minutes, or until reduced by a quarter.

5 Cook the pasta according to the package instructions until nearly al dente. Drain, reserving about ¼ cup of the pasta water.

6 Add the pasta and peas to the sauce and cook for about 2 minutes, or until the pasta is al dente. Add a little pasta water, if needed, to thin or loosen the sauce. Pour the hot pasta and sauce into a serving bowl and stir in the egg yolks so that they cook evenly. Top with the grated cheese, season to taste with salt and pepper, toss again, and serve.

the sommelier recommends
The winery Falesco, which is a Riccardo Cotarella project, can be found in the Lazio region of Italy. Its "Vitiano Rosso" is a blend of Merlot, Cabernet Sauvignon, and Sangiovese, and the smoky character is a lovely echo for the traditional pancetta element in this dish.

stracci with red wine–braised duck

stracci con anitra brasata

braised duck legs
6 duck legs
About 1 cup kosher salt
3 cups quartered button mushrooms
1½ cups diced carrots
1 cup diced celery
¾ cup diced onions
4 tablespoons tomato paste
2½ cups red wine

2 sprigs fresh thyme
1 bay leaf
6 cups chicken stock
1½ cups veal stock or chicken stock

stracci
1½ pounds fresh stracci

assembly
½ cup unsalted butter
2 cups Stewed Tomatoes (page 57)
2 tablespoons sherry vinegar
4 tablespoons chopped fresh basil
Kosher salt and freshly ground black pepper
2 ounces Parmigiano-Reggiano cheese, shaved

Stracci means "rags" in Italian, and I suppose the pasta got its name because it looks like little pieces of torn dough, each roughly 2 inches square. I imagine that hurried home cooks used to rip pasta dough into pieces for cooking when they ran out of time to cut it into more elegant strands and shapes and then shrugged it off with "Oh, it's just little rags of dough!" It's similar to farfalle, but not pinched in the center, so it tends to cook a little more evenly. Use farfalle or another small pasta if you can't find stracci.

I have had the privilege of eating in private homes during my travels through Italy, and I recall one meal where the hostess put a big pot of duck legs braised in red wine and tomatoes on the table along with a bowl of pasta tossed with olive oil. You put the duck on top of the pasta and then spooned the braising liquid right from the pot and poured it over both. This is my version of that memorable meal.

❦ *serves 4*

1 To prepare the braised duck legs, lay the legs on a flat pan and cover with salt. Set another flat pan on top of the duck and weight with some cans or a brick. Refrigerate for about 3 hours.

2 Preheat the oven to 300°F.

3 Allow an ovenproof stockpot to warm over medium heat while you rinse the salt off the duck legs. Put the legs in the pot, skin side down, and cook over medium-low heat for about 20 minutes, or until all the fat is rendered.

4 Lift the legs from the pot and set aside. Add the mushrooms, carrots, celery, and onions. Cook over medium heat for about 4 minutes, or until slightly caramelized and just beginning to soften. Using a slotted spoon, lift the vegetables from the pot and leave behind the fat.

5 Add the tomato paste to the fat and "fry" it for about 5 minutes, beating it with a whisk. Add the wine, bring to a boil, reduce the heat, and simmer for about 5 minutes, or until reduced by half.

6   Return the vegetables and duck legs to the pot. Add the thyme and bay leaf and then the stocks. Raise the heat to high and bring to a boil. Cover the pot and transfer it to the oven. Cook for about 2 hours, until the duck is fully cooked and tender.

7   Remove the duck legs and set aside to cool. Skim the fat from the sauce.

8   When the duck legs are cool enough to handle, pull the skin off. Reserve the skin. Pick the meat from the bones. Add the meat to the sauce and discard the bones. Discard the duck fat skimmed from the sauce or save for a later use.

9   Lay the reserved duck skin on a baking sheet and bake for about 15 minutes, or until crispy. Chop the cracklings roughly and set aside.

10 Push the vegetables left in the stockpot through a fine-mesh sieve or chinois, pressing on the vegetables as you do so. Return the sieved vegetables to the pot with the duck and the sauce. Set over medium-high heat and bring to a rapid simmer. Cook for about 20 minutes, or until the sauce thickens and reduces by half.

11 Meanwhile, cook the stracci according to the package instructions until al dente. Drain the pasta and add it to the duck sauce.

12 Stir the butter into the sauce until it is incorporated. Stir the tomatoes and vinegar into the pasta and sauce. Toss with the basil and season to taste with salt and pepper. Divide the pasta evenly among 4 serving plates. Garnish with the shaved cheese and the reserved duck cracklings.

the sommelier recommends

This dish is a great place to employ the technique that chefs call "liaison." Pair this dish with the red wine used to make it, and you will have the ultimate food and wine match. We like it with a northern Italian Merlot that has deep fruit and a nice balance of high tones. Try the Cortegiara label, which is owned by the celebrated Allegrini wine family in the Veneto region.

pennette with pancetta and peas

pennette con pancetta e piselli

6 ounces pancetta, diced (about 1 cup)
¼ cup diced yellow onion
2 cups frozen peas
1¼ cups chicken stock
1 pound dried pennetti pasta
6 tablespoons unsalted butter
¾ cup freshly grated Parmigiano-Reggiano cheese
Kosher salt and freshly ground black pepper
¼ cup extra virgin olive oil

Pennetti is small penne, or tubular pasta. I like it here because the peas and small pieces of pancetta in the simple sauce cling to the little noodles when the final dish is enriched with a generous dose of butter and grated cheese. This is easy pasta cooking at its best. ❀

serves 4

1 In a small saucepan, cook the pancetta over low heat until crispy and the fat is rendered. Add the onion and cook for about 6 minutes, or until the onion softens and is slightly caramelized.

2 Add the peas and stock to the pan, stir, raise the heat to medium, and continue to cook gently.

3 Meanwhile, cook the pasta according to the package instructions until nearly al dente. Drain, reserving about ¼ cup of the pasta water.

4 Add the pasta to the sauce and cook for about 2 minutes, or until the pasta is al dente. Add a little pasta water, if needed, to thin or loosen the sauce.

5 Add the butter to the pasta and stir until the butter is incorporated. Stir the cheese into the pasta and season to taste with salt and pepper. Finish with a drizzle of olive oil.

the sommelier recommends
This is a pasta dish for white wine lovers. The flavor components to consider here are salty Parmigiano, green tones from the peas, and the smoky pancetta. Try a ripe, round Inzolia from Sicily produced by Baglio di Pianetto. The grape varietal is indigenous to the island and was originally primarily used to make Marsala.

mezzi rigatoni with roasted cauliflower and anchovy

mezzi rigatoni con cavolfiore e acciughe

anchovy bread crumbs
One 8-ounce loaf ciabatta bread
1 tablespoon extra virgin olive oil
Kosher salt and freshly ground black pepper
6 anchovy fillets

rigatoni
1 pound cauliflower florets
4 anchovy fillets
1 cup (2 sticks) unsalted butter plus 1 tablespoon
4 garlic cloves, minced
4 teaspoons crushed red pepper flakes
Kosher salt and freshly ground black pepper
1 pound mezzi rigatoni
2 cups Parmesan Broth (page 57)
4 teaspoons chopped fresh flat-leaf parsley
½ cup extra virgin olive oil

1   Preheat the oven to 350°F.

2   To prepare the anchovy bread crumbs, cut the bread into ½-inch cubes. In a bowl, toss the bread cubes with the olive oil and salt and pepper to taste. Spread in a single layer on a baking sheet and toast for about 10 minutes, or until lightly browned. Set aside to cool completely.

I first had a similar dish in Milan and came home raving about it and determined to develop something very much like it. It couldn't be simpler or better.

Mezzi rigatoni is a short, stubby-ridged, tubular pasta that measures less than an inch long and about half an inch in diameter. Its ends are cut straight. ❧ *serves 4*

3   Using paper towels, pat 6 anchovy fillets dry and roughly chop them.

4   In the bowl of a food processor fitted with the metal blade, process the bread until the cubes turn into large crumbs. Add the anchovies and pulse until well mixed with the crumbs, which should be crumbly.

5   To prepare the rigatoni, bring about 2 gallons of water to a boil in a large pot over high heat. Add the cauliflower and cook for about 5 minutes, or until it just begins to soften. Drain and set aside.

6   Smash 4 anchovy fillets with a rolling pin.

7   In a large sauté pan, heat the cup of butter over medium heat and add the blanched cauliflower. Cook until the butter foams and the cauliflower begins to brown. Add the garlic, anchovies, and red pepper, cook for a minute or so, and then season to taste.

8   Cook the pasta according to the package instructions until nearly al dente. Drain the pasta and add it to the pan with the cauliflower. Add the Parmesan Broth and bring to a simmer over medium-high heat. Add the remaining tablespoon of butter, raise the heat, and bring to a boil, stirring to emulsify the sauce. Stir in the parsley and season to taste with salt and pepper.

9   Spoon the pasta into shallow serving bowls and sprinkle with the bread crumbs and drizzles of extra virgin olive oil.

the sommelier recommends
The inspiration for this dish is Milan, which is in the Lombardy region of Italy. Its northern climate produces wines that can be sublime. A toasty, rich white wine from Cà dei Frati in the Lugana region takes the Trebbiano di Lugana grape to its highest heights, and is wonderful with the caramelized cauliflower.

ricotta gnocchi with simple tomato sauce

gnocchi di ricotta al pomodoro

gnocchi

1 pound fresh ricotta cheese, drained (see Note)

2 large egg yolks

1 tablespoon kosher salt

1 teaspoon freshly grated nutmeg

About 2½ cups 00 Tipo or all-purpose flour (see Note)

tomato sauce

2 cups Stewed Tomatoes (page 57)

½ cup extra virgin olive oil, plus more for drizzling

¼ cup unsalted butter

2 tablespoons chopped fresh flat-leaf parsley

Kosher salt and freshly ground black pepper

Yes, you read the title of the recipe correctly. I make gnocchi with ricotta cheese, not potatoes as you might expect. My grandmother taught me how to make them this way, and though they are less forgiving than potato gnocchi, I love their soft, delicate texture and flavor. They practically melt in your mouth. It's crucial to find high-quality ricotta cheese from a good Italian market, cheese shop, or gourmet store and then drain it, and to handle the gnocchi gently. Because this is more about the gnocchi than the sauce, the sauce is exceedingly easy to make, but nevertheless very tasty. ✽ *serves 4*

1 To prepare the gnocchi, gently mix the cheese, egg yolks, salt, and nutmeg in a large bowl until blended.

2 Using your hands, fold the flour gradually into the cheese mixture. You may need more or less flour, depending on how well the cheese was drained. Work the dough until it forms a loose ball. Turn out onto a lightly floured surface and knead once or twice. Divide the dough into 4 pieces and roll each one into a long rope about ¾ inch in diameter. Lightly dust each rope with flour to prevent sticking when you cut them into gnocchi.

3 Line a baking sheet with parchment paper and lightly dust it with flour. Cut the ropes into ¾-inch-long pieces and transfer each piece to the baking sheet.

4 You may choose to leave the gnocchi in these pieces or go one step further by rolling each piece into a ball. Use your thumb, the back of a fork, or a small gnocchi paddle to make grooves on 1 side of the balls and a small indentation on the other.

5 Transfer the gnocchi to the baking sheet and refrigerate, uncovered, for up to 24 hours. (Do not cover with a damp cloth or the gnocchi will soften.) After the gnocchi dry for 24 hours in the refrigerator, they can be transferred to a rigid plastic container and frozen for up to 1 week. Let them thaw before cooking.

6 Fill a large saucepan with lightly salted water and bring to a boil over high heat. Gently drop the gnocchi into the water and cook for about 2 minutes, or until the gnocchi bob to the surface. When they do, cook for 1 minute longer and then drain, reserving about ¼ cup of the pasta water.

(continued)

7 To prepare the tomato sauce, heat the tomatoes over medium-high heat. Thin or loosen with a little pasta water. Stir in ½ cup of olive oil and the butter until the butter is incorporated. Toss the gnocchi with the tomato sauce. Stir in the parsley and season to taste with salt and pepper.

8 Divide the gnocchi among 4 serving plates and drizzle with olive oil.

note To drain the ricotta cheese, wrap it in a double thickness of cheesecloth and suspend the cheesecloth ball over a bowl, or put the wrapped cheese in a fine-mesh sieve or chinois rested on the rim of a bowl. Refrigerate overnight to give the whey (liquid) time to drain from the cheese into the bowl. Discard the whey. The cheese will be quite dry.

The 00 Tipo pizza flour used in this recipe is Italian flour suitable for pizza and pasta. (Do not substitute 00 Tipo *pastry* flour!) The number of zeros refers to how finely ground the flour is, with one zero meaning the flour is less finely ground than double-zero flour.

the sommelier recommends
One of Piedmont's reds for daily drinking is Dolcetto (Barbera is the other one), which is ideal for this simple but luxurious dish. Dolcetto produces purple-tinted reds that are the perfect foil for the melt-in-your-mouth gnocchi and tomato sauce. Boschis, Altare, Paitin, and Vajra make some of our favorite red wines from the Dolcetto grape.

orecchiette with braised swiss chard and white beans

orecchiette con bietola e cannellini

white bean confit
1 pound dried white beans
1½ cups plus 2 tablespoons extra virgin olive oil
1 carrot, diced
1 large yellow onion, diced
2 sprigs fresh thyme
1 bay leaf
½ sprig fresh basil
½ sprig fresh rosemary
¼ lemon, sliced
Kosher salt

braised swiss chard
1 tablespoon extra virgin olive oil
½ white onion, sliced
1 bunch Swiss chard leaves (about ½ pound), sliced
Dash of crushed red pepper flakes
Kosher salt and freshly ground black pepper

1 pound orecchiette

lemon butter
1 pound unsalted butter, softened
6 tablespoons fresh lemon juice
1½ tablespoons finely grated lemon zest
Kosher salt

to serve
4 teaspoons Lemon Bread Crumbs (recipe follows)
½ cup freshly grated Parmigiano-Reggiano cheese

We used to call this "greens and beans" when I was young, and although my grandparents also called it "Depression food," it ranks among my very favorites. My maternal grandmother, who came from Naples, made this all the time. I dress up her recipe with a white bean confit and Swiss chard quickly braised in olive oil. I make it with orecchiette, one of my favorite pasta shapes, because they have a chewy texture and their name translates to "little ears," which always makes me laugh. Finally, I enrich the dish with a rich, lemony butter. This is particularly good in winter. ❀ *serves 4*

1 To prepare the white bean confit, put the beans in a bowl or pot and add enough cold water to cover. Set aside to soak at room temperature for at least 8 hours or overnight. Change the water once or twice, if possible. Drain.

2 In a large saucepan, heat 1 cup of olive oil over medium-high heat. Add the carrot and onion and cook, stirring, for about 4 minutes, or until just tender. Add the drained beans and the thyme and bay leaf.

3 Add enough water to cover and bring to a boil over high heat. Skim off any foam that rises to the surface, reduce the heat to low, and simmer gently for 35 to 45 minutes, until the beans are just tender.

4 Drain the beans and discard the cooking liquid.

5 In the same saucepan, heat ½ cup of olive oil over medium-high heat. Add the basil, rosemary, and lemon slices. Stir to release the flavors, and then add the beans. Bring to a simmer and poach the beans for about 10 minutes, or until soft and creamy. Taste and season to taste with salt. Set aside to cool in the oil.

6   To prepare the Swiss chard, set a sauté pan over high heat. When the pan is hot, put the olive oil and onion in the pan. Lower the heat to medium-high and cook, stirring, for 5 to 8 minutes, or until the onion is lightly caramelized.

7   Add the Swiss chard and red pepper and season to taste with salt and pepper. Raise the heat to high and cook for about 6 minutes, or until the Swiss chard fully wilts. Set aside to cool. Measure a generous 1½ cups of chard and set aside; cover and refrigerate the remaining Swiss chard to use at another time. (It will keep for up to 3 days.)

8   To prepare the lemon butter, put the butter in a metal mixing bowl and, using a handheld mixer, whip on medium-high speed until doubled in volume. Or use an electric mixer fitted with the whisk attachment.

9   With the mixer on medium speed, slowly add the lemon juice, mixing until it's emulsified with the butter.

10 Add the lemon zest and salt to taste and, using a rubber spatula, fold until fully incorporated. Measure 1½ cups and set aside; cover and refrigerate the remaining butter to use at another time. (It will keep for up to 1 week and is great over vegetables and pasta.)

11 Cook the pasta according to the package instructions.

12 Drain the pasta, reserving 3 cups of the pasta water (add more water to the cup measure if you don't have quite 3 cups). In a large sauté pan, mix together the pasta, the pasta water, and the lemon butter. Add the reserved Swiss chard. Lift the beans from the oil and add to the pan. Stir and cook over medium-high heat for 5 to 6 minutes, or until the sauce begins to reduce, thickens slightly, and the beans and chard are heated through.

13 To serve, sprinkle the Lemon Bread Crumbs and grated cheese over the pasta and drizzle with the remaining 2 tablespoons of olive oil.

the sommelier recommends

Creamy white bean confit, braised Swiss chard, and lemony butter in this dish are all directing us toward that barrel-aged Chardonnay that we have been wanting to drink. Many winemakers in Italy make the international style that will sing with this dish. Take your pick, but make sure that the wine you choose was harvested ripe and kissed by barrique.

lemon bread crumbs
makes about 1 cup

1 cup fresh bread crumbs (2 large slices)
6 tablespoons finely chopped fresh flat-leaf parsley
Grated zest of 2 lemons

1   Preheat the oven to 350°F.

2   Spread the bread crumbs in a single layer on a baking sheet and toast for about 10 minutes, or until lightly browned. Set aside to cool completely.

3   In a bowl, toss the parsley and lemon zest. Add the toasted crumbs and mix well. Set aside until needed. This will keep, covered and refrigerated, for up to 2 days.

capellini with six summer tomatoes

capellini ai sei pomodori

6 heirloom or other vine-ripened tomatoes (about 2 pounds)
6 fresh basil leaves, chopped
2 garlic cloves, minced
Pinch of julienned fresh flat-leaf parsley
1 pound fresh or dried capellini
Kosher salt and freshly ground black pepper
6 tablespoons extra virgin olive oil

During the few months when tomatoes are really, really good, nothing beats an effortless, uncooked tomato sauce, tossed with the hot pasta and served right away. I recommend a mixture of the wonderful heirloom tomatoes sold at farmers' markets or grown in your own garden—look for red, yellow, purple, and green tomatoes. They should be vine ripened, heavy, and juicy. ❊ *serves 4*

1 Cut the tomatoes in half and gently squeeze the seeds and juice from them through a fine-mesh sieve or chinois into a bowl. Discard the seeds and juice. Dice the tomatoes.

2 In a mixing bowl, toss the diced tomatoes with the basil, garlic, and parsley and set aside.

3 Cook the pasta according to the package instructions until nearly al dente. Drain and transfer to a saucepan. Stir the tomato mixture into the hot pasta and season to taste with salt and pepper.

4 Divide evenly among 4 serving plates. Finish each plate with a drizzle of olive oil.

the sommelier recommends
This summery pasta is best enjoyed with a no-frills, fruity, spicy red wine made from the Primitivo grape. Indigenous to Puglia, the heel of the Italy boot, the Primitivo grape tends to be a bit softer and lower in alcohol than wine made from its descendant, Zinfandel, and can actually be quite refreshing with this dish. Try A. Mano, Torre Quatro, and San Marzano's Primitivo.

fish and seafood

Buying fresh fish is not mysterious or difficult, but it demands a little confidence and common sense. The fish should smell like it just came out of the sea, and nothing else. It should feel firm and look moist, and if it has scales, they ought to be bright and supple. But you need to be flexible. If you have your heart set on halibut or salmon but get to the market and they don't look too good, switch gears immediately and buy the fish that looks best. A good fish purveyor buys product that appears to have been carefully handled from boat to market and then displays the fish on cracked ice.

Like many chefs, I have a tremendous fish repertoire. Fish and seafood lend themselves to so many flavors and preparations, it's hard to stop coming up with ideas for cooking them. When I selected the recipes for this book, I relied solely on the trips to Italy I took to research the book. In Italy's osterias, cooks prepare fish simply, mainly in good, fruity olive oil and lemon juice. There is a beauty, purity, and lightness to the fish that I have attempted to capture with these recipes.

I was not surprised by how many Italians eat fish for lunch, both in restaurants and at home. Often it's as simple as roasted cod with potatoes, similar to the kind of seafood meals I grew up eating. When we could afford fish and when it was fresh, my mother cooked it for dinner, usually pairing it with lemon and olive oil or tomato sauce. From her, I learned never to overcook it and to eat it on the day it's bought. At the restaurant and at home, I like to buy whole fish and butcher them myself, and if you want to take the time to learn to do this, you might be surprised at how often you will eat fish and how much you will enjoy it.

notes from the sommelier
white wine with fish?
debunking the old wives' tale

"Drink white wine with fish, and drink red wine with meat" is a great rule if you eat only in traditional French restaurants. The wine-ordering path was clear when the plates in front of us were of Dover sole meunière, trout amandine, and salmon with sorrel. A bottle of Chardonnay from Burgundy, France, was the surefire match in those situations, but what happens if your tuna is Sicilian-style or the sardines are stuffed with spinach and olives?

Every time that Chef Tramonto requests a wine to pair with one of his dishes, I first ask: What is the sauce? During my long tenure as a sommelier, I have learned that one of the cardinal rules of wine pairing is to ignore the protein; it's all about the sauce. A fish sauced with a lemon butter has a very different dance partner (a citrusy white wine like Pinot Bianco, Orvieto, or Grillo) than that same fish sauced with a black truffled veal jus (a meaty red wine like Cabernet Sauvignon, Aglianico, or Nebbiolo).

So when you plan the wine to accompany this chapter's fish dishes, don't worry about the fact that they are fish dishes. Think of the fish as the courier for the sauce. Try the Sauté of Trout with Pumpkin and Anisette with a spicy red wine from Lombardy like Ca' del Bosco's Carmenero, or serve the Sardines Stuffed with Spinach and Gaeta Olives with an herbal Cabernet Franc from Vignalta in the Veneto. Debunking the old wives' tale may be supersurprising and may freak out your friends, but it will also be much tastier and more fun, I promise!

sauté of trout with pumpkin and anisette

trota con zucca e anisetta

About 1½ pounds peeled pumpkin, cut into large
    dice (about 3 cups)
¾ cup olive oil
Kosher salt and freshly ground black pepper
4 rainbow trout, boned and cleaned
½ cup all-purpose flour
½ cup unsalted butter
1 teaspoon ground star anise
1 teaspoon ground anise seeds
½ teaspoon ground fennel seeds
4 fresh sage leaves, very thinly sliced
Juice of 1 lemon
3 tablespoons Pernod or other anise-flavored
    liqueur
1 cup chicken stock

1 Preheat the oven to 450°F.

2 In a large bowl, toss the pumpkin with ¼ cup of olive oil. Season liberally with salt and pepper. Spread the pumpkin on a baking sheet and roast for 8 to 10 minutes, or until tender and lightly caramelized.

3 Pat the trout with paper towels to make sure they are very dry. Season them on both sides with salt and pepper, and sprinkle the skin side with just enough flour to coat. Pat off any excess flour.

4 Heat two large sauté pans over medium-high heat. Pour ¼ cup of olive oil into each pan. When the oil is hot, carefully lay 2 trout in each pan, skin side down. Cook for about 4 minutes, or until the skin is crispy.

5 Divide the butter between the pans and swirl the pans slightly to encourage melting. Sprinkle the star anise, anise seeds, and fennel seeds over the fish in both pans. If you don't use all the spice mixture—and you probably won't—reserve it.

6 As the butter melts and begins to foam, baste the flesh side of the trout with it. Add the sage, dividing it evenly between the pans. This part of the cooking process will take about 3 minutes. The trout should be cooked through but still moist.

7 Lift the trout from the pans and set aside on plates, loosely covered with foil.

8 Divide the lemon juice and Pernod between the pans and cook over medium-high heat, stirring with a wooden spoon and scraping up any browned bits. Add ½ cup of stock to each pan and bring to a boil. By now, the buttery sauce should be browned and smelling of the spices. It will come together after it boils.

9 Toss the roasted pumpkin in the sauce, spoon the sauce and pumpkin over the trout, and serve.

Come fall, our customers can't seem to get enough of this simple trout dish. Perhaps it's the pumpkin or the allure of anise, or maybe they just like good rainbow trout. And who can blame them? Trout is clean and fresh tasting, without being "fishy," and no one seems to mind it served whole, as fish is prepared throughout Italy. *serves 4*

the sommelier recommends
Maurizio Zanella is one of Italy's wine luminaries; his winery in Lombardy, Ca' del Bosco, produces the full spectrum of what we love to drink. For the trout dish, with its heady brown spices and creamy pumpkin, pair a savory, brown-spiced Ca' del Bosco Carmenero. It will fill out the dish with all the right fruit and herbal notes.

salmon scaloppine
scaloppine di salmone

1½ fresh salmon fillet
Kosher salt and freshly ground black pepper
Olive oil
½ cup roughly chopped toasted almonds
½ cup fresh flat-leaf parsley leaves
½ cup celery leaves
½ cup arugula, torn if large
12 red radishes, shaved
4 tablespoons extra virgin olive oil, plus more for drizzling
Juice of 1 lemon
2 lemons, halved, optional

When I lived in England a number of years ago, I grabbed every opportunity I had to travel, and I recall one trip to the Ligurian coast of Italy, famous for its fishing towns. I took note of how the local cooks sliced fresh, oily fish, such as halibut and tuna, very thin and cooked it as scaloppine. Intrigued, I decided to make a similar dish using perfectly fresh Pacific or Atlantic salmon. The trick is to be very careful not to overcook this delicate fish. ❁ *serves 4*

1 Cut the salmon on the diagonal into four 6-ounce slices. Season to taste on both sides with salt and pepper.

2 Lay a large sheet of plastic wrap on the work surface and rub the plastic with olive oil. Lay the salmon slices in a single layer on the oiled plastic wrap and cover all with another sheet of plastic wrap. Using a mallet or the bottom of a small, heavy skillet, gently pound the salmon until the fillets are about ¼ inch thick. Lift the plastic wrap off the salmon.

3 In a small bowl, mix the almonds, parsley, celery leaves, arugula, and radishes. Add 4 tablespoons of extra virgin olive oil and the lemon juice and toss to mix. Season to taste with salt and pepper and set aside.

4 Heat a large nonstick sauté pan over medium-high heat. When the pan is hot, sauté the salmon slices for about 1 minute on each side, or until golden brown. Be careful not to overcook.

5 Place 1 slice of salmon on each of 4 serving plates. Spoon a quarter of the salad on top of each piece of salmon and drizzle a little olive oil around the edge of the plate. Garnish each plate with a lemon half, if desired.

the sommelier recommends
The wine for this dish must deal with arugula, radishes, and almonds. Choose a fresh, crisp white to tackle the job, such as a Verdicchio dei Castelli Jesi from the Marche region. Umani Ronchi, Laila, and Sartarelli all bottle Verdicchio (the grape) wines that are bright and slightly herbal and have a touch of minerality that shows nicely with a fish like salmon.

salmon

Years ago, salmon was expensive and considered a special-occasion fish, but thanks to the proliferation of salmon farms, we can eat it any day of the week without going broke. Like most chefs, I prefer wild salmon to farmed. It's more expensive and may not be as readily available, but when it is, I suggest you buy it. It is usually paler in color than farmed salmon, but its flavor is more distinct and pleasing and its texture tends to be firmer. Although farm-raised salmon is fattier and therefore rich in valuable omega-3 fatty acids, it also may harbor chemicals from the diet it's fed. Some nutritionists warn about eating farm-raised salmon more than once a month or so. Wild salmon consume a variety of foods that occur naturally in the ocean, and the proof is in the flavor. Salmon is so popular, though, that you can't always trust that the salmon labeled "wild" actually is. Buy it from a fishmonger or market you trust and don't hesitate to ask questions, such as where it's from and how it was caught.

Salmon thrive in both the Atlantic and the Pacific oceans along our northern coastlines and into Canada. The only biological or nutritional difference between the two is that Atlantic salmon spawn several times before they die, while Pacific salmon spawn only once. Both spend most of their adult lives in the ocean, returning to the freshwater rivers of their birth only when they spawn.

Atlantic salmon is called just that, while Pacific salmon sport names like Chinook (also called king), sockeye, Coho, pink, and steelhead. Experts believe that the fight to swim upstream to spawn, when the fish leave the ocean and stop eating as they battle the river, gives wild salmon its amazing flavor and texture. Salmon caught in the Pacific Northwest and Alaska's long, cold rivers is particularly prized.

tuna siciliana

tonno siciliano

2 fennel bulbs
2 oranges, preferably organic
¼ cup extra virgin olive oil
1 teaspoon crushed red pepper flakes
Kosher salt and freshly ground black pepper
1¾ pounds tuna steak, cut into 4 even pieces
1 tablespoon ground fennel seeds
2 tablespoons Clarified Butter (page 147) or
     vegetable oil
1 tablespoon sea salt
4 teaspoons aged balsamic vinegar
4 teaspoons Basil Oil (page 147)

1 Preheat the oven to 375°F.

2 Trim the fronds from the fennel bulbs and
   then cut the bulbs into 8 equal segments.
   Cut each orange (unpeeled) into 8 sections.

3 In a mixing bowl, toss the fennel and
   orange with the olive oil and red pepper
   and season to taste with salt and pepper.

4 Spread the fennel in a shallow baking pan
   and roast for 20 minutes. Remove the pan
   from the oven and add the orange. Roast
   for about 5 minutes longer. Test the fennel
   for doneness by poking it with a small,
   sharp knife. When the fennel is done, the
   knife will meet with no resistance. Set aside
   the fennel and orange.

5 Season the tuna with fennel seeds, salt, and
   pepper.

6 Heat a sauté pan over high heat. When the
   pan is hot, put the clarified butter or oil in
   the pan. When the butter foams or the oil
   is smoking hot, sear the tuna on all sides or
   until rare. This should take 30 seconds on
   each side for perfectly rare tuna. Remove
   the tuna from the pan and slice each piece
   into quarters.

7 Put 4 pieces of roasted fennel and 4 pieces
   of roasted orange on each of 4 serving
   plates. Put 4 tuna slices in the center of
   each plate and season with sea salt. Drizzle
   the vinegar around the edge of each plate,
   followed by the Basil Oil.

On a trip to Palermo, Sicily, I tasted a lot of
fish dishes flavored with some of the
traditional flavors of the island: fennel, orange,
chiles, basil, and sea salt. When you make this
dish, buy high-quality tuna, which can be
bluefin, yellowfin, or bigeye tuna as long as it's
as fresh as can be. Cook it only long enough so
that the center is still red or cooked to medium
rare. Believe me, this won't taste nearly as
good if you cook the tuna any further!

serves 4

the sommelier recommends
Stay with the Sicily theme for the wine you
choose for this dish. The island produces
many styles of red wine, but the one we like
best for the meaty tuna is an Etna Rosso made
from the Nerello Mascalese grape. Producers
like Terre Nerre liken their Etna Rosso to the
Pinot Noirs of Burgundy, France, and with
their red fruit, brilliant acidity, and complexity,
we agree.   *(continued)*

aged balsamic vinegar

Most cooks are inclined to buy balsamic vinegar in the supermarket to use in salads or marinades. This inexpensive product tastes good and mixes nicely with olive oil and other ingredients for a fine vinaigrette or similar sauce. It is a white-grape vinegar, as are all balsamics, with added sugar or caramel to give it flavor and color. But until you try "real" *balsamico*, the product that is so carefully made, aged, and bottled, you are missing the point of balsamic vinegar!

Most true *balsamico* is imported from Italy, and the most famous and authentic comes from Modena. Some good balsamic is made in California now, too. Wherever it is made, most comes from the juice of Trebbiano grapes, which are sweet white grapes. After they are harvested, their juice, also called *must*, is cooked over open flames until it reduces significantly. This is a long, meticulous process that ends when the liquid, called *mosto cotto*, is transferred to wooden casks, most commonly oak, and left to turn into vinegar. Generally, the casks contain some old vinegar, which aids the new as it acidifies. Unlike wine, the vinegar is exposed to oxygen in the casks, which are never filled all the way. During the aging process, the white grape vinegar takes on its characteristic reddish-brown hue.

Young *balsamico* is from 3 to 5 years old, while medium-aged balsamico can range from 12 to 20 years old and is complex enough to use on its own, rather than in concert with olive oil. Old *balsamico* ages for at least 25 years; the older it gets, the more spectacular it is. This vinegar is syrupy and intense and meant to be used in drops to flavor fish, meat, duck, and cheese. But what a treat! It's expensive, but because you use it so sparingly, it pays its own way.

clarified butter
makes about 1 cup

1 cup unsalted butter

1 Put the butter in a small saucepan over low heat. Let the butter simmer slowly for 8 to 10 minutes, during which time water will evaporate and the milk solids will collect on the bottom of the pan.

2 Skim off any foam that rises to the surface. Very carefully, pour the clear liquid butter through a fine-mesh sieve or chinois into a glass measuring cup or jar. Take care that the white milk solids remain in the pan. Discard the milk solids.

3 Cool the golden-colored butter completely before covering and refrigerating. Clarified butter keeps very well for up to 1 week.

basil oil
makes about 1 cup

1 large bunch fresh basil (about 4 ounces)
¼ bunch fresh flat-leaf parsley
1 cup grapeseed oil
1 tablespoon kosher salt

1 Remove the basil and parsley leaves from the stems. Discard the stems.

2 In a large sauté pan, heat ¼ cup of grapeseed oil over medium-high heat. When the oil is hot, add the basil and parsley leaves. Sauté for 1 to 2 minutes, or until the herbs are wilted. Season with the salt. Transfer the herbs to a plate to cool slightly.

3 When cool, transfer to a blender. With the motor running, slowly add the remaining oil and blend for 4 to 5 minutes.

4 Transfer to a glass container and cover. Let it steep in the refrigerator overnight or for up to 24 hours.

5 Strain through a chinois or fine-mesh sieve into a small bowl or glass container. Cover and refrigerate the oil for up to 2 days.

halibut steamed in parchment paper
halibut al cartoccio

Four 6-ounce pieces halibut
Kosher salt and freshly ground black pepper
4 tablespoons unsalted butter
1 fennel bulb, very thinly sliced
4 shallots, very thinly sliced
1 garlic clove, very thinly sliced
½ cup extra virgin olive oil, plus more for drizzling
¼ cup dry white wine
3 lemons, halved, plus more lemon juice for drizzling if needed
1 large or 2 medium tomatoes, peeled, seeded, and diced
¼ cup fresh flat-leaf parsley leaves
¼ cup celery leaves
2 tablespoons snipped fresh chives
2 tablespoons finely sliced fresh basil
1 teaspoon crushed coriander seeds

1 Preheat the oven to 400°F.

2 Cut 4 good-sized pieces of parchment paper or aluminum foil, each about 9 inches long, and shape into heart shapes by folding them in half and then, beginning at the bottom of the fold, cutting a half-heart shape, using most of the paper. When you open the folded paper, it should be in the shape of a heart and about 9 inches long. Lay the open hearts on the countertop.

3 Put a piece of halibut on one side of each heart and season to taste with salt and pepper. Put a tablespoon of butter on top of each piece of fish. Arrange the fennel, shallots, and garlic evenly over and around each piece of halibut. Drizzle 1 tablespoon of olive oil, 1 tablespoon of wine, and the juice of ½ lemon on each fish.

4 Fold the parchment over the fish and crimp any open sides by folding it back onto itself to seal the fish inside the packet. Transfer the packets to a baking sheet or shallow baking pan and bake for 12 minutes.

5 Meanwhile, toss the tomatoes with the parsley, celery leaves, chives, basil, and coriander seeds in a bowl. Season to taste and dress with the remaining ¼ cup of olive oil and the juice of 1 lemon.

6 Remove the baking sheet from the oven. Gently cut open each parchment package, taking care because the steam can be very hot, and set each portion on a serving plate. The fish can stay on the parchment or not.

7 Top each piece of fish with a quarter of the salad. Drizzle with more olive oil and lemon juice, if necessary.

Delicate fish is often cooked in parchment in Italy, which allows it to steam gently in the paper. When you open the parchment, a dramatic whirl of hot, moist steam escapes—a true delight for the senses! For this recipe, I follow another Italian culinary custom and top the fish with dressed salad when I serve it. The hot fish brings out the flavors in the herbaceous salad. ❀ *serves 4*

the sommelier recommends
The delicacy of the white fish and the fresh salad dictate opening a bottle of citrusy-spiked white wine. A refreshing, unoaked, pristine Sauvignon Blanc will keep with the high tones of the dish and cleanse your palate with each sip. We like examples from Venica e Venica in the Collio, Pojer e Sandri in Trentino, and Cabanon in Lombardy.

wood-roasted mussels in white wine

cozze al forno in vino bianco

2 leeks, sliced into rounds
2 carrots, peeled and thinly sliced
2 celery ribs, thinly sliced
2 yellow onions, diced
2 cups heavy cream
2 large egg yolks
4 tablespoons extra virgin olive oil
4 garlic cloves, very thinly sliced
2 teaspoons crushed red pepper flakes
4 pounds fresh mussels, cleaned
4 cups dry white wine
Kosher salt and freshly ground black pepper
2 teaspoons chopped fresh flat-leaf parsley
2 teaspoons chopped fresh tarragon
2 teaspoons snipped fresh chives
2 teaspoons chopped fresh basil

I love to cook this simple mussel dish over a wood or charcoal fire, although you can also make it on a burner. The smoke wafting around the covered skillet as the mussels cook over an open fire is pleasing, and the final dish tastes slightly smoky and just that much more authentically Italian. At the restaurant we cook the mussels in the wood oven.

This dish is prepared all along the coast of Italy and on Sicily, and once you taste it you will know why. It makes a lovely main course but can also be served as a first course or a light meal—if you decide to serve it as a first course, halve the ingredients for 4 servings.

serves 4

1 In a deep skillet filled with salted boiling water, blanch the leeks, carrots, celery, and onions for about 10 seconds. Drain, set aside to cool, and then refrigerate to chill completely until needed.

2 In a small bowl, whisk the cream with the egg yolks. Cover and refrigerate.

3 Prepare a wood, charcoal, or gas grill by spraying the grilling rack with nonstick vegetable spray. Heat the grill until hot. Alternatively, use the stovetop.

4 Heat a large, deep sauté pan over the grill or on high heat. Put the olive oil, garlic, and red pepper in the pan and cook, stirring, just until the garlic browns.

5 Add the mussels to the pan and toss. Pour in the wine and immediately cover the pan to allow the mussels to steam.

6 After 2 minutes, remove the lid. The mussels should be beginning to open. Add the blanched vegetables, cover, and cook, shaking the pan now and then, for about 2 minutes longer, or until the mussels open completely.

7 Remove from the heat and discard any mussels that do not open. Reduce the heat to low and stir the cream mixture into the pan to thicken the sauce. Season to taste with salt and pepper.

8 Transfer the mussels and the sauce to a shallow bowl and sprinkle with herbs.

the sommelier recommends
Choose a solid bottle of dry white wine such as those made from the indigenous grapes of Sicily—Grillo from Arancio, Cataratto from Rapitala, or fruity Fiano from Mandra Rossa—when you make this recipe.

sardines stuffed with spinach and gaeta olives

sarde ripiene con spinaci e olive

¾ cup extra virgin olive oil, plus more for drizzling

1 tablespoon sliced garlic

Pinch of crushed red pepper flakes

1 shallot, minced

1 pound spinach

1 teaspoon sea salt, plus more for sprinkling

Juice and grated zest of 1 lemon plus more lemon juice for drizzling

½ cup pitted and chopped Gaeta olives or other black olives

Freshly ground black pepper

¼ cup chopped fresh flat-leaf parsley

16 fresh sardines (about 2¾ pounds), cleaned (see Note)

1 teaspoon sea salt, plus more for sprinkling

Fresh sardines are wildly popular in Italy, and happily they are becoming so here, too. I couldn't be more pleased, because the small, oily fish are absolutely delicious cooked in a hot oven or over an open grill. If you think only of canned sardines when you hear the word, you have a treat in store. I like canned sardines very much, but the difference between them and fresh is similar to the difference between canned tuna and fresh. I was inspired to stuff these with lemony spinach and salty olives by a dish I had in Venice, where they know their sardines!

serves 4

1 Heat a sauté pan over medium-high heat. When the pan is hot, put ¼ cup of olive oil in the pan. When the oil is hot, add the garlic and red pepper. Reduce the heat to low and cook, stirring, until the garlic is lightly browned.

2 Add the shallot and cook for about 1 minute. Add the spinach and sprinkle with a little kosher salt. Fold the spinach into the warm oil until just barely wilted.

3 Add the juice of 1 lemon to the pan and then immediately remove the pan from the heat. Turn the spinach out onto a baking sheet or shallow pan. Refrigerate the spinach until cool. When it is cool, fold the olives into the spinach and season to taste with kosher salt and pepper.

4 In the bowl of a food processor fitted with the metal blade, process the parsley with ½ cup of olive oil and the lemon zest. Set aside.

5 Preheat the oven to 350°F.

6 Split the sardines along their bellies and remove the interior bones. Leave the top portion of skin connected so the fillets stay attached to both head and tail.

7 Lay the sardines on a work surface, skin side down. Be sure both fillets are facing up and, using a butter knife, scrape the fillets to remove all pin bones.

8 Season the fillets with the sea salt and pepper. Put 1 tablespoon of the spinach filling in the center of each sardine.

9 Grab the tail and fold the fillet over, from tail to head. Slip the tail through the open mouth of the sardine to make a "package."

10 Arrange the stuffed fish on a lightly oiled baking sheet and drizzle each fish with a little olive oil. Bake for 6 to 8 minutes, or until the flesh is cooked through.

11 Put 4 sardines on each of 4 serving plates and sprinkle with sea salt. Squeeze a little lemon juice on each sardine and drizzle a tablespoon of the parsley-lemon oil on each plate. Serve warm.

note Before cutting the sardines, rinse them under cool, running water and, using your fingers, rub off the thin, light scales. Pat the sardines dry with a kitchen towel; any remaining scales will come off with the towel. To remove the innards, pinch the gills together and then pull them out. The guts may come with them. If not, split the sardine open and run your finger along the belly to remove them.

the sommelier recommends
Lucio Gomiero knows his vegetables. He is the worldwide producer of premium Italian vegetables, so it is no surprise that his winery in the Veneto, Vignalta, produces vegetable-friendly red wines. His herbal Cabernet Franc is one of the few red wines that will not wilt in the face of the spinach, olives, and anchovies that dominate this dish. And we understand that sometimes you just gotta have red.

branzino in salt crust

branzino in crosta di sale

1 whole 4-pound branzino, sea bass, striped bass,
    loup de mer, or red snapper, cleaned and scaled
Kosher salt and freshly ground black pepper
½ cup extra virgin olive oil
½ lemon, sliced

½ orange, sliced
3 sprigs fresh tarragon
3 sprigs fresh oregano
1 bay leaf
1 garlic clove, sliced
2 pounds kosher salt
1 tablespoon fennel seeds
1 tablespoon black peppercorns
8 large egg whites
1 tablespoon chopped fresh tarragon
1 tablespoon chopped fresh basil
1 tablespoon chopped fresh flat-leaf parsley
4 lemon wedges or slices

This is one of my all-time favorite recipes—partly because I love the drama of cracking open the salt shell and exposing the fish, but mainly because it tastes so good. The salt case keeps the fish perfectly moist but does not make it especially salty. In fact, the fish is perfectly cooked and flavored. Cooking fish this way is a technique as old as ancient Rome, and for all its tableside drama it's surprisingly easy.

It's important to begin with a 4-pound fish (or one slightly larger). I like this with branzino, a light fish with a clean flavor that lives in both salt and fresh water and is prevalent along the Mediterranean. Happily, it's turning up more and more on this side of the Atlantic, but if you can't find it, use one of the other fish I list. As with all fish, it's a good idea to cook this on the day you purchase it for peak flavor and freshness. When you pull the pan from the oven and crack the hardened salt with a hammer or heavy spoon, everyone will be impressed. I love this little piece of kitchen theater! ❧ *serves 4*

1   Preheat the oven to 375°F.

2   With a pair of shears, cut out the gills of the fish, if necessary, and wash the inner cavity. Season the cavity to taste with salt and pepper and drizzle with about ¼ cup of olive oil. Put the lemon and orange slices, tarragon, oregano, bay leaf, and garlic in the cavity of the fish and gently press the two sides of the fish together.

3   In a large bowl, stir 2 pounds of kosher salt and the fennel seeds, peppercorns, and egg whites to a paste-like consistency. You might find it easiest to mix this with your hands.

4   Spread a ½-inch layer of the salt paste over a shallow baking pan, such as a jelly roll pan, large enough to hold the fish. Put the stuffed fish on top of the salt.

5   Pack the rest of the salt paste around and over the fish so that it is completely encased.

6   Bake the fish for 30 to 45 minutes, depending on the weight of the fish. A full 4-pound fish will require 40 minutes; a fish that weighs a little more than 4 pounds will need 45 minutes. Do not overcook.   *(continued)*

7 Remove the pan from the oven and let the fish rest, still encased in the salt, for 5 to 8 minutes. Using a mallet or the handle of a heavy knife, crack the salt. If the fish is cooked through so that the flesh just flakes and is opaque, remove all the salt using a knife and spoon to lift it off. If the fish needs a little more cooking, rest the chunks of salt back on top of it and return it to the oven for 5 or 6 minutes, or until done. Let it rest again for about 5 minutes before removing all the salt.

8 Drizzle the fish with ¼ cup of olive oil and sprinkle with the chopped tarragon, basil, and parsley. Serve with a wedge or slice of lemon.

the sommelier recommends

The instinctual wine pairing here is a clean white, but if you want to bump up the flavors and be a bit daring, try a red wine. The key is to stay away from ponderous tannins, high viscosity, and high alcohol, and instead steer toward bright red fruit flavors. We love this dish with a slightly chilled glass of Montepulciano d'Abruzzo from Caldora, La Valentina, or Masciarelli. It adds a great dose of richness to each bite of fish. Don't be tempted by their luxury blends if you see them on the shelves—in this case, the simple, most basic cuvée is the best choice.

roasted cod with garbanzo beans and aioli

merluzzo arrostito con ceci e aioli

2 cups cooked garbanzo beans (see page 61)

4 cups Fish Fumet (recipe follows) or low-sodium clam juice

8 white anchovies, cut into 1-inch pieces

¼ cup fresh flat-leaf parsley leaves

4 ounces Oven-Dried Cherry Tomatoes (page 12), cut into large dice

1 teaspoon chopped fresh oregano

12 littleneck clams (see Note)

¼ cup Clarified Butter (page 147) or vegetable oil

Four 7-ounce pieces Atlantic cod

Kosher salt and freshly ground black pepper

4 tablespoons Roasted Garlic Aioli (recipe follows)

¼ cup extra virgin olive oil

1 teaspoon chopped fresh flat-leaf parsley

1 Preheat the oven to 400°F.

2 In a large saucepan, heat the beans, Fish Fumet, anchovies, parsley leaves, Oven-Dried Cherry Tomatoes, and oregano until warm. Remove from the heat, cover, and set aside to keep warm.

3 In another large saucepan, arrange a steaming rack set over about an inch of water. Put the clams on the rack and bring the water to a simmer over medium-high heat. Cover the pan tightly and let the clams steam for about 5 minutes. At this point, the clams will have opened. Drain the clams, discard any that do not open, and hold the others in the hot pan, covered.

4 Heat an ovenproof sauté pan over high heat. When the pan is hot, put the clarified butter or oil in the pan. When the butter foams or the oil is smoking hot, lay the cod in the pan, reduce the heat to medium-high, and sear for 2 to 3 minutes. When the cod no longer sticks to the pan, transfer the pan to the oven. Do not flip the fish over. Roast for 4 minutes.

5 Meanwhile, spoon the bean mixture into 4 shallow bowls.

6 Put a piece of cod on top of the beans, turning the fish over as you transfer it from roasting pan to bowl. Put 3 steamed clams in each bowl. Season to taste with salt and pepper. Top each piece of cod with Roasted Garlic Aioli and garnish each bowl with the olive oil and chopped parsley.

An entire section of Massachusetts was named for cod, and for generations fishermen setting out from the Cape came home with boats bulging with cod, one of the most important food fish in the history of the world. Cod may not be as plentiful as it once was, but its delicate, moist flavor and flaky, light texture make it one of the best fish around. If you can't get cod, use haddock or pollack—very similar and members of the same family. When teamed with the garbanzo beans and aioli, this is an easy company meal. 🍴 *serves 4*

note When you buy fresh clams, it's a good idea to soak them to purge any sand in the shells. This step may not be necessary if you know your purveyor and trust his or her word that the clams are very clean. Otherwise, put the clams in a bowl and cover with fresh seawater (if available) or cold salted water. For every gallon of tap water, add about 5 tablespoons of salt to approximate seawater. Discard any clams that quickly float to the surface of the water. Let the other clams soak for 3 to 4 hours, drain and rinse. *(continued)*

The garlicky aioli and the extra flavor of the sea provided by the clams lead us to the white wines of Liguria, which is home to some of the most dramatic seaside vineyards in the world. The grapes grown here cannot be reached by car or truck; harvesters are transported by boats to reach the chosen fruit. Try wines from the Bisson winery—their "U Pastine" is made from a rare grape, Bianchetta Genovese, and tastes of the ocean.

roasted garlic aioli
makes about 1 cup

1 whole garlic head (about 12 cloves)
1½ teaspoons olive oil
Kosher salt
1 cup good-quality, store-bought mayonnaise
1 teaspoon fresh lemon juice
Cracked black pepper

1 Preheat the oven to 300°F.

2 Remove the outer layers of skin from the garlic head but leave the cloves intact at the root end. Put the head in the center of a sheet of aluminum foil, drizzle with the olive oil, and add a pinch of salt. Fold the foil over the top of the garlic to make a loose package. Put on a baking sheet and roast for 35 minutes, until the garlic is soft. Unwrap and set aside to cool.

3 When cool, squeeze the softened garlic pulp from each clove. Transfer the pulp to the bowl of a food processor fitted with the metal blade. Add the mayonnaise and lemon juice. Process until smooth. Season to taste with salt and pepper. Use immediately or cover and refrigerate for up to 3 days.

fish fumet
makes about 3 quarts

2 pounds cod bones or other nonoily fish bones
1 cup dry white wine
½ onion, chopped
½ fennel bulb, chopped
10 fresh flat-leaf parsley stems
2 sprigs fresh thyme
1 bay leaf

1 Chop the cod bones into manageably sized pieces and rinse with cool running water. Transfer to a bowl and add enough cold water to cover. Refrigerate for at least 6 hours or overnight.

2 Preheat the oven to 350°F.

3 Drain the bones and pat them dry. Spread them on a baking sheet and roast for about 20 minutes, or until they are cooked through but have not colored. There will be no fish remaining on them and the bones will be white.

4 Transfer the bones to a saucepan and add the wine, onion, fennel, parsley stems, thyme, and bay leaf. Add 1 gallon of water and bring to a simmer. Simmer for 30 minutes, remove from the heat, and set aside to stand for 10 minutes. Strain and use immediately or cover and refrigerate. The fumet will keep in the refrigerator for up to 7 days. It also will keep in the freezer for up to 1 month.

mackerel escabeche with new potatoes

sgombro escabeche con patate

marinade and vegetables

1¼ cups cider vinegar

1¼ cups dry white wine

3 tablespoons sugar

1 tablespoon kosher salt

4 garlic cloves, thinly sliced

4 shallots, thinly sliced

2 celery ribs, cut on the diagonal into ¼-inch pieces

1 red bell pepper, thinly sliced

1 carrot, thinly sliced

½ fennel bulb, very thinly sliced

½ cup chopped green Cerignola olives or other green olives

8 saffron threads

1 sprig fresh thyme

1 bay leaf

1 teaspoon freshly ground black pepper

potatoes

1 pound new potatoes

1 bay leaf

¾ cup crème fraîche

2 tablespoons snipped fresh chives

Kosher salt and freshly ground black pepper

mackerel

¾ cup extra virgin olive oil

Four 6-ounce skin-on mackerel fillets

to serve

2 tablespoons chopped fresh flat-leaf parsley

1 To prepare the marinade, bring the vinegar, wine, sugar, and ¾ cup water to a boil in a pot over high heat. Add the salt and bring the liquid to a boil. Cook at a rapid boil for about 5 minutes, or until reduced by a quarter.

2 Remove the pot from the heat and add the garlic, shallots, celery, bell pepper, carrot, fennel, olives, saffron, thyme, bay leaf, and black pepper to the liquid. Let the marinade cool to room temperature, and then let it stand for 4 hours at room temperature.

3 To prepare the mackerel, heat a sauté pan over medium-high heat. When the pan is hot, put ½ cup of olive oil in the pan.

4 When the oil is hot, sear the mackerel, skin side down, for 2 minutes. Turn the fish and cook for 1 or 2 minutes longer, or until cooked through.

5 Put the mackerel, skin side down, in a shallow nonreactive glass or ceramic dish and season to taste with salt and pepper. Spoon about 1 cup of the marinade over the fish or enough to cover it, cover with plastic wrap, and refrigerate for at least 1 hour.

This is my version of escabeche, or as it's known in Italy, *scapece*. The mackerel, which is an oily fish that is simply delicious, is first cooked and then soaked in a lovely marinade flavored with cider vinegar, white wine, olives, fennel, and fresh herbs and then served with potatoes mashed with crème fraîche. It's a luscious pairing. *serves 4*

6   To prepare the potatoes, without peeling them, cut the potatoes into large dice and put them in a large saucepan. Cover them with lightly salted cold water and add the bay leaf. Bring the water to a simmer over medium-high heat and cook the potatoes for about 15 minutes, or until just tender. Drain the potatoes, remove and discard the bay leaf, and return the potatoes to the pan.

7   Add the crème fraîche and chives and mix well, lightly crushing the potatoes. Season to taste with salt and pepper and set aside, covered, to let the potatoes cool to room temperature.

8   Divide the potatoes among 4 serving plates. Lift the fish from the marinade and put a mackerel fillet on top of the potatoes. Spoon the vegetables on top of the mackerel. Drizzle some of the marinade and 1 tablespoon of olive oil around each plate. Garnish with the parsley and serve.

the sommelier recommends

Mackerel has a very pronounced flavor, and with this dish, the wine choice also has to contend with cider vinegar, olives, herbs, and saffron! The wine must have high tones (the nice way to say acidity) and not clash with the complex flavors of the dish. The solution? Pinot Bianco. This white wine is produced all over Italy, but our favorite versions come from the northern regions of Friuli and the Alto Adige. Maculan in the Veneto makes a cool, sophisticated blend of Pinot Bianco, Tocai, and Pinot Grigio called "Pino e Toi" that will delight.

₿ braises

I dedicate a chapter to braises for a number of reasons. First, braised dishes are popular in osterias throughout Italy, particularly in the cooler months, and therefore belong in this book. Second, braising is my favorite cooking technique, and over the years I have spent a good amount of time perfecting it. Third, braises are just so completely delicious, warm, and comforting that I wanted to spread the word about how great they are. They used to be considered a kind of peasant food, or at the very most, casual meals for every day. That was when the so-called lesser, tougher cuts of meat—the shanks and short ribs and lamb shoulders—were far less expensive than the roasts, chops, and steaks. They required long, slow cooking, with liquid added to help tenderize them as they simmered for hours on the back of the stove or in the oven. Nowadays, all meat is expensive and the lesser cuts, which have grown in popularity, are no longer a bargain, but they still taste wonderful when braised.

The sauce from a braise is richly redolent of all the flavors in the pot and is the very essence of comfort food. I like braises best when the liquid is partially absorbed by the meat as it cools in it. When the braise is reheated, the sauce is that much more full flavored, proving that stews really are better the next day. You will notice that in all the recipes (except the last two in the chapter, one for rabbit and the other for monkfish), I recommend that you cool and then reheat the braise. It's a good cooking technique to have in your toolbox and also makes these surefire winners for dinner parties, as they can be cooked well ahead of time. I studied with great braise masters in France and Italy who had a significant influence on me and my cooking. I learned a lot from them and from my own experience, and one of the things I am most proud of in my life as a chef is that I am a really good braiser. Enjoy my recipes!

notes from the sommelier
obsessed with amarone

So much love goes into a braised dish: slow, gentle heat; the luxury of lengthy cooking; rich foods that when done, seem to melt in your mouth. Likewise, a lot of love goes into the production of one of our favorite red wines in the world, which also happens to be an excellent partner to the dishes in this chapter. We have a soft spot for everything Amarone and Amaronesque from the Veneto region of Italy. This inimitable red wine is made from Corvina, Rondinella, and Molinara grapes that are left to dry on *graticci* (straw mats) once harvested.

The dehydrated grapes, now raisinated and very high in sugar content, are then fermented into that heady elixir called Amarone. The often inky red can be redolent of blueberry, blackberry, cherry, licorice, tar, chocolate, and espresso. It is a brilliant wine for aging, but who can wait? We can't resist! Bertani, Cesari, Quintarelli, oh my! For anyone looking for an Amaronesque experience without the Amarone-sized credit card bill, try Valpolicella Ripasso, as it's almost Amarone—same grapes but slightly less raisinated. Or try Bardolino, which is a lighter style, again, made from Corvina and Molinara grapes. We also cellar a few of the rebellious wines that defy the Amarone standards, like "Osar" from Masi. Nothing is going to warm your heart like braised oxtail with a glass of one of these treats. Richness on richness, luxury on luxury—you deserve it!

veal osso buco
ossobuco di vitello

Four 12-ounce veal shanks
Kosher salt
Freshly ground black pepper
1 cup vegetable oil
1 cup all-purpose flour
2 carrots, peeled and diced
2 celery ribs, diced
1 yellow onion, diced
6 garlic cloves, sliced
1 cup dry red wine
4 cups veal stock or chicken stock
3 cups chicken stock
3 cups canned plum tomatoes, drained and
   crushed
2 sprigs fresh thyme
1 sprig fresh rosemary
1 bay leaf

1 tablespoon grated fresh horseradish (see Note)
2 tablespoons grated lemon zest
2 tablespoons chopped fresh flat-leaf parsley

1 Lay the veal shanks in a shallow baking pan and sprinkle liberally on both sides with salt. Refrigerate for 2 hours.

2 Rinse the veal shanks of their salt and pat dry with paper towels. Wrap each veal shank once around the circumference so that it holds the bone and meat together in the center. Tie the twine with a good knot. Season the veal shanks with pepper.

3 Preheat the oven to 350°F.

4 Heat a large, ovenproof casserole over high heat. Put the oil into the casserole and let it heat.

5 Meanwhile, put the flour in a shallow bowl, dredge the veal shanks in it, and pat off the excess. Brown the veal shanks in the hot oil for about 5 minutes on each side, or until browned on all sides. Remove from the pan and set aside. If the oil turns dark during the process, discard it and heat a fresh cup of oil.

6 Add the carrots, celery, onion, and garlic to the pan and cook over medium-high heat for 2 to 3 minutes, stirring constantly. Add the wine, bring to a boil, and cook for about 2 minutes, or until reduced by half.

7 Add the stocks, tomatoes, thyme, rosemary, and bay leaf to the pan. Return the veal shanks to the pan and bring to a boil over high heat. Once the liquid boils, cover, transfer to the oven, and cook for 2½ hours, until the meat is fork tender and falling off the bones.

I open the braising chapter with one of Italy's most renowned braises: osso buco. It's a classic Milanese dish usually made with veal shanks cooked in a rich broth that includes tomatoes and wine. I salt the meat before cooking it, a technique that tenderizes the veal. The dish is finished with lemon zest and parsley, which stand in for the more common gremolata that often accompanies it, along with saffron risotto.

The term *ossobuco* roughly translates to "hole in the bone" or "pierced bone." I suggest you tie the shanks before cooking them so that they hold together—and don't forget to dig into the bones for the luscious bone marrow.

serves 4

8   Remove the herbs from the braising liquid and discard. Let the veal shanks come to room temperature in the braising liquid. Remove the veal shanks and set aside. Strain the liquid through a fine-mesh sieve or chinois into a large saucepan. Bring to a boil over medium-high heat, reduce the heat, and simmer for 10 to 15 minutes, or until reduced by a quarter. Using a skimmer or large spoon, skim off any grease or foam that rises to the surface. Return the strained vegetables to the liquid and taste for seasoning.

9   To serve, cut and discard the twine, put a single osso buco (veal shank) in a bowl, and ladle about ¾ cup of the sauce and vegetables over it. (If the sauce and the meat are not still warm, heat them together very gently over low heat for 8 to 10 minutes.)

10 Garnish each osso buco with the fresh horseradish, lemon zest, and chopped parsley and season with pepper.

note If you cannot find fresh horseradish, you can use prepared. It will taste stronger, so it's a good idea to wrap the horseradish in a double thickness of cheesecloth and squeeze out the excess liquid.

the sommelier recommends
Lombardy is home to fashion-obsessed Milan and wine-obsessed Lake Garda. The La Prendina winery in this region produces an Amaronesque red from 100 percent Merlot grapes called *faial*. Half of the grapes are raisinated in straw baskets to accentuate the decadent flavors and textures that the drying process can create. Dark, black fruited, silky on the palate—the veal could not be in better company!

braised veal cheeks
guancie di vitello brasate

2 pounds veal cheeks
Kosher salt and freshly ground black pepper
½ cup plus 2 tablespoons olive oil
1 carrot, cut into large dice
1 yellow onion, cut into large dice
1 celery rib, cut into large dice
2 teaspoons ground coriander seeds
2 sprigs fresh thyme
1 bay leaf
1 quart veal stock or chicken stock
2 tablespoons sherry vinegar
1 cup all-purpose flour
2 large eggs
2 cups panko
½ pound baby arugula
3 tablespoons extra virgin olive oil, plus more for
    drizzling
Juice of 2 lemons
2 ounces Parmigiano-Reggiano cheese, shaved
    (about 2 tablespoons)

You may not have considered veal cheeks, but don't let their unfamiliarity stop you! They are moist, flavorful nuggets of meat with an almost perfect balance of fat and meat. This recipe is a twist on veal Milanese, made with the cheeks, which taste rather like boned short ribs once they are braised, breaded, and then fried. I serve the rich veal cheeks with an arugula salad dressed with lemon juice, which cuts their intensity. You will have to special-order veal cheeks at most butchers, and be sure to ask the butcher to clean them for you.

serves 4

1 Preheat the oven to 300°F.

2 Season the veal cheeks with salt and pepper.

3 Heat 2 tablespoons of olive oil in a large, ovenproof casserole over high heat.

4 Add the veal cheeks and sear for about 4 minutes on each side, or until golden brown. Add the carrot, onion, celery, coriander seeds, thyme, and bay leaf and cook, stirring, for about 10 minutes, or until lightly caramelized.

5 Add the stock, bring to a boil, and cover with parchment paper cut to fit inside the pan. Roast for 45 to 60 minutes, until the meat is fork tender. Remove the pan from the oven, lift off and discard the parchment paper, and let the veal cheeks cool to room temperature in the braising liquid. Stir the vinegar into the cooling liquid. Once they have reached room temperature, remove the veal cheeks and set aside.

6 Strain the liquid through a fine-mesh sieve or chinois into a large saucepan and discard the vegetables. Bring the strained liquid to a boil over medium-high heat and simmer for about 15 minutes, or until reduced by half. Using a skimmer or large spoon, skim off any grease or foam that rises to the surface. Season to taste with salt and pepper.

7 Put the flour in a shallow bowl. Whisk the eggs with ½ cup of water in a second bowl. Put the panko in a third bowl. Season the flour with salt and pepper. Dredge the cooked veal cheeks in the flour, then dip them in the egg wash and finally the panko to coat.

8 Heat a sauté pan over medium-high heat and put ½ cup of olive oil in the pan (if you prefer, substitute vegetable oil). When the

oil is hot, panfry the veal cheeks for about 3 minutes on each side, or until golden brown. Let the cheeks drain on paper towels and season lightly with salt and pepper while hot.

9   In a mixing bowl, toss the arugula with about 3 tablespoons of extra virgin olive oil and the lemon juice and season to taste with salt and pepper.

10 Ladle about ⅓ cup of the reduced braising liquid on each of 4 serving plates and top with a quarter of the veal cheeks. Pile arugula over the veal cheeks, drizzle with extra virgin olive oil and a good squeeze of lemon juice, and top with a generous amount of the shaved cheese.

the sommelier recommends

The winemakers in Lombardy have a trick up their sleeves that they may have picked up from the Amarone producers: They use the Chiavennesca grape, the local name for Nebbiolo, and put it through the drying process to intensify flavors and add body and texture to the resulting wine. The producer Rainoldi bottles a cuvée called "Ca' Rizzieri." It's a Sforzato di Valtellina, and it's a bottle of pure hedonistic pleasure.

braised pork shanks with borlotti beans
stinco di maiale brasato con fagioli borlotti

The pork foreshank is the leg section of the hog that is connected to the shoulder, and the hindshank is the portion that connects to the rump. I prefer the meatier hindshank and suggest you use it here—although either will taste mighty good. More important, try to buy heirloom pork from hogs that are raised responsibly by farmers who treat them humanely. They might be called Large Blacks, Berkshire, Red Wattle, Tamworth, or Gloucestershire Old Spots, which are breeds that were common in bygone days.

Just as is the case with free-range chickens, hogs raised on relatively small farms are fed a varied diet free of subtherapeutic antibiotics and growth hormones and therefore taste better. The movement to reclaim breeds of hog that are not factory farmed is an important one for the good of the animal, the farmers, and our health. And it really makes a difference when it comes to flavor; I can't emphasize enough how deliciously juicy and tender the meat is. Seek it out at farmers' markets, independent butchers, and online. I serve this braise with beans, as is the custom in central Italy and was the practice in the Tramonto household when I was growing up. Why stray from a good thing? *serves 4*

beans
½ pound dried borlotti (cranberry) beans
1 whole garlic head, cloves separated
1 cup extra virgin olive oil
1 Onion Brûlée (recipe follows)
1 carrot, peeled and diced
1 celery rib, diced
4 ounces bacon, cut into large dice
5 fresh flat-leaf parsley stems
3 sprigs fresh thyme
2 sprigs fresh rosemary
Pinch of crushed red pepper flakes
1½ quarts chicken stock
1 tablespoon kosher salt
2 tablespoons sherry vinegar

brine
1 pound kosher salt
1 cup honey
1 sprig fresh rosemary
5 juniper berries

pork
Four 1-pound pork hindshanks
½ cup vegetable oil
1 carrot, peeled and cut into large dice
1 celery rib, cut into large dice
2 cups dry white wine
½ cup Stewed Tomatoes (page 57)
1 quart veal stock or chicken stock

to serve
1 tablespoon unsalted butter
2 tablespoons chopped fresh flat-leaf parsley

1 To prepare the beans, in a large pot, soak the beans in enough cold water to cover by 2 or 3 inches for 6 to 12 hours. Change the water two or three times during soaking, if possible. Drain and set aside.   *(continued)*

2 Use a broad knife to crush the garlic cloves, still in their skins.

3 Heat a saucepan over medium heat. Add the olive oil, onion, carrot, celery, bacon, parsley, thyme, rosemary, red pepper, and half of the garlic cloves to the pan and cook, stirring, for about 7 minutes, or until the vegetables soften.

4 Add the drained beans and the stock and bring to a boil over high heat. Reduce the heat and simmer for about 40 minutes, until the beans are tender but not so soft that they lose their shape.

5 Add the salt and vinegar. Stir to mix, remove the beans from the heat. Taste the cooking liquid and season to taste with salt. Let the beans cool in the cooking liquid and then refrigerate until ready to use.

6 To prepare the brine, in a large pot, mix 1 gallon of water with the salt, honey, rosemary, and juniper berries. Bring to a boil over high heat and cook until the salt and honey dissolve. Remove from the heat and let the brine cool to room temperature.

7 To prepare the pork, submerge the pork shanks in the cool brine, cover, and refrigerate for 3 hours.

8 Preheat the oven to 300°F.

9 Lift the shanks from the brine and pat dry.

10 Heat a large ovenproof casserole or braising pan over medium-high heat. When the pan is hot, put the vegetable oil in the pan and sear the pork shanks for 6 to 8 minutes on each side, or until golden brown.

11 Add the carrot, celery, and wine and the remaining garlic cloves and bring to a boil. Cook over medium-high heat for 8 to 10 minutes, or until reduced by half. Add the tomatoes and stock and bring to a boil.

12 Cover, transfer to the oven, and cook for 2 to 3 hours, until the meat is fork tender. Remove from the oven and let the pork and its juices reach room temperature.

13 Heat the beans and enough of their cooking liquid to keep them moist over medium heat until heated through. Stir in the butter and cook until melted. Add the parsley and stir gently to mix. Taste for seasoning.

14 Reheat the pork shanks over medium-high heat until heated through and taste for seasoning. Put 1 pork shank in each of 4 shallow serving bowls and ladle about 1 cup of sauce over each. Spoon beans on top of each shank and include any vegetables and bacon still intact.

the sommelier recommends
Corvina is the member of the Amarone trio of grape varietals that shines well even without its partners Rondinella and Molinara. We have found great examples of approachable Corvina bottlings from wineries like Cortegiara and Falasco that satisfy our need for dark red without straining our credit cards.

onion brûlée
makes 2 or 4 onion halves

1 or 2 yellow or white onions

1 Slice each onion in half lengthwise (from stem end to tip).

2 Put a sauté pan over high heat. When the pan is hot, put the onion halves in the pan, cut sides down, and cook for about 15 minutes, or until the cut sides are deeply caramelized but not quite burned. Remove from the pan and use as required.

braised lamb shanks
stinco d'agnello brasato

Four 12-ounce lamb shanks
Kosher salt and freshly ground black pepper
1 cup vegetable oil
2 carrots, peeled and diced
2 celery ribs, diced
1 yellow onion, diced
2 cups dry red wine
3 cups lamb stock or beef stock
2 cups chicken stock
2 sprigs fresh thyme
1 sprig fresh rosemary
1 clove

Lamb shanks are not the easiest cuts of meat to find, and so when I see them I buy them in some quantity and freeze them at home. This way, I can make braised lamb shanks any time I want, which is a bonus because nothing tastes better. Look for meaty ones, as they tend to be bony. Like most of the braises in this chapter, I cool the meat in the braising liquid and then reheat it, either the same day as cooking it or a day or two later. This way the moisture and flavor get absorbed right back into the meat, and it tastes best. *serves 4*

1 Preheat the oven to 300°F.

2 Season the lamb shanks on both sides with salt and pepper.

3 In a large casserole or braising pan, heat the oil over high heat. When the oil is hot, sear the lamb shanks for 6 to 8 minutes on both sides, or until they are dark brown. Remove the lamb shanks and set aside.

4 Add the carrots, celery, and onion to the pan and cook over medium-high heat, stirring, for about 8 minutes, or until tender. Add the wine and stir with a wooden spoon, scraping up any browned bits. Let the wine come to a boil and cook for about 10 minutes, or until reduced by half.

5 Return the lamb shanks to the pan and add the stocks, thyme, rosemary, and clove. Bring to a boil, cover, and transfer to the oven. Cook for 4 hours, until the meat is fork tender and nearly falling off the bone.

6 Remove the pan from the oven and let the lamb shanks cool to room temperature in the braising liquid.

7 Reheat the lamb shanks in the liquid over medium heat until heated through and taste for seasoning. Put 1 lamb shank in each of 4 shallow serving bowls and top with a generous cup of sauce and the vegetables. The lamb shanks can also be covered and refrigerated in their braising liquid for up to 4 days; remove the fat that has hardened on top of the lamb before reheating.

the sommelier recommends
Red wines from Valpolicella come in many styles and with many adjectives. We enjoy these wines from Ca' la Bionda and Buglioni with the lamb shank.

braised lamb shoulder with panelle
spalla d'agnello brasata con panelle

lamb
4 tablespoons fennel seeds
1 cup plus 2 tablespoons kosher salt
2 tablespoons freshly ground black pepper
One 3-pound boned lamb shoulder
1 cup olive oil
1 Onion Brûlée (page 169)
2 celery ribs, coarsely chopped
1 fennel bulb, trimmed and coarsely chopped
1 carrot, peeled and coarsely chopped
4 shallots, halved
2 whole garlic heads, crushed
½ cup sherry vinegar
2 quarts chicken stock
Stems from 1 bunch flat-leaf parsley
2 sprigs fresh thyme
1 sprig fresh rosemary

panelle
2½ cups chickpea flour
Kosher salt
1 tablespoon freshly ground black pepper
½ cup semolina flour

to serve
1 cup olive oil
1 cup pitted green Cerignola olives or other green olives

Panelle are little chickpea fritters that used to be cooked as street food in Sicily. I've seen guys make them in frying pans they set over wood fires lit in barrels. The fritters often are used to make some sort of simple sandwich, but I have brought them inside and teamed them with braised lamb shoulder. No one seems to make the little cakes anymore, so let's change that here and now!

We ate lamb shoulder quite often when I was growing up, as it was a lot cheaper than leg of lamb and, when braised, just as delicious. Curing it with a salt rub makes it more tender and flavorful, but be sure to rinse the salt off the lamb after 4 hours. Otherwise, the meat might taste salty. ❧ *serves 4*

1 Spread the fennel seeds in a dry skillet and toast over low heat for 1 to 2 minutes, or until they darken a shade and are fragrant. Transfer to a spice or coffee grinder. Add 2 tablespoons of salt and grind to a fine powder.

2 Put 1 cup of salt in a bowl. Add the pepper and the fennel mixture and stir well.

3 Rub the salt mixture into the lamb shoulder so that the meat is well permeated with it. Put the lamb shoulder in a shallow baking pan and cover with parchment paper or plastic wrap. Refrigerate for 4 to 6 hours. If the lamb shoulder sits for any longer, it will taste salty.

4 Preheat the oven to 325°F.

5 Rinse the lamb shoulder with cool water to remove the salt and pat dry with paper towels.

6 Heat a roasting pan over medium-high heat. When the pan is hot, put the olive oil in the pan. When the olive oil is hot, add the lamb shoulder and sear on all sides until golden brown. Total cooking time will be about 20 minutes. Remove the lamb shoulder from the pan and set aside.

7 Add the onion, celery, fennel, carrot, shallots, and garlic. Reduce the heat to

medium and cook, stirring, for 8 to 10 minutes, or until the vegetables are nicely browned and caramelized.

8   Pour the vinegar into the pan and bring to a boil, stirring with a wooden spoon and scraping up any browned bits. Add the stock, parsley stems, thyme, and rosemary and then return the lamb shoulder to the pan. The liquid should come about halfway up the meat.

9   Raise the heat to medium-high and bring the liquid to a boil. As soon as it boils, cover with parchment paper and transfer to the oven. Cook for about 2 hours, until the meat is fork tender.

10 Remove from the oven, discard the parchment, and let the lamb shoulder reach room temperature in the braising liquid.

11 Lift the lamb shoulder from the pan and strain the braising liquid through a fine-mesh sieve or chinois into a deep roasting pan or large ovenproof pot. Skim the fat from the liquid.

12 Cut the lamb into manageable serving pieces and put in the pan with the strained braising liquid. Cover and refrigerate until ready to serve, or if ready to serve, reheat right away.

13 Increase the oven temperature to 350°F.

14 Put the pan with the lamb and the braising liquid in the oven and cook for 20 to 30 minutes, until heated through.

15 To prepare the panelle, combine the chickpea flour with 3 cups of warm water in a large saucepan, using a handheld mixer. When blended, add 1 tablespoon of salt and the pepper and mix well.

16 Cook the batter over low heat, stirring constantly, for about 20 minutes, until

heated through and any raw flour flavor has dissipated. If the mixture gets too thick, add water, little by little.

17 Line a jelly roll pan with parchment paper and spread the batter evenly on it, smoothing it with a spatula. Cover with another sheet of parchment and refrigerate for about 45 minutes, or until set and completely cooled.

18 Flip the panelle onto a large cutting board and cut into 3-inch squares. Coat the squares with a dusting of semolina flour to prevent sticking.

19 To serve, heat the olive oil in a sauté pan over medium-high heat and panfry the panelle for about 2 minutes on each side, or until golden brown and crispy. Drain on paper towels, blotting the tops with towels, too. Season with a little salt while hot.

20 Put a panelle in each of 4 shallow serving bowls. Spoon a portion of lamb on top.

21 Stir the olives into the hot braising liquid and let them warm through. Spoon about ½ cup of the sauce over the lamb and serve immediately.

the sommelier recommends
Modern Valpolicella producers have a new trick to make their wines labeled "ripasso" tasty. Ripasso indicates that an already-vinified Valpolicella is "repassed" over Amarone lees, and this second fermentation gives the Valpolicella an Amarone kick. It's baby Amarone, the A-word at a fraction of the price. We have found delicious examples from Cesari, Zenato, and Bertani.

red wine–braised short ribs with garlic mashed potatoes

costatine con purè di patate

Four 12- to 14-ounce boneless beef short ribs
Kosher salt and freshly ground black pepper
1 cup vegetable oil
2 carrots, cut into large dice
2 celery ribs, cut into large dice
1 yellow onion, cut into large dice
2 tablespoons tomato paste
One 750-ml bottle dry red wine
2 cups port
3 sprigs fresh thyme
1 sprig fresh rosemary
1 bay leaf
2 quarts veal stock or chicken stock
2 tablespoons sherry vinegar
2½ cups Garlic Mashed Potatoes (page 174)
2 tablespoons chopped fresh flat-leaf parsley

This is a signature dish at Osteria di Tramonto for two big reasons: First, I love this dish and therefore it always finds its way onto my menus, regardless of where I am cooking; second, our customers love its deep, rich flavor and gorgeous aroma. You will, too. Short ribs can be cut from the shoulder or the back, and both cuts are good. Most commonly, they come from the beef rib roast and the plate, and are layered with lean meat and fat, which cover a flat rib bone. They usually are cut crosswise into short sections and may be called *flanken*, but you can ask for the bone to be left longer, as for this recipe. When you serve this slow-cooked braise with garlic mashed potatoes, you have a taste of heaven on earth!

serves 4

1   Lay the short ribs in a single layer in a shallow baking pan and season generously on both sides with salt. Cover and refrigerate for 2 hours.

2   Preheat the oven to 375°F.

3   Rinse the salt off the ribs and pat them dry with paper towels. Season the ribs with pepper and a light sprinkling of salt.

4   Heat a casserole or braising pan over high heat. When the pan is hot, put the oil in the pan. When the oil is hot, sear the short ribs on both sides until golden brown. Lift the short ribs from the pan and set aside. If the oil is dark, discard it and replace with fresh oil.

5   Reduce the heat to medium-high and add the carrots, celery, and onion to the pan. Cook, stirring, for about 8 minutes, or until the vegetables brown and caramelize.

6   Stir in the tomato paste. Reduce the heat to medium and cook for 2 to 3 minutes. Add the wine and port, raise the heat to medium-high, and cook for about 5 minutes, or until the liquid reduces by half.

7   Return the short ribs to the pan and add the thyme, rosemary, and bay leaf. Pour the stock into the pan. Bring to a boil over medium-high heat. Lay a sheet of parchment paper directly on the food and transfer the pan to the oven. Cook for about 2 hours, until the meat is fork tender.

8   Remove the pan from the oven and discard the parchment paper. Add the vinegar. Let the short ribs come to room temperature in the braising liquid.   *(continued)*

9   Lift the short ribs from the liquid and set aside on a large plate or bowl, covered, to keep warm.

10 Strain the braising liquid through a fine-mesh sieve or chinois into a saucepan. Bring to a simmer over medium-high heat, reduce the heat to low, and cook for about 15 minutes, or until reduced by a quarter. Using a skimmer or large spoon, skim off any fat that rises to the surface. Season to taste with salt and pepper and pour the sauce over the ribs.

11 Serve immediately or allow to cool to room temperature and then cover and refrigerate for up to 5 days. (If you are serving immediately and the ribs and sauce are not hot enough, reheat gently over medium-low heat for about 10 minutes.)

12 Spoon the Garlic Mashed Potatoes onto each of 4 serving plates. Top with a short rib, spoon on ¼ to ½ cup of sauce, garnish with the chopped parsley, and serve hot.

the sommelier recommends

We have never opened a red wine that we did not love with Chef Tramonto's braised short ribs. Any Amarone will layer more decadence onto your palate (try Sant Antonio, Speri, or Santi), *or* you can bust out the Barolo and take the experience to a different, more refined place. Something about earthy Nebbiolo and the layering of flavors makes this pairing a real wow! Any older Barolo will do: Ceretto, Conterno, Cogno—make it a dusty bottle, please.

garlic mashed potatoes
makes about 2½ cups

Kosher salt
1½ pounds Yukon Gold potatoes
¼ cup heavy cream
1 tablespoon Roasted Garlic Purée (page 112)
¼ cup extra virgin olive oil
Freshly ground black pepper

1   Preheat the oven to 350°F.

2   Spread a layer of salt over the bottom of a shallow baking pan. Lay the potatoes on top of the salt and bake for about 40 minutes, until fork tender.

3   When the potatoes are cool enough to handle, peel and discard the skins. Push the potatoes through a potato ricer or food mill into a saucepan set over low heat. Add the cream a little at a time, stirring to mix well. Stir in the Roasted Garlic Purée and olive oil and season to taste with salt and pepper. Stir the potatoes until smooth and all the ingredients are well incorporated.

roman braised oxtail
brasata di coda di bue

3 oxtails (about 5 pounds)
Kosher salt and freshly ground pepper
1 cup extra virgin olive oil
4 ounces pancetta, diced
6 celery ribs, diced
1 carrot, diced
1 yellow onion, diced
2 tablespoons tomato paste
Stems from ½ bunch flat-leaf parsley
2 cloves, crushed
1 bay leaf
1 teaspoon crushed red pepper flakes
2 cups dry red wine
2 cups canned crushed tomatoes, drained
3 cups beef stock
2 tablespoons sherry vinegar
¼ cup celery leaves, from the heart
¼ cup pine nuts
2 tablespoons grated lemon zest

Oxtail is an underutilized meat, at least in this country. Europeans are more apt to appreciate its rich, full flavor. If you've ever tasted good oxtail soup, you know what I mean. Oxtail is a humble ingredient, to be sure, but full of flavor. This is a simple, straightforward recipe that, like many braises, has a long list of ingredients with an easy method and a satisfyingly mouthwatering end result.

serves 4

1 Chop the oxtails into 6-inch-long pieces. Using a paring knife, score the length of each oxtail piece so that each one has about 6 cuts going all the way around it. This will loosen the tendons and make the meat easier to remove.

2 Lightly sprinkle the oxtail pieces with salt and pepper and set aside at room temperature for 1 hour.

3 Preheat the oven to 350°F.

4 Heat a roasting pan over medium-high heat. When the pan is hot, put ½ cup of olive oil in the pan. When the olive oil is hot, sear the oxtail pieces in the pan and brown on all sides. Remove the oxtails from the pan. Drain and discard the olive oil.

5 Add ½ cup of olive oil to the pan and cook the pancetta for 3 to 4 minutes, or until it is lightly browned and has rendered most of its fat.

6 Add the celery, carrot, and onion to the pan and cook, stirring, for about 8 minutes, until they begin to soften and brown. Stir the tomato paste into the pan and when heated through add the parsley stems, cloves, bay leaf, and red pepper.

7 Add the wine and bring to a boil, stirring with a wooden spoon and scraping up any browned bits. Let the wine boil for about 10 minutes, or until reduced by half.

8 Return the oxtail pieces to the pan. Add the tomatoes and stock. The oxtail pieces should just be covered by the liquid. Bring to a boil over medium-high heat, cover, and transfer to the oven. Cook for 1 hour, until the meat is easy to pull from the bone.

9 Stir in the vinegar and let the oxtail pieces cool in the braising liquid to room temperature. Lift the oxtail pieces from the

cooled liquid and cut all the meat from the bone. Discard the bones and set the meat aside.

10 Remove and discard the parsley stems and bay leaf and then return the meat to the braising liquid. Stir in the celery leaves, pine nuts, and lemon zest. Refrigerate for up to 4 days or reheat right away and serve.

the sommelier recommends

When we see the bottle with the dark black, flowery script against a tan or green label, we automatically start to salivate! There is no wine in the world that provides a total sensory experience like the Amarone from Giuseppe Quintarelli. He releases his dark, heady, smoky, chocolaty elixir sometimes 10 years later than his competitors, and patience is rewarded in the glass of the drinker.

chicken "hunter's style"
pollo alla cacciatore

8 chicken legs with thighs attached

Kosher salt and freshly ground black pepper

1 cup all-purpose flour

1 cup extra virgin olive oil, plus more for drizzling

2 ounces guanciale, thinly sliced

2 yellow onions, thinly sliced

1 whole garlic head, peeled to expose the cloves and then sliced

1 tablespoon capers, rinsed

1 tablespoon chopped fresh basil

1 teaspoon chopped fresh oregano

1 teaspoon crushed red pepper flakes

2 Calabrian chiles or other small, hot chiles

1 bay leaf

½ cup red wine vinegar

1 cup dry red wine

3 roasted red bell peppers, thinly sliced (see page 11)

3 roasted yellow bell peppers, thinly sliced (see page 11)

1 cup sliced cremini, shiitake, or other forest mushrooms

3 cups chicken stock

3 cups Pomodoro Sauce (page 16)

1 tablespoon chopped fresh flat-leaf parsley

In the old days, hunters spent every autumn making sure they had enough game to feed their families during the cold winter months. This dish is reminiscent of the stews hunters made with mushrooms they could gather in the woods as well as the birds they shot. Although they were originally made with game birds, most versions these days use chicken. Try to use full-bodied "wild" or forest mushrooms to add to this dish's outdoorsy flavor and appeal. Every fall, I prepare chicken "alla cacciatore" at home at least two or three times for the family—at popular request! ✹

serves 4

1 Preheat the oven to 350°F.

2 Season the chicken legs with salt and pepper and then coat in flour. Shake off any excess flour.

3 Set a roasting pan over medium heat. When the pan is hot, put 1 cup of olive oil and the guanciale in the pan and cook for about 4 minutes, or until the meat is translucent and the fat is rendered. Be careful not to burn the thin slices. Remove the guanciale from the pan and set aside.

4 Put the chicken legs, skin side down, in the pan and cook, undisturbed, over medium heat for 10 to 12 minutes, or until golden brown on one side. Turn and brown evenly on the other side. Remove from the pan and set aside.

5 Add the onions and garlic to the pan and cook for about 3 minutes, or until the onions are translucent. Add the capers, basil, oregano, red pepper, chiles, and bay leaf. Add the vinegar and bring to a boil over medium-high heat, stirring with a wooden spoon and scraping up any browned bits. Let the vinegar boil for about 3 minutes, or until it evaporates.

6 Add the wine, bring to a boil, and cook for about 6 minutes, or until reduced by half.

7 Return the guanciale and chicken to the pan. Add the bell peppers and mushrooms

and then pour the stock and Pomodoro Sauce over the chicken and vegetables.

8   Bring to a boil over medium-high heat. Lay a sheet of parchment paper directly on the food and transfer the pan to the oven. Cook for about 1 hour, until the meat is fork tender.

9   Remove the pan from the oven and discard the parchment paper. Let the meat rest for 30 minutes. Serve at this time or refrigerate and reheat just before serving. The braise will keep in the refrigerator for 5 days.

10 To serve, put 2 chicken legs on each of 4 serving plates and spoon about ½ cup of sauce and vegetables over them. Garnish with the parsley and a drizzle of olive oil.

the sommelier recommends

This stew is chock-full of vegetables and mushrooms, and the right red wine will put it all together. A juicy, bright red Bardolino from the Veneto is almost the polar opposite of dark, dense Amarone, though it is made from the same grapes. A basic bottling from the Cavalchina winery will do equally well with the earthy mushrooms and the piquant Pomodoro.

braised rabbit with porcini mushrooms
brasato di coniglio con porcini

1 whole, cleaned rabbit, cut into 4 pieces
Kosher salt and freshly ground black pepper
½ cup extra virgin olive oil
1½ cups pitted Castelvetrano olives or other whole
    large, green olives
½ cup whole black olives
3 garlic cloves, sliced
4 porcini or cremini mushrooms, sliced about
    ¼ inch thick
3 tablespoons red wine vinegar
1 cup dry white wine
2 sprigs fresh rosemary
1 fresh bay leaf
2 cups chicken stock
4 sprigs fresh thyme
4 sprigs fresh rosemary

I came to appreciate rabbit when I lived in England and worked at Stapleford Park, a country-house hotel in Leicestershire. The gamekeeper on the grounds, Malcolm, often turned up at the kitchen door with a fresh rabbit, and I had no choice but to cook it. It didn't take me long to come to like it very much—these days rabbit appears frequently on my menus—and I particularly like it braised. I tasted rabbit braised with porcini mushrooms in Umbria, where the heady braise is some-thing of a classic. Unlike the other braises in the chapter, this one is best eaten soon after cooking. If you let it cool and then reheat it, the meat tends to dry out a little. ❁ *serves 4*

1 Season the rabbit with salt and pepper.

2 Heat the olive oil in a sauté pan over medium heat. When the olive oil is hot, brown the rabbit for about 5 minutes on each side, or until lightly browned. Lift the rabbit from the pan and set aside.

3 Add the olives, garlic, and mushrooms, reduce the heat to medium-high, and cook, stirring, for about 10 minutes, or until the mushrooms are golden brown.

4 Pour in the vinegar, bring to a boil, adjust the heat, and cook at a rapid simmer for about 4 minutes, or until the smell of vinegar vanishes.

5 Return the rabbit to the pan, add the wine, rosemary, and bay leaf, and bring to a boil over medium-high heat. Cook for about 20 minutes, or until the liquid has reduced by about a third.

6 Add the stock, cover the pan, and let the rabbit simmer for about 45 minutes, until the meat is falling off the bone. Let the meat rest for about 30 minutes and then garnish with the thyme and rosemary and serve with the pan juices.

the sommelier recommends
This braise is a lot of fun to pair with wine, as both white and red are nice partners. A white will lighten up the dish, while a red wine will make it seem richer. Our favorite wine to drink with this dish, though, is a zippy, mouth-filling Bardolino Chiaretto. It is a dry, pink wine made from Corvina, Rondinella, and Molinara grapes in the Veneto, and it is the perfect pairing. Try the version from Masi.

monkfish osso buco
ossobuco di coda di rospo

4 bone-in, 10-ounce monkfish steaks

Kosher salt and freshly ground black pepper

1 cup all-purpose flour

4 ounces pancetta, diced

24 pearl onions, peeled

2 celery ribs, diced

1 carrot, diced

6 cups chicken stock

1 cup Oven-Dried Cherry Tomatoes (page 12), cut
　　into large dice

4 sprigs fresh thyme

1 sprigs fresh rosemary

2 tablespoons sherry vinegar

3 tablespoons finely sliced fresh flat-leaf parsley

2 tablespoons grated lemon zest

Just as I opened the chapter with a traditional osso buco, I close it with a version that may not be familiar. It earns the moniker because I leave the bone in the fish, but whatever you call it, this braise is a winner. Monkfish is also called angler fish and bellyfish, and in France they call it *lotte*. When it's braised, the mild-flavored white fish with the texture of lobster meat becomes even more tender and brighter white, and it absorbs the flavors of the braising liquid for a delicious final result. Cook the braise slowly and steadily in a heavy pan (I like cast iron), but do not overcook it and don't expect it to flake, as other fish do. Eat it soon after cooking; the fish turns mealy if you let it cool and reheat it later. You will be rewarded with a moist, clean tasting, and absolutely spectacular dish. ❧ *serves 4*

1　Preheat the oven to 375°F.

2　Liberally season the monkfish steaks with salt and pepper. Dredge the steaks in the flour and shake off any excess.

3　Heat a large ovenproof skillet over medium heat. When the skillet is hot, cook the pancetta for about 5 minutes, or until most of the fat is rendered.

4　Add the monkfish, raise the heat to medium-high, and sear for about 4 minutes, or until browned on one side. Turn the fish and cook for about 4 minutes longer, or until browned on both sides.

5　Add the onions, celery, and carrot and cook, stirring occasionally, for about 2 minutes, or until the vegetables caramelize and are nicely browned. Add the chicken stock and bring to a boil over high heat. Add the tomatoes, thyme, and rosemary.

6　Transfer the pan to the oven and roast for 15 minutes. Remove the pan, stir in the vinegar, and discard the thyme and rosemary.

7　To serve, put a steak in each of 4 shallow serving bowls. Ladle sauce over the fish and garnish with parsley and lemon zest.

the sommelier recommends

We have enjoyed this dish in each of the four seasons in Chicago. When you want to be refreshed in the summer, try a zippy, clean Sauvignon Blanc, which elevates the high tones and citrus notes in both the dish and the wine. In contrast, when the wind chill is negative and you need to be enveloped in warmth and reassurance, order a seductive Cabernet Sauvignon from Tuscany or from the Veneto.

poultry and meat

Without a doubt, I am part of the meat generation. I grew up eating juicy steaks, big roasts, and huge turkeys for the holidays. I have a great respect for the meat I cook and for the farmers and ranchers who make the effort to raise it humanely and carefully. I urge you to buy meat from a reputable butcher and ask about its origins. This is why throughout the book, I refer to heirloom pork and free-range chickens. Look, too, for grass-fed beef and organically raised lamb. You won't be sorry. Unfortunately, the days of the neighborhood butcher shop are long gone, but meat counters in many supermarkets are quite good, and gourmet and specialty shops often have a butcher on staff, too. Talk to the butcher. He or she will be pleased to help you and the more you learn, the better you will be at cooking meat.

Italian cooks pair meat with all sorts of wonderful flavors; drawing on these ideas and my own love of meat, I have come up with some absolutely showstopping recipes. I am a brining and marinating kind of guy and like big, bold, audacious flavors. And yet, as much as meat cookery is about flavor, it is more about technique. Cook the meat carefully, let it caramelize on the outside, and never cook it longer than you should. Let it rest before slicing to give the juices time to run through it again. Meat, whether it's beef, pork, lamb, poultry, or game, is the centerpiece of most meals. Treat it right and you will be well rewarded.

notes from the sommelier
where are you going with my bottle?

In our osteria, we love to decant your wine. On any given evening, our guests are witnesses to sommeliers in all corners of the restaurant pouring streams of dark red wine over sparkling candles into voluptuous glass jugs. Is it all for show? Or does decanting really make a difference in your dining and drinking experience? Ask Chef Tramonto whether his pork chop with rapini would be different without the brining, or whether the lamb chops wouldn't be as tasty without the marinade, and he would answer yes. Ask me whether decanting changes your wine-drinking experience, and I would answer yes. We decant wines in the osteria for many reasons: to "take the wine off of the sediment"—no one really likes chunky sediment in their wine glass; to aerate the wine—that imperial or 6-liter bottle of aged Cesari Amarone from the Veneto that you ordered has been oxygen-starved for a long

time and will blossom in the decanter; to temper the wine—bring it to room temperature; or perhaps you just want to decant it. Just about every red from our wine list benefits from decanting, and the bottle of Monsanto Chianti from Tuscany, Marzemino Battistotti from Trentino, even Barbera from Prunotto in Piedmont will be given "the treatment."

Don't fret if after your wine is presented to you, it is walked away. We always open and decant our guests' bottles of wine away from the table. If the whole point of the exercise is to remove the wine from the sediment, for example, then shaking that bottle around as we try to balance and open the bottle in the air isn't the right course of action. To prevent the jostling of the baby (the living and breathing wine), we open bottles on the credenzas and decanting tables in the center of the restaurant. That's where we make the magic happen, and we'll be right back.

roast chicken piccata-style

pollo alla piccata

Two 3-pound whole chickens
Kosher salt and freshly ground black pepper
½ cup Clarified Butter (page 147) or vegetable oil
2 lemons, sliced about ¼ inch thick
2 cups dry white wine
½ cup unsalted butter
3 tablespoons drained capers
Juice of 2 lemons
2 tablespoons chopped fresh flat-leaf parsley

1. Split the chickens in half and remove the breast section of one half with the wing attached. Leave the skin between the breast and the leg attached, cracking the thigh joint of the chicken and cutting through to separate the leg from the body while it remains attached to the breast by a thin strip of skin. Remove the drumstick completely, trying to leave as much skin from the leg intact as possible. Make an incision in the thigh along the thigh bone and remove the thigh bone. Repeat on the other side and with both chickens. Ask your butcher to do this for you, if you like. (Reserve the drumsticks and carcass for stocks.)
2. Preheat the oven to 400°F.
3. Season the chicken with salt and pepper.
4. Heat 2 large ovenproof sauté pans over medium-high heat. Put ¼ cup of clarified butter or oil in each pan and cook the chicken halves, skin side down, for about 4 minutes. Transfer the pans to the oven and cook for about 12 minutes, or until the chicken is cooked through. Remove the chickens from the pans and let them rest for about 5 minutes.
5. Put the lemon slices in the pans and let them cook over high heat for about 1 minute so that they caramelize. Add the wine and cook, stirring with a wooden spoon and scraping up any browned bits, for 2 to 3 minutes, until reduced by half.
6. Add the unsalted butter and capers and stir the sauce to emulsify the butter with the pan juices. Squeeze the lemon juice into the sauce, remove from the heat, and continue stirring until blended. Stir in the parsley.
7. Put a chicken half on each serving plate, skin side up, and spoon equal amounts of sauce over each. Serve immediately.

Roast chicken is one of life's simpler pleasures, and because I am so enamored with it, I am always on the lookout for new and interesting ways to cook it. *Piccata* usually refers to thin cutlets served with a lemony sauce, but for this I use partially boned chickens—and boning the birds is the only difficult part of the recipe. But you can have your butcher do it. Everything else is straightforward. I love the flavors of lemon, capers, and a good confetti of parsley with the roast chicken—a simple pleasure made even more gratifying when cooked this way. *serves 4*

the sommelier recommends

Lemon, butter, and capers are the ultimate white wine accoutrements, and the rule is not excepted here. Choose a fuller-bodied style of wine, enveloped in oak, and your meal will be perfectly matched. Chardonnay is the obvious grape to choose, but these days winemakers are doing Chardonnay-like things to other grapes. Vie di Romans in Friuli makes an oak-aged Pinot Grigio called "Dessimus."

chicken scaloppine with fried polenta and dandelion greens

scaloppine di pollo con polenta fritta

1 recipe Creamy White Polenta (page 227)
½ pound Taleggio cheese, cut into strips ½ inch wide
6 fresh sage leaves, thinly sliced
Freshly ground black pepper
1 pound dandelion greens or other bitter greens, torn into bite-sized pieces
1 shallot, minced
2 tablespoons balsamic vinegar
Four 12-ounce chicken cutlets, pounded to ½ inch thick
Kosher salt
½ cup all-purpose flour
2 tablespoons extra virgin olive oil
½ cup unsalted butter
Juice and grated zest of 2 lemons

1 Preheat the oven to 350°F.

2 Follow the recipe for Fried Polenta on page 227, but pour only half of the polenta into an 8-inch round cake pan about 2 inches deep, the bottom lined with parchment paper. (Use the rest of the polenta for another dish.) Let the polenta stand for about 2 minutes to stiffen up and then layer with enough cheese strips to cover completely. Sprinkle the sage over the cheese and season with pepper to taste.

3 In a small bowl, toss the dandelion greens and shallot. Drizzle with the vinegar and set aside for at least 5 minutes.

4 Season the chicken with salt and pepper and lightly pat with flour on both sides.

5 Heat a sauté pan over medium-high heat. Put the olive oil and ¼ cup of butter in the pan and when the butter melts, sauté the chicken for about 3 minutes on each side, or until golden brown and cooked through. Remove the chicken from the pan and set aside.

6 Add ¼ cup of butter to the pan and let it brown lightly. Add the lemon juice and zest and season to taste with salt and pepper. Drizzle 2 tablespoons of the sauce over the dandelion greens and toss gently.

7 Cut the polenta into 2- or 3-inch squares and fry for about 3 minutes, according to the directions on page 227. Drain the polenta cakes and put 1 cake in the center of each of 4 serving plates.

8 Top each polenta cake with the dandelion salad and then with a sautéed chicken cutlet. Spoon sauce around the dish and over the chicken, making sure some lemon zest is on each plate. Serve piping hot.

Dandelion and other bitter greens are great favorites in Lombardy, where I had a dish similar to this one. Their natural but pleasing bitterness is offset by the relative mild flavors of the chicken and polenta. One of the most tantalizing aspects of this dish is that the sauce is meant to be sopped up by the polenta—and there is plenty of sauce to satisfy the most enthusiastic "sopper upper"! *serves 4*

the sommelier recommends
We have a friend who is always looking for an excuse to drink wine from Sardegna—it reminds her of a great vacation. It is Cannonau (the local name for Grenache). It and the other varietal, Monica di Sardegna, both play nice with the chicken. Look for these easy red wines from Argiolas and Sella & Mosca producers.

chicken milanese
pollo alla milanese

Two 3-pound chickens
Kosher salt and freshly ground black pepper
2 cups all-purpose flour
2 large eggs
2 cups fresh bread crumbs (see Note)
1 cup extra virgin olive oil
4 tablespoons unsalted butter
8 ounces arugula
1 cup sliced cucumber (one 6-ounce cucumber)
¼ cup pitted black olives, such as Gaeta
1 cup cherry tomatoes
¼ cup fresh lemon juice, plus more for drizzling

1   Split the chickens in half to separate them. Remove the bones from the breasts and legs. You may want to ask the butcher to do this for you. Put each half, skin side down, on a cutting board, cover with plastic wrap, and gently pound with a meat mallet or the back of a heavy skillet until about ½ inch thick. Season the pounded halves with salt and pepper.

2   Put the flour in a shallow bowl and season it with salt and pepper. Whisk the eggs with ½ cup of water in a second bowl. Put the bread crumbs in a third bowl.

3   Dredge the chicken in the flour and pat off any excess. Dip the chicken in the egg wash and then coat with the bread crumbs.

4   Heat 2 large sauté pans over medium-high heat. When the pans are hot, heat ¼ cup of olive oil and 2 tablespoons of butter in each pan. When the butter melts, put the chicken in the pans, skin side down, and cook over medium-high heat for about 4 minutes, or until golden brown and crispy. Turn the chicken and cook on the other side for about 4 minutes, or until cooked through. Lift the chicken halves from the pans and drain on paper towels.

5   In a mixing bowl, toss the arugula, cucumber, olives, and tomatoes with the lemon juice and ½ cup of olive oil. Season to taste with salt and pepper.

6   Put the chicken on a large platter and top with the salad. Drizzle a little extra lemon juice on the chicken and serve piping hot.

note To make the bread crumbs, begin with day-old or stale bread and grind it to crumbs in a food processor or blender. Do not toast the bread first. For 2 cups, you will need about 4 slices of bread.

the sommelier recommends
The cucumber and arugula salad really brightens up this dish and takes it into white wine territory. Falanghina is a lesser-known grape varietal and wine that is found in the Campania region of Italy. It is not quite as full bodied as Chardonnay, nor quite as racy as Sauvignon Blanc, but we have tasted great examples from Mastroberardino and Terradora that were instant refreshers.

Butter is what makes this in the style of Milan. The butter gives the breaded chicken rich yet clean flavor, perfect as a summer dish served with the cucumber and arugula salad. The salad is dressed simply with lemon juice and olive oil, which complement the buttery chicken with piquant clarity. *serves 4*

veal parmesan

vitello parmigiano

1 cup fresh bread crumbs (see page 189)
1 cup freshly grated Parmigiano-Reggiano cheese
1 cup all-purpose flour
2 large eggs
3 pounds veal top round, sliced into four 12-ounce
   cutlets, pounded thin
Kosher salt and freshly ground black pepper
4 tablespoons Clarified Butter (page 147) or
   vegetable oil
3 tablespoons unsalted butter
4 cups Pomodoro Sauce (page 16)
4 ounces provolone cheese, sliced
2 tablespoons chopped fresh flat-leaf parsley
2 tablespoons finely sliced fresh basil

1 Preheat the oven to 400°F.

2 In a small bowl, mix the bread crumbs and
Parmigiano-Reggiano.

No one really thinks this crowd-pleaser is an authentic Italian dish, but instead was a creation of Italian-Americans when they moved here and different regional specialties were borrowed from to create new dishes. The name probably owes more to Parma, a city where breaded veal was panfried and then served—but without red sauce or cheese—while the addition of cheese and sauce owes more to Naples. Put it all together, and it's pretty all-American, in a melting-pot kind of way. It can't be beat when it's well made and served with a side of spaghetti and red wine.

serves 4

3 Put the flour in a shallow bowl. Whisk the eggs with ½ cup of water in a second bowl. Put the bread crumb mixture in a third bowl.

4 Season the veal cutlets with salt and pepper. Dredge them in the flour to coat on both sides and shake off any excess. Dip them in the egg wash, let the excess drip off, and then coat with the bread crumbs.

5 Heat 2 large ovenproof sauté pans over medium-high heat. When the pans are hot, heat 2 tablespoons of clarified butter or oil and 1½ tablespoons of unsalted butter in each pan. When the butter foams and the oil simmers, put 2 veal cutlets in each pan and cook for about 4 minutes, or until golden brown on one side. Turn and cook for about 4 minutes longer, or until golden brown on the other side.

6 Drain any excess fat from the pans. Add the Pomodoro Sauce, splitting it evenly between them. Lay the provolone on top of the cutlets, transfer the pans to the oven, and cook for 2 to 3 minutes, or until the provolone melts and the sauce is heated through.

7 Put 1 cutlet on each of 4 serving plates, sprinkle with the parsley and basil, and spoon any pan sauce over the meat. Serve piping hot.

the sommelier recommends
Sangiovese di Romagna is the lesser-known clone of Sangiovese, as Emilia-Romagna is a little less wine obsessed than its gold coast neighbor, Tuscany, where Sangiovese Toscana is king. Fattoria Paradiso and Terragens both bottle excellent Sangiovese di Romagna wines.

grilled veal chop with apple and mint salad
costolette di vitello con mele e menta

marinade
2 cups olive oil
2 sprigs fresh thyme
Juice and grated zest of 1 orange
1 tablespoon coarsely chopped fresh rosemary
2 garlic cloves, crushed
About 1 teaspoon kosher salt
About 1 teaspoon freshly ground black pepper

chops
4 bone-in 12-ounce veal chops
Kosher salt and freshly ground black pepper

salad
2 Granny Smith or other tart apples, cored, peeled, and julienned (see Note)
1 tablespoon finely sliced fresh mint
1 tablespoon finely sliced fresh basil
1 cup extra virgin olive oil
Juice of 2 lemons

1 To prepare the marinade, whisk the olive oil, thyme, orange juice and zest, rosemary, garlic, salt, and pepper in a nonreactive glass or ceramic bowl. Add the veal chops and turn to coat. Cover and refrigerate for 1 hour. Turn the veal chops and marinate for 1 to 24 hours.

2 Prepare a charcoal or gas grill by spraying the grilling rack with nonstick vegetable spray. Heat the grill until hot.

3 To make the salad: in a nonreactive glass or ceramic bowl, toss the apples, mint, and basil. Add the olive oil and lemon juice, toss until mixed.

4 Lift the veal chops from the marinade and pat dry with paper towels. Lightly season the veal chops with salt and pepper and grill for 4 minutes. Turn the veal chops and grill for about 4 minutes longer, or until there is a browned crust.

5 Move the veal chops to the cool side of the grill for 3 to 5 minutes, or until cooked to the desired degree of doneness. If you use an instant-read thermometer, the veal chops will register 150°F to 155°F when done.

6 Put 1 veal chop on each of 4 serving plates. Spoon a quarter of the salad next to each one and spoon some of the dressing in the bottom of the bowl over each veal chop.

Because few cuts of meat surpass center-cut veal chops on the grill, it is worth the effort to search out the best grade of veal, if possible, and to buy meat that is from animals that have been responsibly and humanely raised. The veal would be fantastic without the marinade, but the light flavors of fresh herbs and orange juice spike its flavor into the "wow" category. I like this with tart Granny Smith apples and clean-tasting fresh mint leaves. ❈ *serves 4*

note To keep cut apples from turning brown, soak them in lemon-lime soda. Or, of course, you can soak them in acidulated water (water mixed with a little lemon juice).

the sommelier recommends
There is a nice brightness to this veal dish, so choose a wine that follows suit. If you are a white wine drinker, a Pinot Bianco from the Alto Adige will add to the zip. Try Hofstatter or Alois Lageder. If you are a die-hard red wine drinker, however, try an ultraclean Pinot Nero (Pinot Noir) from San Michele in the same northern region.

fennel-glazed veal loin with braised fennel

sella di vitello con finocchio brasato

½ cup Pernod or other anise-flavored liqueur

1 cup fresh orange juice

1 cup chicken stock

½ cup honey

3 tablespoons fennel seeds, toasted and ground (see Note)

2½ pounds veal loin

Kosher salt and freshly ground black pepper

1 cup extra virgin olive oil

3 fennel bulbs, cut into eighths

16 cipolline onions

1 quart whole milk

1 Spanish onion, sliced

Although Italians are known for cooking pork in milk for a classic dish called *maiale al latte*, I employ the same technique with veal with outstanding results. I confess, I might have developed this recipe because it tastes so good with braised fennel, which is one of my all-time favorites. I like fennel any way it is prepared. When I was a kid, we sometimes ate a casserole of baked fennel accompanied by a green salad for a summer supper. ❀ *serves 4*

1 To prepare the fennel glaze, heat the Pernod in a small saucepan over medium heat for about 3 minutes, or until the alcohol is burned off. Add the orange juice, stock, and honey and 2 tablespoons of fennel seeds and cook for about 4 minutes, or until reduced by half. Set aside, covered, to keep warm.

2 Preheat the oven to 350°F.

3 Season the veal loin generously with salt and pepper and 1 tablespoon of fennel seeds.

4 Heat a large roasting pan over medium-high heat. Put the olive oil in the pan and when the olive oil is hot, sear the veal loin until golden brown on all sides. Total cooking time will be at least 8 minutes. Remove the loin from the pan and set aside, covered, to keep warm.

5 Add the fennel pieces and onions to the pan and cook for 4 to 5 minutes, or until lightly caramelized on both sides. Return the veal loin to the pan, insert a meat thermometer, and add the milk to the pan. Brush a layer of the reserved glaze over the veal and roast for 15 to 20 minutes, painting the meat with the glaze every 5 minutes.

6 When the internal temperature of the loin reaches 135°F, increase the oven temperature to 450°F. Paint the veal loin with the glaze once again and roast until the internal temperature registers between 140°F and 145°F, depending on the desired degree of doneness, and the veal's crust is deep brown. This will take only 3 or 4 minutes.

7 Remove the veal from the pan and let it rest for at least 10 minutes before slicing.

8 Meanwhile, remove half of the fennel pieces and all of the onions and set aside, covered, to keep warm.

9 Put the sliced Spanish onion, the fennel slices left in the pan, and about half of the milk from the pan in the jar of a blender and purée until smooth. Season to taste with salt and pepper.

10 Put a spoonful of the purée on each of 4 serving plates. Put 4 onions and a few fennel pieces next to the purée. Slice the veal loin into 4 portions and season the cut sides with salt. The veal will be medium at this point. Put on the plates and serve.

note To toast the fennel seeds, spread them in a single layer in a small, dry sauté pan or skillet and toast over low heat for 1 to 2 minutes, or until the seeds are fragrant and darken a shade. Remove from the heat and cool. Transfer to a mortar or spice grinder and pound with a pestle or grind until coarsely ground.

the sommelier recommends

When choosing wine for this dish, think fennel. I like Cortese as a white wine choice, as that grape varietal often has a texture and palate that play nicely with the vegetable. Try a Piedmontese Gavi di Gavi from La Scolca. Or if you are opting for red, Sangiovese often displays an anise character that would be interesting with the veal. Open a simple Tuscan Rosso or a Rosso di Montalcino or Rosso di Montepulciano. All Sangiovese, all good, solid drinking.

veal saltimbocca
vitello saltimbocca

3 pounds veal loin, sliced into four 12-ounce cutlets, pounded thin
4 fresh sage leaves, julienned
4 slices prosciutto di Parma
1 cup all-purpose flour
2 large eggs
2 cups fresh bread crumbs
4 tablespoons Clarified Butter (page 147) or vegetable oil
4 tablespoons unsalted butter
4 ounces provolone cheese, sliced
½ cup Marsala or sweet white wine
2 cups chicken stock
2 cups Caramelized Onions (page 106)
Kosher salt and freshly ground black pepper
2 tablespoons thinly sliced fresh basil

1   Preheat the oven to 400°F.

2   Sprinkle one side of the veal cutlets with the sage. Put a slice of prosciutto directly on top of the sage and, using a meat mallet or the bottom of a small, heavy pan, lightly pound it into the veal.

3   Put the flour in a shallow bowl. Whisk the eggs with ½ cup of water in a second bowl. Put the bread crumbs in a third bowl.

4   Dredge the veal cutlets in the flour to coat on both sides and shake off any excess. Dip them in the egg wash, let the excess drip off, and then coat with the bread crumbs, patting the crumbs into the meat.

5   Heat 2 ovenproof sauté pans over medium-high heat. Put 2 tablespoons of clarified butter or oil and 1½ tablespoons of unsalted butter in each pan. When the butter foams and the oil shimmers, put 2 veal cutlets in each pan and cook for about 4 minutes, or until golden brown on one side. Turn and cook for about 4 minutes longer, or until golden brown.

6   Put a slice of cheese on top of each veal cutlet and let it melt just a little into the meat. Lift the veal cutlets from the pans.

7   Drain any excess grease. Add the Marsala to one of the pans and cook for about 1 minute, stirring with a wooden spoon and scraping up any browned bits. Add 1 tablespoon of unsalted butter and swirl until melted. Stir in the stock and onions and cook for about 1 minute. Season to taste. Divide the juices between the pans.

8   Return the veal cutlets to the pans, transfer to the oven, and cook for about 2 minutes, or until the veal is very hot and the cheese is melted.

9   Put a cutlet on each of 4 serving plates and garnish with the pan juices and onions. Sprinkle with the basil and serve.

Associated with Rome, saltimbocca must include sage, prosciutto, and Marsala (or white wine). It's a rich, quick dish that tastes best with very high-quality veal and salty, fat-streaked prosciutto. When all the elements are in place, it's superb. My recipe is based on one my aunt made, and so far it's the best I've ever tasted. 🍴 *serves 4*

the sommelier recommends
Grillo, Catarratto, and Inzolia are the Sicilian white wine grapes used to make Marsala, and it is fun to use them in their naked state. Winemakers are exploiting the fresh, fruity, aromatic sides of these varietals to make very versatile food wines. Look for top Sicilian producers Planeta, Donnafugata, and Regaleali for a great bottle of white wine.

veal polpettone with tomato conserva
polpettone di vitello con conserva di pomodoro

conserva
¼ cup extra virgin olive oil
½ cup diced yellow onions
1 garlic clove, very thinly sliced
Pinch of minced fresh rosemary
1 teaspoon kosher salt
Pinch of sugar
2 cups canned tomatoes, drained and chopped
1 roasted red bell pepper (see page 11), cut into
  large dice
1 tablespoon chopped fresh flat-leaf parsley

veal
2 cups panko
2 cups (4 sticks) unsalted butter, melted
4 large eggs, beaten

2¼ cups freshly grated Parmigiano-Reggiano
  cheese, plus more for garnish
1¼ cups whole milk
2 tablespoons chopped fresh flat-leaf parsley
2 tablespoons minced garlic
1½ tablespoons kosher salt
1½ tablespoons freshly ground black pepper, plus
  more for garnish
2½ pounds ground veal
2½ pounds ground pork

1 Preheat the oven to 350°F.

2 To prepare the conserva, heat an ovenproof
   sauté pan over medium-high heat. When
   the pan is hot, heat the olive oil until warm.
   Cook the onions for 5 to 7 minutes, or until
   translucent. Add the garlic, rosemary, salt,
   and sugar, and cook for about 3 minutes
   over medium heat.

3 Add the tomatoes, transfer to the oven, and
   cook, stirring every 5 minutes, for about
   20 minutes, or until fairly dried out and
   thick. After the first 10 minutes, stir the bell
   pepper into the conserva. Remove the
   conserva from the oven, stir in the parsley,
   and set aside to cool.

4 To prepare the veal, stir the panko and
   butter in a bowl.

5 In a large bowl, whisk the eggs, cheese,
   milk, parsley, garlic, 1½ tablespoons of salt,
   and 1½ tablespoons of pepper. Add the
   panko and mix well. Add the veal and pork
   and, using your hands and a wooden
   spoon, mix with the other ingredients until
   well incorporated.

When I was a kid growing up in Rochester,
New York, my grandmother made polpettone
several times a month and I was never sorry to
see it on the table. Later, when I heard someone was cooking meat loaf, I was curious
about it. Something new I had never tried! But
when it came to the table I realized it was
polpettone. Some people call this a butcher's
meat loaf because it uses various meats
(originally these were scraps), ground and then
cooked together. Don't rush meat loaf; the
longer it takes to cook, the moister it is, so
don't increase the oven temperature in an
effort to hurry it along. And don't forget to
save the leftovers for killer sandwiches!

serves 4

6   Spoon the meat mixture into a terrine mold or loaf pan, or line a baking sheet with parchment paper and make a free-form loaf about 4 inches wide.

7   If using a terrine mold or loaf pan, put the smaller pan in a larger roasting pan and add enough water to come about halfway up the sides of the terrine or loaf pan. Cook the meat loaf, whether in a pan or a free-form loaf, for 50 to 60 minutes, until the internal temperature reaches 165°F.

8   Slice the loaf into 1-inch slices and arrange on a plate. Spoon the conserva over the veal, garnish with the cheese and black pepper and serve.

the sommelier recommends

The conserva brings out the fruity character of the tomatoes, and we love to serve an ultrafruity red with this dish. This means a red wine where the character of the grape varietal really shines through and is not masked by oak or high alcohol. A Rosso Piceno from the Marche region made mostly from Montepulciano grapes will fit the bill. Boccadigabbia and Cocci Griffoni are two producers that make the required style.

pork porterhouse with pancetta–dried cherry vinaigrette

bistecca di maiale con vinaigrette di pancetta e ciliegie

pork chops

½ cup extra virgin olive oil

1 lemon, thinly sliced

4 sprigs fresh oregano

1 teaspoon crushed red pepper flakes

Pinch of fresh thyme leaves

Eight 5-ounce pork porterhouse chops, about
   ½ inch thick

Kosher salt and freshly ground black pepper

vinaigrette

1 cup extra virgin olive oil

½ cup diced pancetta

4 shallots, sliced into rings

½ cup apple cider vinegar

¼ cup dried cherries

1   To prepare the pork chops, stir the olive oil, lemon slices, oregano, red pepper, and thyme in a nonreactive glass or ceramic dish. Sprinkle the pork chops with salt and pepper and put them in the dish with the marinade. Turn to coat with the marinade, cover, and refrigerate for 6 to 12 hours or overnight.

2   To make the vinaigrette, heat 1 tablespoon of olive oil in a sauté pan set over low heat. When the olive oil is hot, add the pancetta and cook for about 5 minutes, or until the fat is rendered and the pancetta is crispy. Add the shallots, vinegar, and cherries and cook for 6 to 8 minutes, or until reduced by half.

3   Add the remaining olive oil, stir well, and set aside to cool.

4   Prepare a charcoal or gas grill by spraying the grilling rack with nonstick vegetable spray. Heat the grill until very hot.

5   Lift the pork chops from the marinade and wipe off any excess oil. Season lightly with salt and pepper and grill for 1 to 2 minutes. Turn the chops and cook for about 1 minute longer, or until cooked through. The thin chops do not take long to cook over a hot fire.

6   Arrange the chops on a large platter and dress with the cooled vinaigrette. Serve immediately.

the sommelier recommends

The dried-cherry vinaigrette for this dish screams for the classic Tuscan quaff: cherry-scented Chianti. Forget about the straw-wrapped bottles of yore; today's modern producers make a much more sophisticated drink. These days Chianti producers are even allowed by law to add a percentage of international varieties like Cabernet, Merlot, and Syrah. Our favorite producers include Isole e Olena, Monsanto, and Melini.

If you can find good heirloom pork, as I discuss on page 167, this dish will be even more delicious. Heritage pork is tender and juicy with silky, buttery meat that tastes unlike any you have had before. Look for it at farmers' markets and good butcher shops. Pork's natural sweetness makes it a natural to pair with fruit, which is why the dried-cherry vinaigrette is such a sure thing here.

serves 4

grilled pork chops with broccoli rabe
costolette di maiale con rapini

Four 12-ounce pork chops
About 1 quart Brine for Pork (recipe follows)
2 bunches broccoli rabe
¼ cup extra virgin olive oil, plus more for
    drizzling
4 garlic cloves, shaved
2 Calabrian chiles or other small, hot chiles
Juice of 1 lemon, plus more for garnish
Kosher salt and freshly ground black pepper
2 tablespoons unsalted butter

1   In a nonreactive glass or ceramic dish,
    submerge the pork chops in enough brine
    to cover and refrigerate for 45 to 60
    minutes. Remove the pork from the brine
    and pat dry.

2   Prepare a charcoal or gas grill by spraying
    the grilling rack with nonstick vegetable
    spray. Heat the grill until hot.

3   Meanwhile, in a saucepan filled with lightly
    salted water, blanch the broccoli rabe for
    3 to 4 minutes, or until bright green. Drain.

4   In a sauté pan, heat the olive oil over
    medium-low heat and then cook the garlic
    and chiles for about 2 minutes, or until the
    garlic begins to brown. Add the broccoli
    rabe, turn the heat to high, and sauté for
    2 to 3 minutes, or until cooked through and
    hot. Toss with the lemon juice and season
    to taste. Cover and set aside.

5   Sear the pork chops over the hot grill for
    3 minutes. Turn and put ½ tablespoon of
    butter on top of each chop. Cook for 4 to
    5 minutes longer, or until the pork is
    cooked through but not overcooked. The
    internal temperature should be 155°F.

6   Spoon some sautéed broccoli rabe on each
    of 4 serving plates. Top each with a pork
    chop and garnish with lemon juice and a
    drizzle of olive oil. Serve immediately.

the sommelier recommends
With its soft tannins and gobs of black fruit,
the Oltrepo Pavese Buttafuoco from Bruno
Verdi in Lombardy is a treat with this dish.
The fruit in this red wine seems to take the
edge off of the bitter greens.

If you haven't tried brining, here's a good
recipe to start with, and if you are already sold
on the technique, add this to your repertoire. I
brine the pork chops for only 45 to 60 minutes,
as any longer will toughen them. The short
soak in the brine makes them moist and tender
and provides a good flavor boost. They also
firm up a little and taste great with the sautéed
broccoli rabe. This pairing is similar to a meal
I once had in the Lombardy region of Italy on
a hot summer night. ❊ *serves 4*

brine for pork
makes about ½ gallon

8 ounces kosher salt
½ cup honey
1 small sprig fresh rosemary
3 juniper berries

In a large pot, mix all the ingredients with
½ gallon of water and bring to a boil over
high heat. Cook, stirring, just until the salt
dissolves. Remove from the heat and set aside
to cool to room temperature. Use as directed.

lamb porterhouse with salsa verde
bistecca d'agnello con salsa verde

salsa verde
1 tablespoon minced Spanish onion

1 teaspoon kosher salt

1 cup extra virgin olive oil

¼ cup finely chopped fresh flat-leaf parsley

2 tablespoons finely chopped fresh mint

2 tablespoons finely chopped fresh basil

5 garlic cloves, minced

2 tablespoons capers, rinsed

1 tablespoon pitted and finely chopped green olives

Grated zest of 1 lemon

1 teaspoon freshly ground black pepper

Juice of 2 lemons

3 cornichons, chopped

2 salt-packed anchovy fillets, rinsed, patted dry, and
    chopped or mashed

Fronds from ½ fennel bulb, chopped

lamb
Four 10-ounce lamb porterhouse steaks, or eight
    5-ounce lamb porterhouse steaks

Kosher salt and freshly ground black pepper

to serve
Juice of 1 lemon

You may think of porterhouse as a beef cut but it's an equally flavorful cut of lamb (also known as loin chops). I love it with a classic salsa verde (green sauce), which tastes amazing with just about any grilled meat or chicken during the summer months. If you begin by salting the onions, they will be a little milder and mellow out the salsa. I tend to keep it on hand in the refrigerator, as it lasts about 1 week.

serves 4

1 To prepare the salsa verde, gently stir the onion and salt in a small bowl and set aside for about 15 minutes.

2 In a nonreactive glass or ceramic bowl, mix the olive oil, parsley, mint, basil, garlic, capers, olives, lemon zest, pepper, and the onion mixture. Add the lemon juice, cornichons, anchovies, and fennel fronds and stir gently to mix. Set aside at room temperature for at least 4 hours before serving.

3 To prepare the lamb, prepare a charcoal or gas grill by spraying the grilling rack with nonstick vegetable spray. Heat the grill until very hot.

4 Season the lamb with salt and pepper and grill for 2 to 3 minutes to sear one side. Turn and sear the other side for 3 to 4 minutes, or until both sides are nicely browned. Move the steaks to a cooler part of the grill and cook for about 4 minutes longer, or until cooked to the desired degree of doneness. For medium rare, the internal temperature should be 140°F.

5 Remove the steaks from the grill and let them rest for 4 to 5 minutes.

6 Serve each steak with a heaping spoonful of salsa verde and a squeeze of lemon juice.

the sommelier recommends
The smokiness from the grilling, the richness of the lamb, and the fresh spike from the salsa verde all call for a dark red that can handle the green element. Aglianico is the answer. It is a grape varietal that can do amazing things in southern Italy, and one of the most ageworthy wines made from Aglianico is Taurasi from Campania. It is not unusual to see decades-old bottles of Taurasi at reasonable prices. Look for Struzziero, Molettieri, and Caggiano for a mature treat.

lamb chops with garlic jus

costolette d'agnello con salsa di aglio

1 whole garlic head
¼ cup olive oil
12 fingerling potatoes (about 1 pound)
2 tablespoons kosher salt
5 coriander seeds
1 bay leaf
Four 6- to 8-ounce double-cut lamb chops
Kosher salt and freshly ground black pepper
½ cup vegetable oil
2 tablespoons unsalted butter
2 sprigs fresh rosemary, about 4 inches long
2¼ cups lamb jus or beef stock (recipe follows)
2 tablespoons sherry vinegar

The key to most meat dishes in Italy is simplicity. Meats are panfried, roasted, or grilled and served plain with very little fanfare. This dish fits that description, constructed as it is with panfried lamb chops—which I am mad for—and boiled potatoes. I sampled a dish similar to this at a vineyard in Emilia-Romagna, and even though it was as down-to-earth as could be, the flavors lingered in my memory. The lamb is served with whole cloves of softened garlic, because everyone knows how much lamb and garlic love each other!

serves 4

1   Preheat the oven to 400°F.

2   Separate the garlic head into cloves and put the cloves, still with their skins on, in a small saucepan and cover with the olive oil. Cook over medium-low heat for 20 to 25 minutes, or until the garlic softens but the pulp does not burst through the skins. Set aside, covered.

3   In a saucepan, cover the potatoes with cold water. Add 2 tablespoons of salt, the coriander seeds, and the bay leaf. Bring to a simmer over medium heat and cook for about 20 minutes, or until fork tender.

4   Drain the potatoes, return to the hot pan, cover, and set aside to keep warm.

5   Season the lamb chops with salt and pepper. Heat an ovenproof sauté pan over high heat. When the pan is hot, heat the vegetable oil until hot. Sear the lamb for 2 to 3 minutes on each side, or until well browned.

6   Transfer the pan to the oven and bake for about 7 minutes. Remove the pan from the oven and add the butter and rosemary. Off the heat and out of the oven, let the butter melt and as it does so, baste the chops with the melted butter. Remove the butter and the chops from the pan. Add the jus and garlic cloves to the pan and cook over medium-high heat for 2 to 3 minutes, or until the jus is reduced by three-quarters.

7   Meanwhile, let the lamb rest for 3 to 5 minutes before serving while the jus reduces.

8 Put 3 potatoes in the center of each of 4 serving plates and split each one down the center. Cut the lamb chops in half and arrange 1 chop on each plate with the cut side facing up.

9 Stir the vinegar into the pan sauce and drizzle about ½ cup of sauce on each plate.

10 Garnish with the garlic cloves, still in their skin.

the sommelier recommends

Emilia-Romagna is one of the most celebrated regions for cuisine. It is the home of Parmigiano-Reggiano, Prosciutto di Parma, and Aceto Balsamico. The lamb chops are such a simple and elegant dish, based on excellent ingredients, that you should follow the same road for the wine. Umberto Cesari makes its version of a luxury Sangiovese called "Tauleto" that would be fine with the chops. On the more decadent side of Emilia-Romagnan winemaking, there is "Valbruna" from Castel Sismondo, an inky blend of Sangiovese with Cabernet Sauvignon and Montepulciano, also a great match.

lamb jus
makes about 2 cups

½ cup vegetable oil or Clarified Butter (page 147)
½ pound lamb scraps (see Note)
¼ cup unsalted butter
2 whole garlic heads, cloves removed, skin on and crushed lightly
2 shallots, peeled and sliced ¼ inch thick
2½ cups veal stock or beef stock

1 Heat a saucepan over high heat and then heat the oil in the pan. When the oil is hot, cook the lamb scraps for about 12 minutes, or until deeply browned.

2 Drain the fat from the pan and add the unsalted butter. When the butter foams, add the garlic cloves and shallots and cook for about 6 minutes, or until the garlic and shallots brown and soften. Do not let the garlic burn or let the pulp burst through the skins. Use a wooden spoon to scrape up any browned bits.

3 Add ½ cup of water and cook, scraping the bottom of the pan, for about 20 minutes, or until the water evaporates.

4 Add the stock and let it come to a simmer. Simmer for about 30 minutes, until the stock reduces by a quarter.

note Ask the butcher for lamb scraps, but if you can't get them that way, buy lamb stew meat. Cut the meat, and any bones you can get, into pieces to use for the scraps.

stuffed leg of lamb
coscia d'agnello ripiena

8 ounces fresh basil leaves

¾ cup pitted black olives, coarsely chopped

1 salted anchovy, chopped

1 teaspoon capers, drained

2 tablespoons plus ½ cup extra virgin olive oil

One 3-pound boneless leg of lamb

Kosher salt and freshly ground black pepper

3 garlic cloves, very thinly sliced

4 Oven-Dried Cherry Tomatoes (page 12)

½ cup julienned roasted red bell peppers (see page 11)

2 celery ribs, coarsely chopped

1 carrot, coarsely chopped

1 large Spanish onion, coarsely chopped

For this intoxicating roasted leg of lamb, you make your own olive tapenade with salty black olives, an anchovy, some capers, and olive oil, which is used to stuff the leg along with oven-dried tomatoes, garlic, basil, and roasted red bell peppers. My dad made this dish often, and always on Easter Sunday. It was his favorite, and for good reason. *serves 8*

1. Preheat the oven to 350°F.

2. In a saucepan filled with boiling water, blanch the basil for 45 to 60 seconds, or until bright green. Drain and immediately plunge the basil into a bowl of iced water to cool. Drain and set aside.

3. In a small bowl, stir the olives, anchovy, and capers. Using a fork, mash the mixture to a paste-like consistency. Slowly add 2 tablespoons of olive oil, mashing as you do so, to emulsify the tapenade further. This can also be done in a mortar and pestle.

4. Lay the leg of lamb, skin side down, on a cutting board and spread it open as wide as you can, like a book. With a paring knife, cut small, ½-inch-deep slits into the meat about 1 inch apart. Make the cuttings diagonally both ways across the meat. Season the scored meat with salt and pepper and then tuck the garlic slivers into the slits.

5. Spread the olive tapenade over the meat, covering it entirely. Line the tomatoes along the center of the leg, from top to bottom, and top them with individual basil leaves. Lay the bell peppers over the basil and then top them with more basil leaves.

6. Beginning at the thin side of the leg, fold it inward on top of itself toward the center. Continue to roll into a cylinder and then set on a cutting board, seam side down, so that the thin end faces away from you.

7 Cut butcher's twine to a length of 3½ to 4 feet. Tie a loop around the thin layer, just at the end of the leg, and secure it with a knot. Using your hand, form a loop with the string and pull the loop underneath the leg from the back to the front, encasing the next inch of leg in butcher's twine. Using the excess twine, tighten that loop, making sure it is centered on the leg of lamb.

8 Repeat this process about ten more times so that there is a new loop about every inch along the leg of lamb: form a loop, pull it under the leg, and tighten by pulling on the straight length of twine. Once you have reached the end nearest you with about an inch to spare, flip the leg over with the seam side up and weave the leftover twine through every other loop, pulling taut each time. At the other end, tie the last of the string to the very beginning of your first knot, securing the leg of lamb in its own tight netting.

9 Season the lamb generously with salt and pepper.

10 Heat a large roasting pan over medium-high heat. Put ½ cup of olive oil in the pan and heat it until almost smoking. Sear the roast on all sides until nicely browned. Total cooking time will be 10 to 12 minutes. Remove the lamb from the pan and set aside.

11 Add the celery, carrot, and onion to the pan and cook for 10 to 12 minutes, or until lightly caramelized. Return the roast to the pan, setting it on top of the vegetables. Transfer to the oven and roast for 40 to 45 minutes, or until the internal temperature is 135°F to 140°F for medium rare or 145°F to 150°F for medium.

12 Let the roast rest for about 20 minutes before snipping the twine and discarding it. Slice the lamb across the leg to expose the bright beautiful filling and serve immediately.

the sommelier recommends

We can only imagine how your kitchen smells as the lamb is roasting in the oven, and the only thing that would complete the perfect picture is you sipping a glass of Barolo as you wait for the lamb to cook. Sandrone, Fontana-fredda, and Gaja make bottles that can be for now instead of later. If your bank account is screaming "no!" then make it a Langhe Nebbiolo day. Same producers, same grape, same technology, better price.

balsamic skirt steak with pickled red onion
bistecca con cipolle

1 cup red wine vinegar
¾ cup sugar
Kosher salt and freshly ground black pepper
1 bay leaf
Pinch of crushed red pepper flakes
2 red onions, thinly sliced
Four 10-ounce skirt steaks
1 cup balsamic vinegar
1 cup extra virgin olive oil, plus more for drizzling

1   In a heavy saucepan, heat 3 cups of water with the wine vinegar, sugar, 1 teaspoon of salt, 1 teaspoon of black pepper, the bay leaf, and the red pepper for 2 to 3 minutes, or until the salt and sugar are dissolved.

2   Immediately pour the pickling liquid over the onions, cover, and allow to come to room temperature before refrigerating for at least 24 hours.

3   Put the steaks in a shallow nonreactive glass or ceramic dish and add the balsamic vinegar and 1 cup of olive oil. Turn the steaks to coat evenly with the marinade. Cover and refrigerate for 3 to 6 hours.

4   Lift the steaks from the marinade, pat off most of the olive oil with paper towels, and season well with salt and pepper.

5   Heat a cast-iron skillet over medium-high heat. Sear the steaks for 2 to 3 minutes on each side, or until they form a nice crust and are medium rare. The steaks should not be cooked any further, as they can toughen. Let the steaks rest off the heat for 4 minutes before slicing.

6   Slice the steaks against the grain and divide among 4 serving plates. Put a nice pile of pickled red onions alongside the steaks, drizzle each plate with olive oil, and serve.

When marinated and carefully cooked, skirt steak makes one of the best cuts of beef. It has great flavor and although it may not be as tender as filet, it's totally delicious. The balsamic adds a lot of flavor, even if it's not a superexpensive aged balsamic. To add to the overall deliciousness of this dish, you could finish the steak with truffle oil. No work, just a little expense! ❧ *serves 4*

the sommelier recommends
A vinegar component, as in the red onions, can make choosing a red wine for this dish tricky. Just be certain to choose one that can handle the acidity, though, and your palate will be safe. We like the almost-black Teroldego grape that can be found in the Trentino region. It has deep, dark jammy fruit and adds a nice peppery component to the dish as well. Elisabetta Foradori is considered a master artist of making wines from the Teroldego grape.

beefsteak florentine with arugula

bistecca di manzo fiorentina con rucola

Two 24- to 32-ounce beef porterhouse steaks, at
    room temperature
Sea salt and freshly ground black pepper
1 pound fresh arugula
Juice of 2 lemons
About 1 cup extra virgin olive oil
2 lemons, halved

1   Prepare a charcoal or gas grill by spraying
the grilling rack with nonstick vegetable
spray. Heat the grill until very hot.

2   Season the steaks liberally with salt and
pepper and press the seasoning into the
meat. Sear 1 side of the meat for about
5 minutes or until caramelized, leaving at
least 2 to 3 inches between each steak. Do
not move the steaks unless they ignite.
Turn the steaks and sear the other sides.

3   Move the steaks to a cooler part of the grill
and continue to cook for 3 to 4 minutes
longer, or until cooked to the desired
degree of doneness. The internal
temperature should be 135°F to 140°F for
medium rare. Total cooking time will be
10 to 15 minutes, depending on the size of
the steak. Let the steaks rest off the heat
for at least 5 minutes before slicing.

4   In a small bowl, toss the arugula with the
lemon juice and season to taste with salt
and pepper. Dress it with enough of the
olive oil to coat and toss again.

5   Cut the steaks from the bones and slice the
meat into 1-inch-thick slices.

6   Pile the salad on one end of a serving
platter. Put the steak bones on the platter
and arrange the sliced meat along the
bones. Drizzle the meat with the remaining
olive oil and sprinkle with salt. Garnish
with the lemon halves and serve
immediately.

For many, this dish is the pinnacle of Tuscan
cooking. When really good beef is finished
with peppery olive oil, good salt, and fresh
pepper and accompanied by a glass of full-
bodied Italian red wine, you can see why.
There is more to this dish, which is also about
an ancient breed of cattle in central Italy called
Chianina and which made the first *bistecca*
possible. It's a breed that is being saved by
farmers in both Italy and the United States,
which I applaud. I don't expect anyone to find
Chianina porterhouse, but look for prime beef
to really get the most from this dish, which
may be made with spinach instead of my
choice, arugula. ❀ *serves 4*

the sommelier recommends
This is the classic Italian version of the
steakhouse dinner, and we all love the big,
bigger, and biggest reds with our grilled
porterhouse. Check out the reds of Tuscan
neighbor Umbria, where you will find some
real bang for your buck, relatively speaking, in
the wines of Montefalco made from the
weighty, black-fruited, nuanced Sagrantino
grape. If you are looking for palate impact,
you will not be disappointed in these reds
from Paolo Bea, Adanti, and Scacciadiavoli.

licorice-dusted venison loin

sella di cervo in liquirizia

fig glaze
8 dried figs, halved
3 cups dry red wine
2 tablespoons honey
1 sprig fresh thyme

farro
2 cups uncooked farro
6 tablespoons extra virgin olive oil
2 shallots, thinly sliced
3 tablespoons unsalted butter
1 tablespoon kosher salt
1 gallon chicken stock
1 bay leaf

venison
1 tablespoon star anise
1 tablespoon anise seeds
1 tablespoon fennel seeds
1 licorice root, grated (see Note)
1½ teaspoons coriander seeds
2½ pounds venison loin
Kosher salt and freshly ground black pepper
2 tablespoons olive oil
1 teaspoon unsalted butter

It's no surprise that this dish originated in northern Italy, where game is more prevalent than in the south and farro, an ancient grain sometimes mistaken for spelt, is prized. Farro is nutritious, with a pleasing nuttiness that has caught the attention of chefs in Europe and the United States in recent years. Today, you can buy farro in many supermarkets and most natural-food stores. The licorice flavor comes from licorice root, found wherever a good selection of spices are sold, as well as fennel and star anise and showcases the mild gaminess of the venison. This is a full-bodied and earthy dish, enhanced even further with the sweet fig glaze. ❈ *serves 4*

1 To prepare the fig glaze, soak the figs in the wine in a nonreactive glass or ceramic bowl for at least 8 hours or overnight.

2 To prepare the farro, put the farro in a bowl, add enough cold water to cover, and soak for at least 8 hours or overnight. Drain.

3 When the figs have soaked, strain the wine into a small saucepan, reserving the fig halves. Add the honey and thyme to the pan and bring to a boil over high heat. Reduce the heat to low and simmer for about 25 minutes, or until the mixture is reduced by two-thirds and is the consistency of a light glaze. Cover and set aside.

4 To cook the farro, heat a large pot over medium heat. When the pot is hot, heat the olive oil and the shallots for 3 to 4 minutes, or until the shallots are translucent. Add the butter and when it foams, add the farro and salt.

5 Stir the farro vigorously to prevent sticking until its color deepens slightly and it emits a heavy, nutty aroma. Add the stock and bay leaf and bring to a simmer. Reduce the heat to low and cook, stirring frequently, for about 45 minutes, or until the farro is tender with only a little "bite." Remove from the heat and cover to keep warm.

(continued)

6 Preheat the oven to 350°F.

7 To prepare the venison, in a small, dry skillet, toast the star anise, anise seeds, fennel seeds, licorice root, and coriander seeds over low heat until they begin to emit a heavy aroma. Transfer to a spice or coffee grinder and grind to a fine powder.

8 Season the venison loin with salt and pepper and then generously rub the spice mix into the meat.

9 Heat a large sauté pan over high heat. Heat the olive oil in the pan until smoking and sear the venison on both sides until well browned. Because the spices will smoke, turn the meat often. Total cooking time will be about 4 minutes.

10 Transfer the venison to a roasting pan and roast for 10 to 15 minutes, or until the internal temperature reaches 130°F for medium rare. Let the venison rest for 10 to 15 minutes before slicing.

11 Return the figs to the glaze and add 1 teaspoon of butter. Gently stir the butter into the sauce until it's incorporated and the figs are warm. Put 4 fig halves on each plate and drizzle the glaze around the plate. Serve immediately.

note Licorice root is sold in stores that sell a lot of spices or that are dedicated to selling only spice. You can also order it online. See page 266. To grate licorice root, use a microplane grater.

the sommelier recommends
Sweet figs, star anise, and full-flavored venison all make this a dish not to be trifled with by a wimpy red wine. Go down to your wine cellar or open your dark, cool closet, and grab any wine whose name ends in -aia. High-octane Cabernet Sauvignon or Merlot is best suited to be poured with this serious meat dish. One of our favorites is "Saffredi," made by Elisabetta Geppetti at Fattoria Le Pupille in Tuscany; up to 100 percent Cabernet Sauvignon in some vintages, it is a great drink!

calves' liver with pancetta

fegato di vitello con pancetta

One 3-pound calves' liver

About 2 cups whole milk

1 pound caul fat

2 ounces pancetta, thinly sliced or shaved (12 to 15 slices)

Kosher salt and freshly ground black pepper

About 2 cups fresh thyme leaves

2 tablespoons canola or vegetable oil

1 cup Caramelized Onions (page 106)

1 cup chicken stock

2 cups Creamy White Polenta with Parmigiano-Reggiano (page 227)

1 tablespoon aged balsamic vinegar

My mother cooked liver at least once a month when I was growing up. Admittedly, this was not one of the meals my friends begged to be invited to, but as far as I was concerned, their absence left more for me. Just as all good Italian cooks do, my mom soaked the calves' liver in milk to mellow its flavor, and the result is an enticing dish that might surprise you, especially if you are like my old friends and run at the mention of liver! I like to caramelize sweet Spanish onions and sometimes add a little garlic for more depth. You will probably have to order the caul fat from the butcher, but even if he or she can't get one for you, don't neglect to make this dish, with the liver simply wrapped in the pancetta. So good! ❀ *serves 4*

1 Put the calves' liver in a bowl large enough to hold it easily and pour the milk over it. Be sure the liver is covered by the milk. Cover and refrigerate for 6 to 24 hours. The longer you soak the liver, the milder its flavor. Many people like to soak it for 24 hours to lessen its ironlike taste.

2 Rinse the caul fat under cold running water until the water runs clear, and then transfer it to a bowl. Add enough cold water to cover and let it soak for about 1 hour to rid it of any remaining blood.

3 Lift the liver from the milk and let the excess drain. Pat dry with paper towels. Cut into ¾-inch-wide slices and set aside. Spread the caul fat on a cutting board.

4 "Unwrap" or gently stretch the pancetta slices into strands and lay them on top of the caul fat. Make sure there is enough pancetta to wrap all the liver.

5 Put a liver slice on top of the pancetta, season with salt and pepper, and sprinkle with the thyme. Repeat with all slices.

6 Wrap the pancetta around the liver slices, overlapping it as needed to swaddle the liver. Wrap the 4 sides of the caul fat up and over these bundles, with the edges slightly overlapping each other. Season the wrapped caul fat with salt and pepper.

7 Heat a sauté pan over medium heat and very lightly coat it with canola oil. Sauté the caul fat bundle, folded side down, for 3 to 5 minutes, or until golden brown and the seams seal closed. Flip the caul fat package and cook for another 3 to 5 minutes, or until golden brown on both sides. Most of the fat will remain in the pan, but a thin layer of caul fat will remain around the liver slices. Remove from the heat and let the caul fat package rest for about 3 minutes. Drain the fat from the pan.

8 Return the pan to the heat, add the caramelized onions, and use a wooden spoon to scrape up any browned bits. Add the stock, raise the heat to medium-high, and bring the stock to a boil. Reduce the heat and simmer for about 3 minutes, or until reduced by half.

9 To serve, spoon about ½ cup of polenta on each of 4 serving plates. Put 2 slices of liver on each plate and spoon about ¼ cup of the juicy caramelized onions over the liver. Drizzle with the vinegar and serve.

the sommelier recommends

Rich calves' liver is made even richer with the addition of caramelized onions and balsamic vinegar, so choose a red that will lighten and brighten up the whole package. In some of its Tuscan incarnations, Sangiovese can be a light, bright, red-fruited delight. Try a soft style from Conti Contini, a Capezzana label; it will help cut right through the richness.

side dishes

Many people overlook side dishes when they plan a meal. I have an expansive repertoire of side dishes and an abiding passion for them, many of which are interchangeable with antipasti. With both, I find a lot of room for creativity and improvisation. You might want to serve the potato chips as an antipasto, or serve the chilled artichoke or heirloom beets in the antipasti chapter as sides. When you prepare a side dish, there's the possibility of changing it just a little to go with a certain meat or fish dish.

Nothing makes me happier than poking around a farmers' market and buying the freshest and most gorgeous-looking vegetables I can find and then going home and figuring out ways to prepare them. This way, too, I cook with the seasons and support local farmers.

When I was young, my mother or grandmother cooked two starches and two vegetables with almost every meal, and also served a salad. It's the same way in Italy, where there are always a few side dishes on the table, both in osterias and in private homes. The meal is almost like an upside-down pyramid that begins with an expansive antipasti course, goes to smaller servings of meat and vegetables, and ends with fruit or some kind of light dessert.

notes from the sommelier
on the side: our
winemakers' wall

Don't tell the chef, but in some ways, an osteria is defined by what people drink there. The definition of an osteria that I have always liked is "a tavern or humble restaurant where wine is served as the main attraction and food is prepared to wash it down. . . ." So at our restaurant, we have always venerated the Italian winemakers and winery owners who keep our cellars stocked to the rafters and our glasses filled to the brim with tasty reds, pinks, and whites. As you are enjoying your Barolo from winemaker Scavino, or your Vino Nobile di Montepulciano made by winemaker

Catarina Dei, it is fun to know that the people who crafted those wines have visited the restaurant as well. It's a tradition in our osterias to celebrate these fine people when they honor us with a visit by asking them to sign our winemakers' wall. We know that often the last thing that an Italian wants to do is eat at another Italian restaurant, so we are especially glad to see them. We are happiest when our walls are adorned with autographs from the likes of Angelo Gaja, Paulo Scavino, Alois Lageder, Nino Franco (he always draws a picture of two sparkling wineglasses toasting), and Elena Walch. Armed with a big, black Sharpie marker, the visiting winemakers are free to write whatever they like, and wherever they would like to on the wall, but those who visit us first get the best spots.

cauliflower agrodolce
cavolfiore "agro dolce"

1 pound cauliflower, separated into large florets
1 cup golden raisins (about 5 ounces)
½ cup sherry vinegar
3½ anchovies, drained
3½ tablespoons drained capers
½ cup unsalted butter
Kosher salt and freshly ground black pepper
¼ cup fresh flat-leaf parsley, finely chopped
2 cups Anchovy Bread Crumbs (recipe follows)

1 In a large saucepan filled with boiling salted water, blanch the cauliflower for 5 to 7 minutes, so it is still al dente. Do not overcook; it will cook further later. Drain and set aside.

2 In a saucepan, simmer the raisins and vinegar over medium heat for 20 to 25 minutes.

3 Meanwhile, rinse the anchovies and capers and transfer to the bowl of a food processor fitted with the metal blade. Add the raisins and any liquid in the pan and process until the ingredients form a paste.

4 In a large ovenproof sauté pan, melt the butter over medium heat. Add the cauliflower and cook for 4 to 5 minutes, or until the cauliflower softens and starts to brown. Season to taste with salt and pepper.

5 Preheat the broiler.

6 Spoon 3 tablespoons of the anchovy paste over the cauliflower and rub it with the back of a spoon, a knife, or your fingers so that it will sink into the cauliflower evenly when heated. Broil for about 4 minutes, or until golden brown. Garnish with the parsley and Anchovy Bread Crumbs and serve hot.

The poor cauliflower! It's so white and creamy and sits in a pretty cup of green leaves in the supermarket, but so few people actually buy it. I find it takes on a whole new meaning when paired with this piquant sweet-and-sour sauce agrodolce made from raisins, capers, and anchovies. The sauce is originally from Rome and versions of it hark back to the Renaissance, but you can find it now all over Italy, particularly in the south. The remaining sauce will keep in a tightly lidded glass jar for up to 2 weeks. You can use the sauce with other vegetables, but it's especially good with white or purple cauliflower or green broccoflower. *serves 4*

anchovy bread crumbs
makes about 2 cups

4 large slices day-old or stale bread, torn into pieces
3 anchovies, drained, patted dry, and coarsely chopped
2 tablespoons extra virgin olive oil

1 In the bowl of a food processor fitted with the metal blade or the jar of a blender, process the bread until coarse crumbs form. Add the anchovies and process for 1 to 2 minutes longer.

2 With the motor running, add the olive oil in a steady stream until the bread crumbs are moist and roughly chopped. Use immediately.

creamed green and red chard

bietola con mascarpone

1 tablespoon extra virgin olive oil
½ white onion, sliced
1½ teaspoons minced garlic
½ pound green chard leaves (about ½ bunch), sliced
½ pound red chard leaves (about ½ bunch), sliced
Pinch of crushed red pepper flakes
¾ cup mascarpone cheese
½ cup heavy cream
Kosher salt and freshly ground black pepper

1   Heat a large sauté pan over medium-high heat. Put the olive oil and onion in the pan and cook for about 3 minutes, or until the onion begins to caramelize. Add the garlic and cook for another 2 minutes, or until the garlic softens and the onion is slightly caramelized.

2   Add the green and red chard and red pepper and cook, stirring, until the chard wilts completely.

3   Meanwhile, in a small bowl, whisk the cheese and cream. Pour into the pan and stir to mix with the wilted chard. Simmer the mixture for 2 to 3 minutes, or until well incorporated. Season to taste with salt and pepper and serve.

I grew up eating and cooking greens, and because I love seeing them in the farmers' market in all their magnificent leafy, colorful glory, this side dish combines the best of my childhood with the best of how I cook today. I really like creamed spinach, and this is my version made with green and red chard. If you see rainbow chard, try it, too. Just be sure to buy full heads of chard with firm stems and no wilting. Serve this with chicken or lamb. I particularly like it with the Braised Lamb Shanks on page 170. *serves 4*

braised red cabbage

brasato di cavolo rosso

4 slices bacon or pepperoni, diced
1 yellow onion, thinly sliced
1 red cabbage, thinly sliced
3 sprigs fresh thyme
1¼ cups chicken stock
2 tablespoons red wine vinegar
Kosher salt and freshly ground black pepper

1   In a large saucepan, cook the bacon over medium-low heat until the fat is rendered and the bacon is crispy. Add the onion and cook for about 5 minutes, or until the onion is translucent.

2   Add the cabbage and thyme and cook for about 15 minutes, or until the cabbage wilts. Pour the stock over the cabbage and bring to a simmer over medium heat. Cover and cook for about 10 minutes.

3   Season with the vinegar and salt and pepper to taste.

If you haven't tried braised cabbage in a while, it's well worth another look. The cabbage cooks only for about 25 minutes, just until tender and wilted. It is a simple and delicious dish that belies the old tales about the sulfurous odor of cabbage cooked for hours. Not this! It smells warm and earthy.

In the summer, the leaves on cabbage heads are more open, whereas the cabbage heads you buy in the winter are more tightly wrapped. When you prepare it, pull off the outer leaves only if they look wilted or browned; otherwise, just start slicing. I like the color of red cabbage but you could use green cabbage here, or try savoy, napa, or bok choy. All are good, mild, and sweet and should never be overcooked. I pep the cabbage up with a little red wine vinegar here and also mix it with bacon, an appealing combination of flavors and textures. ❈ *serves 4*

brussels sprouts with crispy pancetta
cavolini di bruxelles con pancetta

24 Brussels sprouts, soaked for 15 minutes in ice water
1 tablespoon olive oil
3 tablespoons ¼-inch diced pancetta
1 Spanish onion, julienned
1 garlic clove, minced
1 teaspoon crushed red pepper flakes
1 cup chicken stock
2 tablespoons unsalted butter
Kosher salt and freshly ground black pepper
1 tablespoon chopped fresh flat-leaf parsley
1½ teaspoons chopped fresh marjoram
¼ cup freshly grated Parmigiano-Reggiano cheese

Don't neglect Brussels sprouts in the fall and winter and, if you possibly can, buy them fresh off the stalk. One of our best and yet most humble vegetables, they don't get the respect they deserve. Among the last vegetables to be harvested in the fall garden, they are crisp and green tasting and especially welcome when other vegetables tend to be lackluster. I serve these with crispy pancetta, which dresses them up very nicely. Try this with the Red Wine–Braised Short Ribs with Garlic Mashed Potatoes on page 173 or the Roast Chicken Piccata-Style on page 187. *serves 4*

1 In a saucepan filled with lightly salted boiling water, blanch the drained Brussels sprouts for 5 to 8 minutes, or until tender. Drain and immediately submerge in ice water. Drain again and cut in half.

2 In a sauté pan, heat the olive oil over medium heat. When the olive oil is hot, add the pancetta and sauté for about 4 minutes, or until it begins to brown. Add the onion and sauté for 4 to 5 minutes, or until the pancetta is browned and the onion is soft and lightly colored. Add the garlic and red pepper and cook for about 1 minute, or until the garlic is softened but not colored.

3 Add the Brussels sprouts and cook for 5 to 8 minutes, or until lightly browned. Add the stock, bring to a boil, reduce the heat, and simmer briskly until reduced by half.

4 Add the butter and heat until incorporated. Season to taste with salt and pepper.

5 Divide the Brussels sprouts among 4 serving plates. Garnish with the parsley and marjoram and sprinkle each serving with the grated cheese. Serve.

broccoli rabe with chiles and brown garlic

rapini con peperoncini e aglio

1 pound broccoli rabe, thick or fibrous pieces
   removed
1 Spanish onion, sliced into half moons
½ cup extra virgin olive oil
4 garlic cloves, sliced
4 whole Calabrian chiles or other small hot chiles
Kosher salt and freshly ground black pepper

Happily, increasing numbers of home cooks
are learning to appreciate what I call a "green
with attitude." Broccoli rabe is a little bitter, a
little mild, and a little crunchy, and though it
can be served simply, I like to dress it up with
chiles and garlic. My grandmothers cooked it
every which way when I was a kid and called it
rapini. I just call it one of the best, most
versatile of the green vegetables anywhere.
This is delicious with the Roasted Cod with
Ceci Beans and Aioli on page 155 or Chicken
"Hunter's Style" on page 177. ❀ *serves 4*

1 Bring a large saucepan filled about halfway
with salted water to a boil over high heat.
Add the broccoli rabe and onion and blanch
for about 2 minutes, so the broccoli rabe
does not soften. Drain and set the
vegetables aside.

2 In a saucepan, heat the olive oil over
medium heat. Add the garlic and chiles and
sauté for 3 to 4 minutes, or until the garlic
and chiles soften and the garlic turns light
brown. Add the broccoli rabe and onion,
season to taste with salt and pepper, and
serve hot.

roasted parmesan-creamed onions

cipolle arrostite a legno

4 medium yellow onions
¼ cup extra virgin olive oil
Kosher salt and freshly ground black pepper
1 cup heavy cream
¼ cup dry white wine
2 ounces Parmigiano-Reggiano cheese, shaved
  (about 2 tablespoons)

Talk about succulent! The yellow onions are pretty pungent when you slice them, but surrender their kick when they are roasted and become sweet and tender. When they reach this point, the cream sauce is poured over them, they are topped with shaved cheese, and then the whole thing is returned to the oven for a slow melt. I like to cook these in a wood oven to get some smoke on them, which makes them even better—if that's possible. Great with chicken, lamb, beef—you name it! I also like it served as a first course. *serves 4*

1 Preheat the oven to 350°F.

2 Slice the onions into ¼-inch-thick rings and lay them in a shallow baking pan, such as a sheet pan or jelly roll pan. Drizzle with the olive oil and season to taste with salt and pepper. Roast for 15 to 18 minutes, or until lightly browned.

3 Meanwhile, in a medium saucepan, bring the cream and wine to a simmer over medium-high heat. As soon as the liquid starts to bubble around the edges, remove from the heat.

4 Spoon about a tablespoon of the cream mixture over each onion slice. Cover with aluminum foil, return to the oven, and cook for about 25 minutes. Increase the oven temperature to 450°F.

5 Remove the foil and top the onions with the shaved cheese. Return the pan to the oven and cook for 4 to 5 minutes, or until the edges caramelize. Serve hot.

eggplant caponata
caponata alla siciliana

2 medium eggplant, sliced lengthwise

1 Roma tomato, halved

1 red onion, cut into wedges

1 celery rib

1 cup extra virgin olive oil

Kosher salt and freshly ground black pepper

½ cup golden raisins

¼ cup toasted pine nuts (see page 46)

¼ cup balsamic vinegar

2 tablespoons pitted and sliced green olives

2 garlic cloves, minced

1 tablespoon sugar

1 tablespoon unsweetened cocoa powder

Eggplant is the primary component in caponata, a tangy, salty spread or condiment that shows up on antipasto platters and as a side dish for meat, poultry, and fish. It's a rustic food first served in Sicilian bars, and it may have gotten its name from the word *caupo*, which means "tavern" in Latin. It's one of my favorite ways to use a dark purple eggplant, although any eggplant will do—white, striped, lavender; slender or bulbous—as long as it is smooth, glossy, and firm and feels heavy. If it feels light when you heft it, the flesh will be spongy and bitter. I like to grill the eggplant, but you could broil, roast, or panfry it. And don't forget the cocoa powder. It adds depth of flavor and is not a mistake in the recipe! Serve this with Lamb Chops with Garlic Jus on page 202 or Beef Steak Florentine with Arugula on page 208. *serves 4*

1 Prepare a charcoal or gas grill by spraying the grilling rack with nonstick vegetable spray. Heat the grill until medium-hot.

2 In a large bowl, coat the eggplant, tomato, onion, and celery with ¾ cup of olive oil. Season with salt and pepper to taste.

3 Lay the vegetables on the grill and cook each vegetable for 2 to 3 minutes, or until grill marks appear on one side. Using tongs, turn the vegetables over and grill until grill marks appear on the other side and the vegetables are cooked through.

4 Remove from the grill and let the vegetables cool. When they are cool, cut them into large dice.

5 Transfer the vegetables to a bowl and add the raisins, pine nuts, vinegar, olives, garlic, sugar, and cocoa powder. Add ¼ cup of olive oil and mix thoroughly. Adjust the seasonings and refrigerate for at least 4 hours or overnight. Serve at room temperature.

calabrian potatoes
patate calabrese

Kosher salt
1¼ pounds small Red Bliss potatoes
Vegetable oil for deep-frying
¼ cup Calabrian Marinade (recipe follows)
Freshly ground black pepper

1 Preheat the oven to 400°F.

2 Sprinkle about 1 cup of salt over a dry baking sheet to cover. The salt prevents the potatoes from burning. Lay the potatoes on top of the salt and bake for about 30 minutes, or until tender.

3 Smash the hot potatoes on a counter with the heel of your hands. They will break into small pieces along their natural fault lines, and the pieces should be about 2 inches long.

4 Pour enough oil into a deep skillet to a depth of 4 inches (leave at least 2 inches between the oil and the top of the pan) and heat over medium-high heat. When the air above the oil shimmers and a piece of bread sizzles when dropped in it, lower the potato pieces into the oil with a slotted spoon and fry for 2 to 3 minutes, or until very lightly browned. Remove and drain on paper towels.

5 Let the oil regain its heat. Lower the potatoes into the hot oil again and fry for about 1 minute longer, or until crispy.

6 Remove and drain again on paper towels. Put the potatoes in a bowl and pour the marinade over them. Season to taste with salt and pepper. Serve hot.

calabrian marinade
I love this marinade, made with my favorite chiles—Calabrians. They are packed in oil and about as big as your pinky, and because they are sweet and hot at the same time, they don't set your palate on fire. Look for them in Italian markets and specialty stores.
makes about 2½ cups

2 cups extra virgin olive oil
2 garlic cloves, minced
1 cup chopped fresh flat-leaf parsley
3 Calabrian chiles or other hot chiles, chopped
2 tablespoons chopped fresh thyme
1 tablespoon chopped fresh rosemary

1 In a large saucepan, heat the olive oil and garlic over medium-high heat until the garlic sizzles. Remove the pan from the heat and set aside to cool.

2 When the oil is cool, stir in the parsley, chiles, thyme, and rosemary. Set aside. If not using within 1 hour, cover and refrigerate for up to 5 days. Let the marinade reach room temperature before using.

When these small potatoes—no larger than a Ping-Pong ball—are fried for the second time, they crisp up in a way that defies any preconceived notion you might have about what a crispy potato should be. You just can't stop eating them, particularly when they are tossed with a spicy marinade that acts as a dressing. They taste good with anything—meat, fish, poultry, or dipped in aioli as an appetizer. Try them. You will thank me!

serves 4

creamy white polenta with parmigiano-reggiano

polenta con parmigiano-reggiano

2 quarts chicken stock

1 quart heavy cream

Kosher salt

4 cups white or yellow polenta or stone-ground
    cornmeal

1 cup semolina

1 cup plus 2 tablespoons freshly grated
    Parmigiano-Reggiano cheese

¼ cup extra virgin olive oil

2 tablespoons unsalted butter

Freshly ground black pepper

1 In a large, heavy pot, bring the stock, cream, and 1 quart of water to a boil over high heat. Season to taste with salt.

2 Add the polenta and semolina, reduce the heat to medium, and cook gently for about 10 minutes, or until the cornmeal has absorbed all of the liquid and begins to resemble wet sand. As it cooks, its grittiness will lessen and the polenta will thicken. Be careful when you taste it; it's very hot and can burn your mouth.

3 Stir in 1 cup of cheese and the olive oil and butter. Season to taste with salt and pepper and serve hot, garnished with 2 tablespoons of grated cheese.

I have written a lot about polenta and cornmeal on page 101, and to make this creamy, satisfying dish, I suggest you buy locally produced, stone-ground cornmeal. Imported polenta works very well, too, but I like using products close to the source to ensure freshness and full flavor. I add semolina for texture. In Italy, home cooks often have a copper pot designated as the polenta pot that is never used for anything else. If you don't happen to have a copper polenta pot, I find that enameled cast iron works very well.

serves 4

variation To make Fried Polenta, *Polenta Fritta*, spread the hot, cooked polenta in a jelly roll or shallow baking pan and refrigerate for at least 1 hour and up to 24 hours. Cut the chilled polenta into squares. Heat about an inch of olive oil in a deep skillet and fry the polenta squares over medium-high heat for 2 to 3 minutes a side, or until golden brown. Drain on paper towels and season to taste with salt and pepper.

truffled garlic-parmesan potato chips
patatine fritte con parmigiano e tartufo

1 cup finely grated Parmigiano-Reggiano cheese
2 tablespoons kosher salt
1 teaspoon granulated garlic
2 pounds russet potatoes
Canola oil or vegetable oil for deep-frying
¼ cup black truffle oil

Here's another potato dish that is over the top. And why wouldn't it be? You are in effect making your own potato chips and seasoning them with a garlicky cheese mixture and a drizzle of truffle oil. Need I say more?

❧ *serves 4*

1 Stir together the cheese, salt, and garlic powder.

2 Slice the potatoes as thinly as you can with a sharp knife. If you have a mandoline, use it, but do not slice the potatoes paper thin, just very thin. As you cut a few slices, drop them into a bowl filled with cold tap water to keep them from discoloring.

3 Pour enough oil into a large, deep skillet to a depth of 4 inches (leaving at least 2 inches from the oil to the top of the pan) and heat over medium-high heat until it registers 350°F on a deep-fat thermometer, or until the air above the oil shimmers and a piece of bread sizzles when dropped in it.

4 Pat the potato slices dry with paper towels and lower them into the hot oil with a slotted spoon. You may have to do this in batches. Fry for 4 to 6 minutes, or until golden brown.

5 Lift the potatoes from the oil and drain on paper towels. While still hot, season with the cheese mixture, using only enough to coat them lightly, and drizzle with the truffle oil to serve.

olive oil crushed potatoes
purè di patate all'olio

Kosher salt
5 Yukon Gold potatoes (about 1½ pounds)
1 cup extra virgin olive oil
3 tablespoons chopped fresh flat-leaf parsley
Freshly ground black pepper

1 Preheat the oven to 350°F.

2 Evenly spread 1 cup of salt on a baking sheet or in a shallow baking pan. Arrange the potatoes on top of the salt and roast for about 45 minutes, until tender.

3 Remove the potatoes from the oven, peel while hot, and transfer to a bowl. Crush the potatoes with a fork and at the same time slowly add the olive oil until incorporated. Stir in the chopped parsley, season to taste with salt and pepper, and serve.

When I studied French cooking, I learned to finish potatoes with butter and cream. These are finished with olive oil, a lighter version of the same idea. I am generous with the olive oil, and I use very good oil, because no other fat is involved. The salt prevents the potatoes from burning on the baking sheet and crisps their skin because it draws moisture from it, although it doesn't mean the potatoes are especially salty. 🍀 *serves 4*

goat cheese scalloped potatoes

torta di patate con formaggio caprino

1 quart heavy cream
1 quart chicken stock
1½ cups dry white wine
1 cup minced shallots
2 tablespoons minced garlic
2 teaspoons chopped fresh thyme
2 teaspoons chopped fresh rosemary
¾ teaspoon kosher salt
8 ounces goat cheese
6 pounds russet potatoes, peeled
Snipped fresh chives

The goat cheese adds intense flavor and creaminess to these rich, gorgeous potatoes. You could use Parmigiano-Reggiano cheese or fontina instead, but if you like goat cheese as much as I do, make these as written.

❧ *serves 4*

1 Preheat the oven to 400°F. Line a large, shallow baking pan with aluminum foil.

2 In a large pot, mix the cream, stock, wine, shallots, garlic, thyme, rosemary, and salt. Bring to a simmer over medium-high heat and then add 4 ounces of goat cheese. Whisk until smooth. Refrigerate the remaining goat cheese.

3 Slice the potatoes as thinly as you can with a sharp knife, about ⅛ inch thick. If you have a mandoline, use it, but do not slice the potatoes paper thin, just very thin. As you cut a few slices, drop them into a bowl filled with cold tap water to keep them from discoloring.

4 Add the sliced potatoes to the pot, bring the sauce to a simmer over medium-high heat, and simmer until warmed through.

5 Transfer the potatoes and the sauce to the lined pan, spreading them evenly in a 3-inch layer. Cover with foil and bake for 15 minutes. Remove the foil and bake for about 50 minutes longer, until the potatoes are very tender and the sauce is bubbling.

6 Dot the potatoes with 4 ounces of goat cheese and bake for about 5 minutes, or until the goat cheese melts. Let the potatoes cool for about 15 minutes before serving, garnished with the snipped chives.

borlotti beans

fagioli borlotti

1½ pounds dried borlotti (cranberry) beans
8 ounces bacon, diced
2 celery ribs, cut into large dice (about 1½ cups)
2 carrots, cut into large dice (about 1½ cups)
1 large yellow onion, cut into large dice
2 garlic cloves, crushed

1 small bunch fresh sage
1 bay leaf
1 teaspoon crushed red pepper flakes
Kosher salt and freshly ground black pepper
1½ gallons chicken stock
1 cup Stewed Tomatoes (page 57)
½ cup sherry vinegar
¼ cup extra virgin olive oil

Dried beans are much loved in many cultures, including Italy. Trouble is, many home cooks shy away from cooking beans "from scratch" and instead buy canned beans. Although I am not opposed to canned beans, I encourage you to try cooking dried beans. Like so many kitchen tasks, it's not hard, it just takes time—but mostly time for the beans to soak and then cook. The beans have much better texture and flavor than those in a can.

I begin with an Italian favorite, the borlotti bean, which in the United States is called roman or cranberry bean and is mottled red and white. When it cooks, it loses its color. Nearly any dried bean will work in this simple but versatile and delicious recipe that includes bacon, tomato sauce, and a pinch of crushed red pepper flakes. Try red beans (also called kidney beans), white beans (also called Great Northern beans, navy beans, and cannellini beans), or garbanzo beans (also called ceci beans and chickpeas). The list goes on, and dried heirloom beans are now showing up at farmers' markets, which just makes the selection that much more exciting. *serves 4*

1 Rinse the beans well and then transfer to a large bowl or pot. Add enough cold water to cover and let the beans soak at room temperature for 8 to 12 hours or overnight. Change the water once or twice, if possible. As they soak they will swell to two and a half to three times their volume.

2 In a heavy pot, cook the bacon until the fat is rendered. Add the celery, carrots, onion, garlic, sage, bay leaf, red pepper, and salt and pepper to taste. Cook over medium-low heat, stirring, for about 10 minutes, or until the vegetables soften but do not color.

3 Drain the beans and add them to the pot. Stir to mix with the vegetables so that the beans absorb the flavors.

4 Add just enough stock to cover the beans and bring to a boil over high heat. Reduce the heat to medium-low and, using a skimmer or large spoon, skim off any foam that rises to the surface. Simmer, adding more stock if necessary to keep the beans covered at all times, for 45 to 60 minutes, until almost fork tender.

5 Add the tomatoes, stir, and then remove the beans from the heat and let them cool in the liquid. When the beans are cool, pick out the large pieces of celery, carrot, and onion. Remove and discard the bay leaf.

6 Serve the beans sprinkled with vinegar and olive oil.

ℬ cheese

When a meal winds down, it's time for one of the most civilized of all culinary traditions: the cheese course. I love cheese and never tire of tasting and learning about it when I travel through Italy, where some of the best are made and cherished. I put together a few recipes for this chapter that showcase some of my favorite selections.

A good cheese can stand on its own, but serving it with bread or crackers and perhaps some fruit, cured meat, or vegetables just enhances its glory. Almost always serve cheese at room temperature, which means remembering to take it from the refrigerator for tempering at least 20 minutes or more before serving it. Never slice the cheese too far in advance, as it will oxidize and lose much of its sensual aroma. Slice hard cheeses with a sharp knife and soft cheese with a thin, flexible one. Use different knives for each cheese and cut them into wedges with some rind left on the end, if at all possible. Some cheeses crumble when cut; others ooze. This is how it should be.

I like to serve cheese accompanied by baguettes or country-style bread. Fruit breads are also nice, as is foccacia. Crackers are another good choice, whether simple wheat, rye, or water crackers. Finally, if you make your own jam or preserves, regardless of the flavor, serve it with the cheese. Magnificent!

notes from the sommelier
what grows together,
goes together!

The servers-in-training during their first few days of Osteria School invariably ask, "When are you going to teach us which wines go with which dishes on the menu?" They are generally overwhelmed by the dishes they need to memorize and daunted by the potential list of "pairings" that I might add to their to cram-and-regurgitate list. That is when I look them all in the eye, smile, and tell them about the beauty of our all-Italian wine list. I recite this mantra for them: "What grows together, goes together."

It couldn't be easier. The cuisines from the Italian regions that we represent on our menus, and that are represented in Chef Tramonto's recipes, all produce outstanding wines. In fact, each region's dishes evolved side by side with the wines. Once you spend some time investigating a regional cuisine and its wines, it all becomes clear.

Tuscany is known for its Chianti, Brunello, and Vino Nobile and its big, rich Super Tuscan reds like Bastianich Morellino di Scansano and d'Alessandro Syrah from Cortona. On Tuscan tables you will find rich white beans, game meats like wild boar, bread soup, and *bistecca fiorentina*—a big old beef porterhouse steak. Put those Tuscan wines and those Tuscan dishes together and you've got yourself a successful marriage of wine and food.

Lombardy is famous for its Grana Padano cheese, Franciacorta, *Bresaola* (cured beef), Rosso di Valtellina, Gorgonzola, and passito-style Erbaluce. So note where these cheeses originate and look for compatible regional wines. You'll have a good time making matches.

some of my favorite cheeses

GORGONZOLA DOLCE I absolutely love this mild, sweet, creamy blue cheese. Anyone with a fondness for blues will gravitate to this lovely cheese, and even those who are not major fans of more pungent blues may fall for this in a big way. My grandparents kept a cheese plate out on the table much of the time, and more often than not the two offerings were Gorgonzola Dolce and Parmigiano-Reggiano. I never thought of either as anything special, although I now respect the years of knowledge that go into the making of each.

Dolce is made in Lombardy near the town of Gorgonzola and aged according to Italy's Denominazione di Origine Controllata (DOC) regulations. The EU based its PDO (protected designation of origin) laws on these and similar regulations in France and Spain. The PDO protects the reputation of regional foods by stipulating their authenticity. I like to pair it with pears and spiced walnuts or with a balsamic jelly, as I do on page 239. It's younger and gentler than sharper blue cheeses and therefore is moister and more ivory-colored than Gorgonzola Naturale. Its texture is soft and spreadable, which makes it perfect for serving with crackers or stirring into risottos, polentas, or dips. It is superb served alongside fruits such as berries, figs, plums, and peaches.

All blue cheeses used to be made by leaving milk curd to cure until it developed a blue-green streak of mold. The environmental circumstances have to be right—as in the famous caves in France where the noble Roquefort is made—for the mold to appear, but when it does, the cheese strikes a chord with those cheese lovers who can't get enough of a good blue. Perhaps Italy's most famous blue is Gorgonzola Piccante, which is an assertive, bold, tangy blue cheese with a strong aroma that may not agree with everyone, although for those who love it, it's ambrosia. Nowadays, the cheeses are injected with mold-producing bacteria, which accelerates the process. To enhance the final flavor of the cheeses, most good blues spend time in cavelike storage areas.

Gorgonzola Dolce wine suggestions: Gorgonzola Dolce can show up in so many different parts of the meal with so many different dance partners that the wine-pairing strategy varies. When served as part of a savory course, a full-bodied red with firm tannins and black fruit, such as a Bordeaux-style blend from Lombardy, will match well. When served alone with black fruits, such as berries, a fortified style of red wine like Recioto della Valpolicella or a Sagrantino Passito will sing. When served with tree fruits, honey, or sweets, try a Passito made from white wine grapes such as Garganega or Fiano.

MOZZARELLA DI BUFALA CAMPANIA You have heard of buffalo mozzarella but may not realize that to be the real thing this mild, adaptable fresh cheese must be made from the milk of water buffalo. Traditionally, it's from Campania and Apulia, east of Naples, although it's now made in many more places. The city of Aversa in the province of Caserta is the birthplace of the cheese. It's a sweet, very mild cheese that is shipped all over the world so that it's available here, fresh and ready to use. Italians buy and eat mozzarella on the same day, although it will keep for about 5 days. I like to eat it within 2 days of purchase for the best flavor. Other mozzarella, made from cow's milk, is less expensive than buffalo mozzarella and, depending on how carefully it is made, can be very good. It, too, should be eaten soon after purchase.

Mozzarella di Bufala Campania wine suggestions: Campanian whites are the classic match with this cheese. A mouthful of the rich mozzarella is lifted by a white wine with good acidity, and the following styles and grape varieties fit that requirement: Aspirinio, Falanghina, Fiano, and Greco from Campania.

PARMIGIANO-REGGIANO I feel passionate about this cheese. To be authentic, it must come from or near the cities of Parma and Reggio-Emilia in north-central Italy and be made as it has been for centuries. It's a *grana,* which is a hard, granular cow's-milk cheese that is cooked but not pressed so that its texture is at once firm and crumbly and its flavor slightly sweet, slightly salty, and totally luxurious, deep, and memorable. Imitator cheeses, often referred to as Parmesan, tend to be drier and saltier than the cheese produced in Italy, and so I urge everyone to seek out the real deal. Many consider Parmigiano-Reggiano the greatest cheese produced in the world—and you know, I have to agree.

Parmigiano-Reggiano wine suggestions: Everyone gives me a hard time, but I am a devout fan of Parmigiano-Reggiano paired with slightly sweet and bubbly Lambrusco! The first thing that we did when we arrived in Bologna, Italy, last March was to drive to the famed Tamborini Deli, order every salumi and cheese, and start in on a bottle of Lambrusco. The *New York Times* hopped on the bandwagon in July 2007 with a feature story about the joys of Lambrusco—but we knew it all along. Try what is available: Ceci, Zonin, and Ca' de' Medici.

PECORINO My all-time favorite pecorinos are from Tuscany, although the cheese is crafted throughout much of Italy. I particularly like the cheeses from near the town of Pienza in Tuscany.

Pecora, the Italian word for "sheep," gives the cheese its name, and the result is an agreeable yet intense, sheepy flavor with a mildly peppery finish. If the cheese is aged for longer than 6 months, I find it becomes a little concentrated for my taste, but perhaps not yours. Pecorinos cut cleanly and easily, and so they are good for snacking or cutting into cubes and tossing with olive oil.

Pecorino Foglie de Noce: This pressed sheep's-milk cheese from Tuscany is aged in wheels wrapped in black walnut leaves and rubbed daily with olive oil. By the time it gets to market, the cheese is both attractive to look at and robust to eat, with a hint of black walnut.

Pecorino Toscano Stagionato: Cheeses with this designation are made from 100 percent sheep's milk. To earn the name, these small, mild cheeses have to be made between September and June.

Pecorino wine suggestions: Much to our amusement, every time we asked what kind of cheese we were eating while we were in Tuscany, the reply invariably was "pecorino." Whether the cheese was soft or hard, wet or dry, the answer was the same. The wine choice should vary as well. Fresher cheeses need a wine with more acidity, while the older, more mellow pecorino cheeses would do well with a more mellow and mature wine. Try whites like Tuscan Vernaccia or Chardonnay with the younger pecorino, and move into mature Brunello or Vino Nobile di Montepulciano for the "cellared" pecorino.

PIAVE I have come to appreciate this cow's-milk

cheese that resembles a young Parmigiano-Reggiano. It lacks some of the depth of that cheese, but has a pleasing nuttiness and fullness that makes it delightful with fruit, wine, and bread. It is made in northeastern Italy in the Piave River Valley region of Bellunao.

Piave wine suggestions: This nutty, northern cheese has the guts to stand up to a full-octane red with either a hint of residual sugar or unabashed amounts of sweetness. Red wine made from raisinated grapes is called for to pair with this cheese, so break out the Amarone, the ripasso, the passito, and the appassimento.

ROBIOLA Many types of robiola cheese are produced in northern Italy; the word refers to a family of cheese (not unlike how *Cheddar* refers to a family of cheese). The mild, semisoft cheeses have beige rinds and mild yet luxurious flavors.

Robiola Rocchetta: This lovely, creamy cheese brings together the flavors of goat's, cow's, and sheep's milk in harmonious balance. It is a semisoft cheese with a silken texture.

Robiola Bosina: As with all robiolas, this one is from the northwest regions of Italy, Langhe and Piedmont, and is a glorious blend of cow's and sheep's milk that is aged just until the young cheese is luxuriously soft and milky. It is best served runny, like a good brie.

Robiola wine suggestions: There are two methods to pairing wines with this category of rich, creamy cheeses. You can go the acid-bubbles route, in which case a vivacious sparkling Franciacorta or even a simple Prosecco will refresh after each bite of the unctuous cheese. Or you may choose to go the fortified-sweet wine route and open a coveted bottle of Vin Santo or Picolit to go rich on rich. Either method will lead you to a pairing that works.

UMBRIACO What I love about this cow's-milk cheese from Lombardy is that it is soaked in red wine, so that its rind turns a deep purple and the cheese tastes ever so subtly of grapes. It sometimes is called *Umbriaco Vin Rosso*, and some Umbriacos are soaked in Prosecco. Though Umbriaco has been compared to Asiago cheese—which is a wonderful, versatile cheese—I prefer the depth and interest of the Umbriaco. The word translates to "drunkard" or "inebriated," and that small fact alone makes the cheese fun to eat and to serve. Don't hesitate to use Asiago if you can't find Umbriaco. Both cheeses are very good with salads and as part of a cheese course.

Umbriaco wine suggestions: Two categories of wine pair well with this cheese. If it is coming at the end of the meal, but before you are ready for a sweet wine, try a dry, full-bodied red from Lombardy such as Cabernet, Merlot, Cabernet Franc, or Chiavennesca. If you are ready to move on to the next phase of the meal and pour an almost portesque style of wine for this cheese, try an off-dry appassimento-style of red from Lombardy like Sfursat di Valtellina. What grows together, goes together, and what an amazing match!

buffalo mozzarella with red bell pepper purée

mozzarella di bufala con purè di peperoni rossi

¼ cup extra virgin olive oil, plus more for
   drizzling
½ yellow onion, diced small
3 red bell peppers, diced small
Sea salt and freshly ground black pepper
9 garlic cloves, skins on
1 teaspoon red wine vinegar
Four 3-ounce balls of fresh buffalo mozzarella or
   other high-quality mozzarella cheese
4 tablespoons buttermilk

When you slice a fresh piece of buffalo
mozzarella, you can see milk dripping from it.
Its soft creaminess is highlighted by an intense
red bell pepper purée, which is the perfect foil
for the cheese. ❧ *serves 4*

1   Preheat the oven to 350°F.

2   In a saucepan, heat 2 tablespoons of olive
    oil over medium heat. When the olive oil is
    hot, add the onion and cook for about
    5 minutes, or until translucent. Add the bell
    peppers and continue to cook for about
    8 minutes longer, or until soft. Season to
    taste with salt and pepper.

3   Remove the skin from 1 garlic clove and
    mince the clove. Add it to the pan and stir
    for about 1 minute, or until cooked
    through. Add the vinegar and cook for
    about 30 seconds, or until evaporated.

4   Transfer the onion and bell peppers to the
    jar of a blender and purée until smooth. Set
    aside.

5   In a small bowl, toss 8 garlic cloves with
    2 tablespoons of olive oil. Spread the
    coated garlic cloves and any oil in a small
    baking pan and bake for 12 to 15 minutes,
    or until the garlic is soft and the skins are
    slightly charred.

6   Put 2 tablespoons of the red bell pepper
    purée on each plate. Slice the cheese into
    ½-inch slices and divide equally among
    the plates. Put 2 charred garlic cloves on
    each plate and drizzle a touch of olive oil
    on the plate. Spoon the buttermilk over the
    cheese and season to taste with salt and
    pepper.

gorgonzola dolce with balsamic jelly

gorgonzola dolce con gelatina di balsamico

1 cup balsamic vinegar
1½ tablespoons sugar
1 teaspoon apple pectin
Pinch of fresh thyme leaves
6 ounces Gorgonzola Dolce
Extra virgin olive oil

1 In a small saucepan, mix the vinegar and sugar and bring to a boil over high heat. Immediately remove from the heat and let the mixture cool until warm.

2 Sprinkle the pectin over the warm vinegar while stirring vigorously. Pour into a shallow container and let the jelly cool to room temperature. Stir in the thyme, cover, and refrigerate for about 1 hour, or until the consistency of soft, loose jelly.

3 Divide the cheese evenly among 4 serving plates. Drizzle the cheese with a little olive oil, put a teaspoon of the jelly next to the cheese, and serve.

Though a drizzle of balsamic would taste wonderful with this cheese, I played around with texture to make a jelly that adds another layer of interest to the soft, indulgent cheese.

serves 4

umbriaco wrapped in bresaola

umbriaco in bresaola

24 thin slices Bresaola
12 ounces Umbriaco cheese, sliced into 24 batons (sticks), each 3 to 5 inches long
About 4 tablespoons extra virgin olive oil
Freshly ground black pepper

1 Lay the slices of Bresaola on a work surface and lay a baton of cheese on one side of each slice. Roll the meat around the cheese, like a cigar.

2 Arrange 6 rolls on each of 4 serving plates. Garnish each plate with olive oil and a turn of the pepper mill.

If you are not familiar with Bresaola, I suggest you make its acquaintance. The salted, aged beef, usually cut from the tender filet, is terrific, and I remember it being front and center of every meat-and-cheese platter when I was growing up. Paired with Umbriaco cheese, it's nothing short of outstanding. *serves 4*

parmigiano-reggiano with aged balsamic

parmigiano-reggiano con aceto balsamico

1 Granny Smith apple, cored but not peeled

1 Anjou pear or other ripe, firm pear, cored but
   not peeled

1 tablespoon extra virgin olive oil

1 tablespoon lemon juice

1 tablespoon thinly sliced fresh basil

Kosher salt and freshly ground black pepper

6 to 8 ounces Parmigiano-Reggiano cheese

4 teaspoons aged balsamic vinegar (see Note)

If you have really good Parmigiano-Reggiano and sweet, syrupy aged balsamic, you have two flavors that marry in blissful harmony. I pair them with a simple apple-and-pear salad to round out the cheese course. ✺ *serves 4*

1 Using a mandoline or very sharp knife, cut the apple and pear into very thin matchsticks. Put in a bowl and toss with the olive oil and lemon juice. Add the basil and toss gently. Season to taste with salt and pepper.

2 Break the cheese into large chunks, each of approximately equal size. You want 1 or 2 chunks per serving.

3 Pile the salad on the side of each of 4 serving plates and set the cheese chunks in the center of each plate. Drizzle the vinegar around the cheese and sprinkle lightly with pepper. Serve at room temperature.

note Aged balsamic vinegar is truly addictive and once you discover its splendor, you will be hooked. I suggest you buy the oldest you can find. You may experience sticker shock, but remember that you need only a very little to make a big statement. For more information, turn to page 146.

pecorino toscano stagionato with fig paste

pecorino toscano stagionato con purè di fico

4 ounces pecorino cheese
½ cup Fig Paste (4 ounces; recipe follows)

1 Slice the cheese into 8 thin slices. Cut the Fig Paste into 16 slices.

2 Arrange the cheese slices in the center of each of 4 serving plates and surround them with the Fig Paste slices.

fig paste
makes about 1½ cups (12 ounces)

¾ pound fresh Mission figs
1 cup port
1 sprig fresh rosemary, 1 inch long
1 tablespoon extra virgin olive oil
1½ teaspoons grated orange zest
Kosher salt and freshly ground black pepper

1 Preheat the oven to 250°F. Put a rack in a shallow baking pan.

2 Slice the stems from the figs and cut the figs in half, from stem to tip. Arrange the figs, cut sides up, on the rack and bake, turning every 10 to 15 minutes, for 40 to 50 minutes, or until dried and shrunk by about a quarter. Remove and set aside.

3 In a saucepan, heat the port and rosemary over high heat until boiling. Let the port boil for about 1 minute to remove most of the alcohol. Remove the pan from the heat.

4 Put 1 cup of the figs into the port, reserving the rest of the figs, and set aside for about 20 minutes, during which time the figs will absorb about a quarter of the port.

5 In the bowl of a food processor fitted with the metal blade, pulse the reserved figs 5 or 6 times or until the figs form a paste. Drop the port-steeped figs, one at a time, through the feed tube of the food processor and pulse after each addition. Scrape the sides of the bowl often to incorporate the figs.

6 When all the figs are mixed into the paste, add the olive oil and orange zest and season to taste with salt and pepper. Pulse to combine. If any port is left in the pan, stir it into the paste.

7 Lay a piece of parchment paper on the countertop and spread the paste across the bottom of the paper. Roll the parchment over the fig paste to form a cylinder about 1 inch in diameter. Once it is rolled, wrap the parchment cylinder in plastic wrap and refrigerate. Unwrap and slice off pieces of fig paste as needed.

I pair the pecorino with a homemade fig paste that takes a little while to make—only because you have to let the figs dry in a warm oven—but is an absolutely spectacular condiment. There's no point making just a little, so the recipe makes about three times as much as you need here, but that's okay; if well wrapped, it keeps in the refrigerator for about 2 weeks and goes well with other cheeses, meats, and poultry. *serves 4*

piave with tomato marmalade

piave con marmellata di pomodoro

6 Roma tomatoes

4 teaspoons extra virgin olive oil, plus more for drizzling

2 tablespoons minced onion

1 teaspoon crushed red pepper flakes

2 garlic cloves, peeled

1 sprig fresh thyme

1 bay leaf

Kosher salt and freshly ground black pepper

4 ounces Piave cheese

Local honey, such as chestnut, or any other honey

I watched Piave cheese being made when I visited the Piave River valley in northern Italy. And when I tasted the cheese I knew it would be impressive with this homemade tomato marmalade. Paired with local honey, it's an impressive cheese course as the flavors burst in your mouth. ❁ *serves 4*

1 Preheat the oven to 300°F.

2 In a large saucepan filled with boiling water, blanch the tomatoes for 45 to 60 seconds and lift the tomatoes from the water. Pull the skin off the tomatoes; it should slide right off. Halve the skinned tomatoes, hold the tomato halves over a bowl, and gently squeeze the seeds from them. Dice the peeled, seeded tomatoes.

3 In an ovenproof sauté pan, heat the olive oil over medium-high heat. When the olive oil is hot, cook the onion, red pepper, garlic, thyme, and bay leaf for about 6 minutes, or until the onion softens. Add the tomatoes to the pan and bring to a simmer. Season to taste with salt and pepper.

4 Transfer the pan to the oven and cook, stirring every 5 minutes, for about 25 minutes, or until the liquid evaporates and the sauce is thick. This can be finished on the burner, if necessary. Set aside to cool to room temperature.

5 If not using right away, transfer the tomato marmalade to a lidded container and refrigerate for up to 6 days. Let the marmalade return to room temperature before using.

6 Slice the cheese into 8 thin slices. Put 2 slices on each of 4 serving plates and garnish with 1 tablespoon of the tomato marmalade. Drizzle the marmalade with olive oil. Drizzle about a teaspoon of the honey on the cheese. Do not drizzle more than just a little honey.

robiola bosina with truffled radish salad

robiola bosina con insalata di ravanello e tartufo

8 ounces Robiola Bosina cheese
4 radishes, thinly sliced
1 celery rib, thinly sliced on the diagonal
1 teaspoon minced shallot
1 teaspoon white or black truffle oil
Pinch of sea salt

1 Cut the robiola into 4 triangles and put 1 triangle on each of 4 serving plates.

2 In a small bowl, toss the radishes, celery, and shallot with the truffle oil. Arrange the salad next to the robiola. Season the robiola with a little salt.

The crunch of the radish salad offsets the creaminess of the cheese for a remarkable cheese course. If you want to take this over the top, buy a single white truffle (available in the late fall) and slice it into the salad. *serves 4*

robiola rocchetta with flat-leaf parsley and dandelions

robiola rocchetta con prezzemolo e cicoria

½ cup seedless red grapes (about 12 grapes)

6 ounces Robiola Rocchetta cheese

1 cup fresh flat-leaf parsley leaves, picked and washed

½ cup dandelion greens, torn into bite-sized pieces

2 tablespoons extra virgin olive oil, plus more for drizzling

1 teaspoon red wine vinegar

Kosher salt and freshly ground black pepper

8 thin slices crusty country bread, toasted

The peppery dandelion greens and the parsley come together in a simple salad dressed with red wine vinegar and olive oil that plays off the smooth, semisoft cheese. The crunchy, dried grapes add the perfect sweet note.

serves 4

1 Preheat the oven to 200°F.

2 Spread the grapes in a shallow baking pan and roast for 6 to 8 hours, during which time the grapes will dry out and turn into raisins. Check the grapes at different stages throughout the drying to determine at which stage you prefer them. Remove them when you are most satisfied. (If the oven has a pilot light, you can leave the grapes in the oven overnight to dry rather than turning on the oven.)

3 Cut the robiola into 4 pieces and set each piece in the center of a serving plate.

4 In a small bowl, toss the parsley and dandelion greens with the dried grapes, 2 tablespoons of olive oil, and the vinegar. Season to taste with salt and pepper.

5 Pile the salad next to the robiola on each plate.

6 Drizzle the toasted bread with olive oil and serve with the robiola and salad.

desserts

My dessert recipe file is short, but the few I make I truly love, and all are easy. My desserts are very much geared to the home cook. I have worked with Gale Gand for the last 20 years; she is one of the most celebrated pastry chefs in the country, and she always does a brilliant job following my meals with perfect desserts. I learned from Gale that when it comes to dessert, simplicity and seasonality are always wonderful. Although this is not the only way to travel down the pastry road, it's the way I chose.

These recipes come from aunts, cousins, and grandmothers as well as my travels through Italy. Italian desserts are not as buttery and fancy as French desserts and almost always include fruit. The key is to find the best apples, peaches, berries, and lemons. These are satisfyingly sweet ends to almost any meal. Enjoy them!

notes from the sommelier
nectar of the gods

Whoever thought that it might be a good idea to toss a bunch of grapes onto a straw mat, let them dry out, and then produce a sweet elixir from them deserves a great big thank-you, because he or she gave us the likes of Recioto della Valpolicella. Whoever thought that people might enjoy a wine for which the grapes are dried and then allowed to ferment in chestnut or oak barrels for more than three years deserves his or her thank-you for Vin Santo, too! And our extraspecial thanks go to the crazy winemaker who thought that people might enjoy a wine made from grapes that were left to hang on the vines until they were attacked by a fungus called *Botrytis*, because he or she came up with Quintarelli's Bandito and Maculan's Torcolato, among others. Anyone who forgoes the pleasure of one of Italy's delicious dessert wines take note: You are missing out on what truly must be as close as we mortals get to the nectar of the gods!

apple crostata with caramel gelato

crostata di mele con gelato al caramello

4 cups all-purpose flour

2 cups (4 sticks) cold unsalted butter, cubed

1 cup granulated sugar, plus more for sprinkling

Grated zest of 1 lemon

3 large eggs

2 large egg yolks

2 quarts apple juice

⅔ cup packed light brown sugar

1 cinnamon stick

4 Granny Smith apples or other firm, tart apples, peeled, cored, and each cut into 16 wedges

Caramel Gelato (recipe follows) or vanilla ice cream

Just about any sort of pie is a winner at the end of a good meal, with its buttery, flaky crust and soft, warm fruit filling. A crostata is more rustic and free-form than a pie, but serves the same purpose. This one has an exceptional crust and reminds me of the open-face tarts I ate with gusto in Rome and Milan. Serve this with ice cream to raves! 🐾 *serves 8*

1 In the bowl of an electric mixer fitted with the paddle attachment, blend the flour, butter, granulated sugar, and lemon zest on medium speed until the mixture resembles coarse sand.

2 In a small bowl, whisk 2 eggs and the egg yolks and add to the bowl of the mixer all at once. Mix on medium speed just until the dough comes together.

3 Turn the dough out onto a lightly floured surface, gently gather into a ball, wrap in plastic wrap, and refrigerate for 2 hours to 2 days.

4 In a medium saucepan, mix the apple juice and brown sugar. Add the cinnamon stick and bring to a low simmer over medium heat. Cook gently for about 15 minutes, or until reduced by half.

5 Add the apples, stir gently, and cook for about 5 minutes, or just until slightly softened and fork tender. Remove from the heat and set aside while you roll the crust.

6 Preheat the oven to 350°F.

7 Remove the dough from the refrigerator. On a lightly floured surface, roll the dough into a large sheet about ¼ inch thick.

8 Carefully transfer the dough to a baking sheet. It should nearly cover it and may overlap the sides. Spoon the apple filling into the center of the dough.

9 In a small bowl, whisk 1 egg with 2 table-spoons of cold water. Brush the egg wash over the exposed edges of the dough and then fold them up and over the apple filling so that the dough encases the apples. It will not cover the apples. Make rough pleats or folds in the dough covering the fruit.

(continued)

10 Brush the remaining egg wash over the dough-covered apples. Sprinkle with granulated sugar. Bake for 15 to 20 minutes, or until the crust is golden brown and the filling is bubbling.

11 Serve with the Caramel Gelato or vanilla ice cream.

caramel gelato

Anyone who has been to Italy remembers the enticing gelato shops on nearly every corner, with tubs of luscious-looking, creamy, icy confections in a rainbow of hues begging you to stop and try a scoop . . . or two or three! Gelato is a little different from ice cream in that less air is whipped into it, so it's a tiny bit denser and seems somewhat richer. You will need an ice cream machine to make this blissfully rich dessert in which the warm undertones of caramel interact with the chill of ice cream as it melts on your tongue.

makes about 1 quart

¾ cup sugar
2¼ cups whole milk
¼ cup heavy cream
1 tablespoon plus 2 teaspoons skim milk powder

1 Pour about half of the sugar into a small saucepan and set it over low heat. Using a wooden spoon, stir the sugar, adding the rest a little at a time until it all dissolves. Stop stirring but continue cooking the sugar for 4 or 5 minutes longer, or until it turns amber. Swirl or tip the pan to keep the caramel from burning. If you use a candy thermometer, the sugar will register about 340°F, although the sugar may be too shallow for a candy thermometer to measure the temperature accurately. Remove the pan from the heat. Take care, as it will be very hot.

2 In a separate saucepan, heat the milk over medium heat until it's very hot but not boiling. Remove from the heat and add the caramel in thirds, stirring well with each addition.

3 Add the cream and skim milk powder and whisk until the powder dissolves and the mixture is smooth and evenly colored. Strain through a fine-mesh sieve or chinois into a bowl.

4 Set the bowl in a larger bowl filled with ice cubes and water. Stir occasionally until the caramel mixture is cool. Cover with plastic wrap and refrigerate for 2 to 24 hours, until very cold.

5 Pour the chilled mixture into a gelato or ice cream machine and freeze according to the manufacturer's instructions. Transfer the gelato to containers and freeze until firm, which can take up to 4 hours, depending on the size and depth of the container.

olive oil cake with passion fruit and mango crema
torta all'olio con crema di frutta tropicale

¾ cup olive oil, plus more for greasing the pan
1 cup cake flour (not self-rising)
Juice and finely grated zest of 1 large lemon
5 large egg yolks
¾ cup plus 1½ tablespoons sugar
4 large egg whites
½ teaspoon kosher salt
Passion Fruit and Mango Crema (recipe follows)

As surprising as it may sound, this is a pound cake made with olive oil, not butter. It is made throughout the Mediterranean region. The olive oil makes it remarkably moist and provides its own mellow flavor. When you serve golden slices of cake with the fruit crema, the soft flavors of the cake reach out and grab the sweet acidity of the crema for a heavenly dessert. I have been known to eat a piece of this cake with a cup of coffee in the morning, sans crema. ❦ *serves 8*

1 Position the oven rack in the center of the oven. Preheat the oven to 350°F. Grease a 9-inch springform pan with olive oil. Line the bottom of the pan with a round of parchment or wax paper. Oil the paper.

2 In a mixing bowl, whisk the flour with the lemon zest and set aside.

3 In the bowl of an electric mixer fitted with the paddle attachment, beat the egg yolks and ½ cup of sugar on medium-high speed for about 3 minutes, or until thick and pale. Reduce the speed to medium and add ¾ cup of olive oil and the lemon juice, beating until just combined.

4 Using a wooden spoon, stir in the flour mixture until just combined and set aside.

5 In the clean, dry bowl of an electric mixer fitted with the whisk attachment, beat the egg whites with the salt on medium-high speed until foaming. Add ¼ cup of sugar, a little at a time, beating continuously, until the egg whites just hold soft peaks.

6 Fold a third of the whites into the batter to lighten it, and then fold in the remaining whites.

7 Transfer the batter to the pan and tap it on the countertop to release any air bubbles. Sprinkle the top of the cake with 1½ tablespoons of sugar and bake for about 45 minutes, or until puffed and golden and a toothpick inserted in the center comes out clean. Cool the cake in the pan on a rack for 10 minutes. Run a knife around the edge of the pan and release the sides of the cake. Let the cake cool for about 1¼ hours, until room temperature. *(continued)*

8 Remove the bottom of the pan and peel off the paper. Transfer the cake to a serving plate and serve with the Passion Fruit and Mango Crema.

passion fruit and mango crema
makes about 2½ cups

½ cup diced fresh mango (about ½ mango)
¼ cup passion fruit juice
1 tablespoon confectioners' sugar
½ teaspoon fresh lime juice
¼ teaspoon pure vanilla extract
2 cups crème fraîche

1 In the bowl of a food processor fitted with the metal blade, combine the mango, passion fruit juice, sugar, lime juice, and vanilla and purée until smooth.

2 Add the purée to the crème fraîche and stir until well mixed and the color is even. Serve right away or cover and refrigerate for up to 2 hours. The flavor and texture will be best if used right away.

tiramisu

6 large organic egg yolks
3 tablespoons sugar
1 pound mascarpone cheese
1½ cups freshly brewed espresso, cooled
1 tablespoon Marsala
24 savoiardi (ladyfingers)
½ cup bittersweet chocolate shavings

1 In the bowl of an electric mixer fitted with the whisk attachment, whisk the egg yolks and sugar on medium speed for about 5 minutes, or until thick and light.

2 Add the cheese and beat on medium-high speed until smooth. Add 1 tablespoon of espresso and mix thoroughly.

3 In a small shallow dish, stir the remaining espresso and the Marsala. Dip each ladyfinger into the mixture for about 3 seconds, just until soaked through but not falling apart.

4 Lay as many of the soaked ladyfingers as needed on the bottom of a 9 × 13-inch baking dish to cover. Break them in half, if necessary, to fit.

5 Spoon half of the cheese mixture over the ladyfingers. Top with another layer of soaked ladyfingers. Top with the remaining cheese mixture, smooth the surface, cover with plastic wrap, and refrigerate for at least 4 hours, or until well chilled. Sprinkle with the chocolate shavings and serve.

Although the word *tiramisu* translates as "pick me up," I think of this heavenly dessert as far more than that. It's a joyful embrace of sweetened mascarpone cheese—which on its own is a lesson in indulgence—and espresso-soaked cake (commonly ladyfingers), sealed with a kiss of chocolate. It has become an extremely popular dessert in the United States, which might surprise some Italian grandmothers, who have been making it for generations to please their grandsons, just as mine did when I was growing up. Although all versions have these same ingredients, the finished desserts vary widely. Without reservation, this is my favorite tiramisu. Because this is made with raw eggs, buy organic ones and don't serve the dessert to anyone with a compromised immune system or the elderly. *serves 4*

spumoni cookies
biscotti di spumoni

8 ounces almond paste, broken into chunks and
    pieces
1 cup unsalted butter, softened
1 cup sugar
4 large eggs, separated
2 cups all-purpose flour
20 drops red food coloring
24 drops green food coloring
¼ cup raspberry jam
¼ cup apricot preserves
½ cup warm Chocolate Glaze (recipe follows)

1 Preheat the oven to 325°F. Grease 3 large
baking sheets or half-sheet pans and spread
parchment or wax paper on each one.
Grease the parchment paper with butter.

2 In the bowl of an electric mixer fitted with
the paddle attachment, beat the almond
paste, butter, sugar, and egg yolks on
medium speed for about 5 minutes, or until
light and fluffy.

3 Using a wooden spoon, stir in the flour
until well incorporated.

4 In the clean, dry bowl of an electric mixer
fitted with the whisk attachment, beat the
egg whites on medium-high speed until soft
peaks form.

5 Fold a third of the egg whites into the
batter to lighten it. Gently fold in the
remaining two thirds of the whites.

6 Divide the batter into three portions and
put each in its own small bowl. Mix one
portion with red food coloring, mix
another with green food coloring, and leave
the final portion white.

7 Spread each portion of batter on one of the
baking sheets, spreading it with a palette
knife or spatula. Spread the batter as thinly
and evenly as you can, so that it covers the
baking sheets. Bake for about 15 minutes,
or until set. Remove from the oven, invert
each baked piece of dough on wire racks,
remove the parchment paper, and let cool
completely.

8 When the layers are cool, spread raspberry
jam on the green layer and top with the
white layer. Spread the apricot preserves on
the white layer and top with the red layer.

9 Cut the cookies into 1-inch-wide rectangles,
2 to 2½ inches long. Dip each into the
warm Chocolate Glaze to coat all sides and
let set on wire racks until the chocolate
cools.   *(continued)*

When I was young, these were my favorite
cookies. My cousin Kathy Abbamonte gave
me this recipe, and the cookies so resemble
the tricolored confections my mother made
and that I loved, I wanted to share it with
everyone. Brava, Kathy!

makes about 40 cookies

chocolate glaze
makes about ½ cup

1 pound semisweet chocolate morsels
2 tablespoons unsalted butter

1 In the top of a double boiler set over barely simmering water, melt the chocolate and butter, stirring gently, until melted and smooth.

2 Remove the top of the double boiler from the heat and set aside to allow the chocolate to cool to room temperature. It is ready when you stick the tip of your finger in it and it does not feel hot. Use immediately. (If there is any leftover glaze, refrigerate it and reheat to drizzle over ice cream or pound cake.)

panna cotta with balsamic, strawberries, and raspberries

panna cotta con aceto balsamico e fragole

2 leaves gelatin
1 cup whole milk
½ vanilla bean, split
½ cup plus 2 teaspoons sugar
1 cup heavy cream
¼ pound fresh strawberries, hulled and halved
    (about 1 cup)
¼ pound fresh raspberries (about ½ cup)
¼ cup aged balsamic vinegar (see Note)
1 teaspoon finely sliced fresh basil
½ teaspoon finely grated orange zest

1 In a small bowl, soak the gelatin in 1 cup of water and let it soften for about 5 minutes.

2 In a saucepan, heat the milk and vanilla bean over medium heat until it simmers. Add ½ cup of sugar and stir until dissolved.

3 Remove the pan from the heat and remove and discard the vanilla bean. Lift the gelatin from the water and squeeze out any excess water. Add to the milk mixture.

4 Set the pan in a bowl filled with ice cubes and cold water and stir occasionally until very cold.

5 In the bowl of an electric mixer fitted with the whisk attachment, whip the cream to medium-firm peaks. Fold the cream into the cold milk mixture.

6 Pour the mixture into 4 small bowls. Cover with plastic wrap and refrigerate for 2 hours to 5 days.

7 Before serving, gently toss the berries with 2 teaspoons of sugar and the vinegar and let stand for 15 minutes. Add the basil and orange zest and toss again.

8 Serve the panna cotta chilled and topped with the berries.

A simple dessert found throughout Italy, panna cotta is a plain custard made without eggs. It literally translates as "cooked cream." Originally the silken pudding was considered a homey dessert, one that could be made a few hours before an everyday meal with ingredients always on hand. Today, of course, this is not always the case. Home cooks make it for special occasions, and restaurant chefs add it to the dessert menu. I have had it served with berries, which is traditional, and also drizzled with sweet, syrupy balsamic. For this recipe, I combine the two for double the flavor. Use whatever berries are in season, or substitute any soft fruit. I like this with strawberries and rhubarb in the spring.

serves 4

note Though the older, more intense, and more syrupy the balsamic vinegar that you use, the better it will taste, for this dessert you don't have to break the bank. But use a good balsamic. For more on balsamic vinegar, turn to page 176.

italian chocolate pudding
budino di cioccolata

pudding
5 ounces bittersweet chocolate, coarsely chopped
1 quart heavy cream
½ cup sugar
8 large egg yolks
Pinch of kosher salt

topping
½ cup heavy cream, whipped to medium-stiff
  peaks
5 Amaretti cookies, coarsely crushed

I am not a chocolate lover, and yet this smooth, rich custard-based pudding is just right whenever I have a craving for it. It's a simple, home-style dessert—nothing fancy or stylish, but instead pure comfort. Use the best bittersweet chocolate you can find; the best has at least 70 percent cocoa solids, which means it's rich and sinfully delicious. *serves 4 to 6*

1 To prepare the pudding, melt the chocolate in the top of a double boiler or a metal bowl set over barely simmering water. Stir it occasionally until smooth. Set aside to cool.

2 In a saucepan, mix the cream and sugar and cook over medium-high heat just until boiling.

3 In a separate bowl, whisk the egg yolks until smooth. Pour about half of the hot cream into the eggs, whisking constantly until smooth. This tempering prevents the eggs from cooking. Return the mixture to the saucepan with the remaining cream.

4 Cook over medium heat, stirring constantly with a wooden spoon, for about 2 minutes, or until the custard coats the back of the spoon. Remove from the heat.

5 Stir in the salt and then strain the custard through a fine-mesh sieve or chinois into the melted chocolate. Using a handheld mixer, blend the pudding until smooth and uniformly colored. If you don't have a handheld mixer, use a strong wire whisk.

6 Refrigerate the pudding for at least 2 hours, or until completely cool.

7 Spoon into small serving bowls and top with the whipped cream and crushed cookies.

winter fruit granita—blood orange, meyer lemon, and pomegranate

granita ai tre frutti

blood orange granita
¼ cup superfine sugar
2½ cups fresh fresh blood orange juice (10 to 12 oranges)
½ cup fresh lemon juice

meyer lemon granita
½ cup superfine sugar
Juice of 3 large Meyer lemons or other lemons

pomegranate granita
2 cups pomegranate juice
1 cup fresh orange juice
1 tablespoon superfine sugar

to serve
12 blood orange segments
1 tablespoon grated lemon zest
1 cup fresh blueberries, optional
Fresh pomegranate seeds

For these three granitas, you will need fruit that are at their best in the winter: blood oranges, Meyer lemons, and pomegranates. Blood oranges, originally from Sicily, are so called because of their crimson flesh and juice and have a mild, berrylike flavor. Meyer lemons, a product of California, are a hybrid developed at the beginning of the twentieth century by a horticulturist named Frank Meyer and have a deeper yellow skin, rounder shape, and slightly sweeter flavor. Pomegranates have a gorgeous sweet-and-sour tang, although getting to the glistening red seeds, which are impregnated with the juicy fruit, is a little tricky and always messy! I wish more people made granitas, which appeal to me more than ice cream because of their clean, bright flavors. They are easy and colorful, particularly refreshing, and similar to sorbets, but with a grainy texture formed when the mixtures are scraped repeatedly during the freezing process.

serves 4

1 To prepare the blood orange granita, heat 1 cup of water in a small saucepan over medium heat and add the sugar. Stir to dissolve the sugar, remove from the heat, and whisk in the orange and lemon juices. Set aside to cool.

2 Pour the cool liquid into a shallow non-reactive metal dish, cover with aluminum foil and freeze for about 1 hour, or until the mixture begins to freeze around the edges and the rest is covered with a thin layer of ice. Remove the pan from the freezer and break the mixture up with a fork. Scrape the icy sides of the pan and mix the shards of ice with the liquid. Cover again and freeze for 25 to 30 minutes.

3 Repeat the scraping and mixing process two or three times, until the granita is grainy and completely frozen. It should be firm and icy, not soft or mushy. The process takes 2 to 3 hours.

4 To prepare the Meyer lemon granita, heat 1 cup of water in a small saucepan over medium heat and add the sugar. Stir to dissolve the sugar, remove from the heat, and whisk in the lemon juice. Set aside to cool.

(continued)

5 Pour the cool liquid into a shallow nonreactive metal dish, cover with aluminum foil, and freeze for about 1 hour, or until the mixture begins to freeze around the edges and the rest is covered with a thin layer of ice. Remove the pan from the freezer and break the mixture up with a fork. Scrape the icy sides of the pan and mix the shards of ice with the liquid. Cover again and freeze for 25 to 30 minutes.

6 Repeat the scraping and mixing process two or three times, until the granita is grainy and completely frozen. It should be firm and icy, not soft or mushy. The process takes 2 to 3 hours.

7 To prepare the pomegranate granita, mix the pomegranate and orange juices in a small bowl and add sugar to taste. Remember that sugar does not taste as sweet when frozen.

8 Pour the cool liquid into a shallow nonreactive metal dish, cover with aluminum foil, and freeze for about 1 hour, or until the mixture begins to freeze around the edges and the rest is covered with a thin layer of ice. Remove the pan from the freezer and break the mixture up with a fork. Scrape the icy sides of the pan and mix the shards of ice with the liquid. Cover again and freeze for 25 to 30 minutes.

9 Repeat the scraping and mixing process two or three times, until the granita is grainy and completely frozen. It should be firm and icy, not soft or mushy. The process takes 2 to 3 hours.

10 Serve the orange granita garnished with the orange segments, the lemon granita garnished with the lemon zest and blueberries, if using, and the pomegranate granita garnished with the pomegranate seeds.

ricotta pie with coconut whipped cream

torta di ricotta con crema di cocco

filling
About 1 cup fresh ricotta cheese
⅔ cup sugar
2 large egg yolks
Grated zest of ½ orange
½ teaspoon pure vanilla extract

pie crust
2½ cups all-purpose flour
⅔ cup sugar
⅔ cup (11 tablespoons) unsalted butter, softened
3 large egg yolks

to serve
Coconut Whipped Cream (recipe follows),
    optional
½ cup toasted coconut, optional

This pie, which resembles cheesecake, is in keeping with my love and respect for simple Italian desserts. My grandmother made it for the family when I was young, and I suspect most children and grandchildren of Italian immigrants could say the same. I have added a lovely coconut whipped cream to dress it up a little—and to pay homage to one of my prime indulgences, coconut cream pie—but if you don't share my passion for coconut, leave it off or serve the pie with plain sweetened whipped cream. ❈ *serves 4*

1 To prepare the filling, put the cheese in a fine-mesh sieve or colander lined with cheesecloth and set over a bowl. Refrigerate for 8 to 10 hours. When the water has stopped dripping through the sieve and the cheese is well drained, transfer the cheese to a bowl.

2 Add the sugar, egg yolks, orange zest, and vanilla. Stir to combine.

3 To prepare the pie crust, whisk the flour and sugar in a large bowl.

4 In the bowl of an electric mixer fitted with the paddle attachment or using a handheld mixer, cream the butter and egg yolks until smooth. Add to the dry ingredients and cut the wet mixture into the dry with a pastry cutter or a fork. Work the dough as little as possible.

5 Turn the dough out onto a lightly floured surface and form into a disk. Wrap in plastic wrap and refrigerate for at least 1 hour.

6 Preheat the oven to 350°F.

7 Divide the chilled dough into 2 portions, one about twice as large as the other. Return the smaller piece to the refrigerator.

8 On a lightly floured surface, roll the larger piece into a circle and drape in a greased 8-inch pie plate. Crimp the edges and cut off any excess with a small, sharp knife. Add the filling and smooth it with a spatula so that it is even.

9 Roll the smaller portion of dough into a circle large enough to cover the pie filling with some overhang and drape over the top of the pie. Crimp the crusts together. Cut a few slits in the top crust.

10 Bake for 45 to 60 minutes, or until the pie crust is lightly browned. Gently lift the pie with a spatula to check the bottom of the crust. It should be lightly browned and firm.

11 Set the pie on a wire rack and let it cool to room temperature before serving. Pass the Coconut Whipped Cream and toasted coconut, if using, to serve with the pie.

coconut whipped cream
makes about 1½ cups

½ cup plus 2 tablespoons heavy cream
½ cup coconut cream
4 teaspoons confectioners' sugar

In the chilled bowl of an electric mixer fitted with the whisk attachment, beat the ingredients on high speed until medium-stiff peaks form. Serve immediately.

peaches in red wine with whipped mascarpone

pesche in vino rosso con mascarpone

4 ripe peaches
2 cups dry red wine
1 tablespoon packed brown sugar
1 sprig fresh thyme
1 cup mascarpone cheese
1 tablespoon granulated sugar
1 teaspoon grated lemon zest
¼ cup toasted walnuts (see Note)

I love peaches. White or yellow, as long as they are ripe and juicy, I am there! I like peaches eaten out of hand, or cooked, as in this recipe. Other stone fruits are on my list of favorites, and so I use this recipe to make the most of the summer's bumper crop of nectarines and plums, too. Here I suggest serving the peaches with whipped mascarpone, which is lush and decadent, but they would be fantastic with ice cream, too. ❧ *serves 4*

1 Bring a saucepan of water to a boil over high heat. Drop the peaches in the water and boil for 6 or 7 seconds. Remove with a slotted spoon and let the peaches rest for about 30 seconds before peeling the skin with a small paring knife. It will slip right off. Halve each peach and remove and discard the pits.

2 In a saucepan, combine the wine, brown sugar, and thyme. Cook over medium heat, stirring, until the sugar dissolves. Raise the heat to high and bring to a boil. Cook for about 10 minutes, or until the poaching liquid is reduced to a syrupy consistency.

3 Put the peach halves in a shallow dish, pour the warm wine over them, cover, and let stand for 4 to 12 hours. If the peach halves are not completely covered with wine, turn them after 2 hours. Turn them several more times during soaking if left in the wine for longer than 4 hours.

4 Using a wire whisk, whip the cheese until the consistency is smoother, lighter, and creamier. Fold in the granulated sugar and lemon zest. Put 2 peach halves in each of 4 serving bowls and spoon a little of the liquid over them. Top each with the toasted walnuts and a dollop of cheese.

note To toast the walnuts, spread them in a small, dry baking pan in a 300°F oven for 5 to 15 minutes. Shake the pan now and then to prevent burning and to turn the nuts. The nuts are done when they are fragrant and a shade darker. Transfer to a plate to cool.

sources
hard-to-find ingredients and equipment

The following are some sources I use in my restaurants for our food and equipment. If there is something you cannot find from local purveyors, one of these merchants may well be able to help you.

SEAFOOD AND FISH

Browne Trading
260 Commercial Street, Stop 3
Portland, ME 04101
Phone: 207-766-2402, 800-944-7848
Fax: 207-766-2404
www.brownetrading.com
All fish

Honolulu Fish
824 Gulick Avenue
Honolulu, HI 96819
Phone: 808-833-1123
Fax: 808-836-1045
www.honolulufish.com
All fish

M. F. Foley Fish Company
24 West Howell Street
Boston, MA 02125
Phone: 800-225-9995
www.foleyfish.com
All fish

Steve Connolly Seafood Company
34 Newmarket Square
Boston, MA 02118
Phone: 800-225-5595
www.steveconnollyseafood.com
Lobsters; shellfish

MEATS, GAME, AND
POULTRY
Jamison Farm
171 Jamison Lane
Latrobe, PA 15650
Phone: 800-237-5262
Fax: 724-837-2287
www.jamisonfarm.com
Lamb

Joseph Baumgartner Company
935 West Randolph Street
Chicago, IL 60607
Phone: 312-829-7762
Fax: 312-829-8791
All meat

Millbrook Venison
499 Verbank Road
Millbrook, NY 12545
Phone: 800-774-3337
Fax: 845-677-8457
Venison

Niman Ranch
1600 Harbor Bay Parkway
Suite 250
Alameda, CA 94502
Phone: 866-808-0340
www.nimanranch.com
Lamb, pork

Stock Yards
340 North Oakley Boulevard
Chicago, IL 60612
Phone: 877-785-9273
Fax: 312-733-1746
www.stockyards.com
All meat and poultry

Swan Creek Farms
10531 Wood Road
North Adam, MI 49262
Phone: 517-523-3308
Lamb, pork, eggs, cheese

PRODUCE
The Chef's Garden
9009 Huron-Avery Road
Huron, OH 44839
Phone: 800-289-4644
www.chefs-garden.com
All vegetables; herbs

Fresh & Wild
PO Box 2981
Vancouver, WA 98663
Phone: 360-737-3657, 800-222-5578
www.freshwild.com
Wild mushrooms

SPECIALTY PRODUCTS
Anson Mills
1922-C Gervais Street
Columbia, SC 29201
Phone: 803-467-4122
Fax: 803-256-2463
www.ansonmills.com
Stone-ground grits

European Imports
2475 North Elston Avenue
Chicago, IL 60647
Phone: 773-227-0600, 800-323-3464
Fax: 773-227-6775
www.eiltd.com
Specialty foods

Spiceland
6604 West Irving Park Road
Chicago, IL 60634
Phone: 773-736-1000
Fax: 773-736-1271
Spices

For information about me, my products, and my restaurants, go to:

Tramonto Cuisine
www.tramontocuisine.com

Cenitare Restaurants
www.cenitare.com

Tru Restaurant
www.trurestaurant.com

index

about the authors

RICK TRAMONTO has been cooking since he was a teenager growing up in Rochester, New York, as part of a large Italian family. He worked at some of the finest restaurants in the United States and Europe before settling in Chicago, where he is chef and partner of five restaurants. He was the founding chef of Trio of Evanston, Illinois, and then in 1999 opened the award-winning Tru restaurant, a Relais & Châteaux property in Chicago, which has received four stars from the *Chicago Tribune*, the *Chicago Sun Times,* and *Chicago Magazine.* Rick has been featured in *USA Today*, the *New York Times*, *The Wall Street Journal, People, Gourmet, Bon Appetit, Food & Wine, Wine Spectator*, and *Conde Nast Traveler*. He has appeared on the *Today Show, Good Morning America, Oprah,* and on PBS. Rick was named Best Chef in the Midwest by the James Beard Foundation for 2002. In 2006, Rick opened Osteria di Tramonto. Tru was awarded the James Beard Best Service in America award in 2007 and was named in the Top 50 Best Restaurants in the World in 2000 by *Conde Nast Traveler.*

MARY GOODBODY is a nationally known food writer and editor. Her credits include *Tru, Amuse-Bouche, Fantastico,* and *Taste: Purse and Simple.* She has contributed significantly to books such as *Back to the Table, The Naked Chef, How to Be a Domestic Goddess,* and *The Morton's Steak Bible,* among others. She lives outside New York City.